Psychology
for
Leaders

The Portable MBA Series

The Portable MBA Series provides managers, executives, professionals, and students with a "hands-on," easy-to-access overview of the ideas and information covered in a typical Masters of Business Administration program. The published and forthcoming books in the program are:

Published

The Portable MBA (0-471-61997-3, cloth; 0-471-54895-2, paper)
  Eliza G. C. Collins and Mary Anne Devanna
The Portable MBA Desk Reference (0-471-57681-6) Paul A. Argenti
The Portable MBA in Finance and Accounting (0-471-53226-6)
  John Leslie Livingstone
The Portable MBA in Management (0-471-57379-5) Allan R. Cohen
The Portable MBA in Marketing (0-471-54728-X) Alexander Hiam and
  Charles Schewe
New Product Development: Managing and Forecasting for Strategic Success
  (0-471-57226-8) Robert J. Thomas
*Real-Time Strategy: Improving Team-Based Planning for a Fast-Changing
  World* (0-471-58564-5) Lee Tom Perry, Randall G. Stott, and
  W. Norman Smallwood
The Portable MBA in Economics (0-471-59526-8) Philip K. Y. Young and
  John McCauley
The Portable MBA in Entrepreneurship (0-471-57780-4)
  William Bygrave
The Portable MBA in Strategy (0-471-58498-3) Liam Fahey and
  Robert M. Randall
The New Marketing Concept (0-471-59576-4) Frederick E. Webster
*Total Quality Management: Strategies and Techniques Proven at Today's
  Most Successful Companies* (0-471-54538-1) Arnold Weimerskirch and
  Stephen George
*Market-Driven Management: Using the New Market Concept to Create a
  Customer-Oriented Company* (0-471-59576-4) Frederick E. Webster
Psychology for Leaders (0-471-59538-1) Dean Tjosvold and Mary Tjosvold

Forthcoming

The Portable MBA in Global Business Leadership (0-471-30410-7)
  Noel Tichy, Michael Brimm, and Hiro Takeuchi
Analyzing the Balance Sheet (0-471-59191-2) John Leslie Livingstone
Information Technology and Business Strategy (0-471-59659-0)
  N. Venkatraman and James E. Short
Negotiating Strategically (0-471-01321-8) Roy Lewicki and Alexander Hiam

Psychology
for
Leaders

❖

Using Motivation, Conflict, and Power to Manage More Effectively

Dean Tjosvold
Mary M. Tjosvold

John Wiley & Sons, Inc.
New York • Chichester • Brisbane • Toronto • Singapore

Library of Congress Cataloging-in-Publication Data:

Tjosvold, Dean.
  Psychology for leaders : using motivation, conflict, and power to
manage more effectively / Dean Tjosvold, Mary Tjosvold.
      p.   cm. — (The Portable MBA series)
  Includes index.
  ISBN 0-471-69755-4
  1. Psychology, Industrial.   2. Personnel management.
I. Tjosvold, Mary M.   II. Title.   III. Series.
HF5548.8.T53   1995
158.7—dc20   94-12760

Printed in the United States of America

10 9 8 7 6 5 4 3 2 1

Preface

Leading and discussing leadership are part of our human heritage. Yet the empirical study of leadership began just a few decades ago. The psychological study of management and organization behavior began on a broad scale in the early 1960s in professional schools of business and administration. We are at the beginning of a journey to develop insights into the psychology of diverse individuals, varied relationships, and complex organizations necessary to understand leadership.

We are fortunate to be able to draw upon the field of psychology as well as leadership research. For over a century, thousands of psychologists have worked hard to develop cogent theories and do the tough empirical research needed to challenge and extend these theories. There are far too many individuals to mention; however, the endnotes include many psychologists whose work is the foundation for this book. We express our deep gratitude to them all.

We are grateful to the many persons who have directly aided writing this book. People in our family business and managers in the Simon Fraser University Executive Masters in Business Administration program and in companies we have worked with have challenged us to extend our ideas and make them more useful. John Mahaney of John Wiley & Sons had confidence in us and Eleanor MacDonald gave us sound advice. Margaret Tjosvold, our mother, continues to demonstrate how psychological insight, caring for people, an inspiring vision, and hard work can be profitably integrated. The Aba-akram family shows us

v

how diverse leadership styles can be effective. Jenny Tjosvold contributed to the writing of the book and with Jason, Wesley, Lena, and Colleen creates a lively, loving family.

Writing a book, like leading, can only be successful with others. When the ideas and perspectives of this book stimulate your thinking, help you re-examine your approaches to leading, and forge more effective ways of working together, the book succeeds. We thank you for giving our book a chance to make a difference for you and the people you work with.

DEAN TJOSVOLD
MARY M. TJOSVOLD

Vancouver, British Columbia
Minneapolis, Minnesota

Contents

Psychology
for
Leaders

INTRODUCTION

Leaders are challenged to ennoble and unite people in a common purpose. Fulfilling that promise in today's pressured, ever-changing, fragmented world requires deep personal integrity, self-awareness, and sensitivity to other people. Leaders must be willing to take risks and experiment, articulate and model new ways of working, and celebrate and use diversity. They must help people feel loyal and plan for the future without the security of long-time employment. Conflicts must be confronted and managed honestly and openly to reduce frustrations and solve problems. To lead today is to be tenacious, open-minded, and savvy, and to help employees be so motivated and skilled.

Leaders are psychologists whether they want to be or not. Their use of finance, engineering, and other disciplines depends on their role and industry, but all leaders must work *with* and *through* other people to accomplish goals. To meet today's leadership challenges requires knowing valid psychological ideas and having the skill and determination to use them. This book presents psychological insights on such vital issues as shared vision, cooperation, power, emotions, and conflict to guide you and your employees on your journey to become a productive, enhancing team.

Leaders are in a special position to make psychological knowledge pay off.[1] Every day leaders are asked to respond to employee concerns, react to their feelings, reassure their doubts, and consider their plans. Leaders demonstrate the honesty and hard work necessary to achieve.

1

They are hardy and show how to cope with stress. Through praise, recognition, and rewards, leaders motivate and energize employees. Leaders stimulate and reinforce an organization's corporate culture.

Employees look to leaders for the group's direction, ethical standards, and ways of working. Are they to be cool and impersonal, friendly and courteous, or direct and honest? Are they to be open with their feelings or circumspect? They want to know whether their leader wants them to work by themselves, compete to see who is best, or work together to accomplish mutual goals.

Leaders can greatly impact employees' everyday lives and their experience of success and acceptance. Employees have strong feelings and opinions about their bosses. Unfortunately, often they are frustrated that their bosses are too arrogant and gruff, or too weak and wishy-washy.

Many managers we have worked with have complained about their bosses, even described them as mean and incompetent. (They are less worried that their own subordinates might be frustrated.) On a radio call-in show a few years ago, our talking about what makes a good boss was met with skepticism after many people had so vividly and bitterly derided their bosses. The host hoped that one day she would stumble upon a good boss!

PUTTING THIS BOOK TO WORK

Psychology is the study of people. Sometimes psychologists restrict themselves to behavior, but actions cannot be understood without considering people's intentions, emotions, ideas, perspectives, and situations. Leadership is much more than the actions a leveler takes. A leader's ability to influence employees depends upon who those employees are as persons, the situation they are in, the corporate culture of the organization, and their relationship with the leader and each other.

Applying Ideas from Psychology

Educators, writers, politicians, and many others have given the basic tenets of psychology away in classrooms, popular books and articles, and television and radio shows. We have been told the shortcomings of punishment, the importance of motivating people to do their best, the value of recognition, and the need to listen with empathy to troubled people. We understand the importance of healthy relationships where people trust one another. We know that stress can be debilitating and that physical exercise and social support can help us cope with stress. That people should feel confident and have high self-esteem is considered fundamental. Many psychological ideas are now so widely accepted that they have the status of common sense knowledge. We know "how to act" in accordance with a large number of sound psychological concepts. But knowing how to act and acting are not always the same thing.

These ideas must be incorporated into a leader's everyday work to have maximum effect. Knowing an idea does not mean that the idea automatically gets translated into action; believing that you should be empathetic does not mean that you are empathetic. This book was written to help leaders build on, extend, and refine their ideas and to encourage discussion and application. Each chapter shows how different psychological ideas can be applied in the office and in stressful situations.

Challenging Common, Misleading Ideas

Conflict may not be the most misunderstood issue in organizations, but it comes close. Traditionally, people have assumed that conflict is destructive and avoidable. Neither assumption, psychological research has demonstrated, is true. Especially now when people are so specialized, the demands to reduce costs and improve quality so intense, and the pressure for innovations so continuous, organizations are filled with conflict. People experience change differently and have opposing ideas about how to respond to it.

Fortunately, conflict can be highly constructive and a valuable ally in learning and adapting to change. We have found, for example, that well-discussed conflict aids effective response to customer complaints, serving customers with quality products and service, the implementation of new technology, and coping with threats to the safety of airplanes. Conflict is not the problem; conflict is part of the solution.[2] Leaders must structure and mediate conflict, not try to suppress it.

Conflict contributes to cooperation and unity. When people work together for common goals, they disagree about how to achieve them, how to distribute the work and the rewards, and how they should treat each other. Unity cannot be decreed but needs to be worked out through honest discussion. A Chinese proverb put it this way: "Begin with certainties, end with uncertainties. Begin with uncertainties, end with certainties."

Open conflict is the path to synergistic teamwork and cooperative unity. However, it must be properly understood and managed. Developing this conflict-positive organization requires a great deal of skilled leadership. Chapter 11 discusses conflict management in detail.

Competition is also much misunderstood. Some theorists argue that competition makes companies productive and effective; it distinguishes us from the discredited economies of the communist world. Other authors believe that though competition is necessary for the company, it is destructive for people. Competition is seldom clearly defined. Does competition mean a free market system, a win-lose battle, striving for excellence, open conflict, or achieving a satisfactory bottom line?

This book reviews the theory and research that clarifies the relationship between competition and cooperation. Considerable research has demonstrated that cooperative, overlapping goals underline the spirited teamwork that helps organizations innovate and adapt.[3] Cooperation within a company helps it compete in the marketplace. Competitive leaders who are committed to a win-lose way of working create mistrust and undermine the coordinated efforts needed for group and company success. Surprisingly, these competitive leaders, doubtful that they can discuss conflict skillfully, have been found to avoid the direct discussion of conflict necessary for a productive, enhancing work place.[4] Chapter 6 defines and discusses the concepts allowing managers to understand cooperation and competition.

Breaking Away from Either/Or Thinking

Conflict versus cooperation, competition versus cooperation, and other trade-offs dominate thinking about organizations. The company must focus on lowering cost or improving quality, on fostering teams or individuality, on efficiency or innovation. Leaders must chose between promoting themselves or employees, between people or productivity, and between control or self-management. But as with cooperation and conflict, either/or thinking masks confusions and makes excuses for ineffective practices.

Since the 1960s, Japanese automobile makers have smashed the myth that there is an inevitable tradeoff between cost and quality and between cost and variety, yet other manufacturers would not admit it for decades.[5] It has become clear that a productive organization is needed for a healthy work place. Being unproductive can be the most stressful of all stresses; people feel bored and ineffectual and worry about their job security.

Today's intense pressures to produce are incentives for leaders to create people-enhancing organizations. However, to do so requires that leaders break away from stereotyped, either or thinking. Psychology does not promise that everyone gets whatever he or she wants, but it does suggest, as Chapters 4 and 5 summarize, how the interests of workers, managers, customers, shareholders, and the community can be integrated to create the organizations needed to survive and flourish in the 1990s and beyond.

Use this book to reaffirm your commitment to using vital, fundamental psychological ideas of building the self-confidence and motivation of individuals, developing trusting relationships, showing empathy, and coping with stress. We also want you to challenge common thinking about conflict and competition and create new ways of leading and organizing.

OUR PSYCHOLOGY, YOUR PSYCHOLOGY

We have developed our psychological ideas through extensive research and writing. We have formally interviewed in depth many hundreds of managers and employees about their experiences, published more than 75 empirical research studies on interdependence in organizations and 35 critical reviews of the literature and chapters summarizing knowledge, and authored 15 books and many conference papers. We have drawn upon the insightful theorizing and vast research of many psychologists in developing our ideas about leadership and organizations.

But, as with you, our experience has affected our psychological perspectives. Since the 1970s, we along with our mother have built our family business so that today it is a successful $12 million company specializing in residential and health services for elderly and handicapped persons. We have worked with a staff to develop enriching relationships with clients and to challenge them to build their abilities. We have invested much in developing a team organization where employees work together to manage themselves and serve their customers. We have debated business decisions and directions and helped each other cope with the risks of new projects and the stress of owning a business. Our family and personal experiences have also shaped our beliefs.

This book is a statement of the ideas, insights, and conclusions that we believe are critical for leading based on our research, writing, and experience. The ideas in this book will help you, the reader, become a more effective leader, whether that is leading a small group or a diversified company. This book does not try to give an overview of psychology that identifies all ideas and issues that psychologists are investigating. Nor does it try to summarize theories of leadership or explore the personalities of leaders. This book will help you develop your psychological competence and confidence as you step up to lead.

Psychology for Leaders is action-oriented; you can use the book to help you lead your team. The book is also research-based. It draws on considerable educational psychology research on learning and social psychology and organizational behavior research on leadership, teamwork, and organizational effectiveness.

TAKING UP THE CHALLENGE

Leaders are asked to break away from the command-and-control, tell-and-sell organization and the suspicion and fragmentation it has left. They are to create new, more integrative ways of working so that organizations continually adapt to the fast-paced marketplace. They are to build teams able to manage themselves without costly, cumbersome supervision. Today's organizations must change or be changed; if they do not get better, they fall behind.

Leaders are asked to help new employees quickly contribute to the organization, not take months of trial and error to find out how things get done. They are asked to make diverse people work together in task forces and new product teams under tight time deadlines. They are to foster communication and teamwork in their ethnically diverse and geographically dispersed organizations.

Leaders must be highly competent. They need to be self-confident and approachable, personal and business-like, honest and controlled, expressive and inhibited, consistent and flexible. Leaders are to build organizations that learn and adapt, serve customers effectively, and deliver quality products. Leaders must show the way for organizations to be lean, cost-efficient, ethical, and just.

Despite these demands, support for leaders is minimal. They are promoted into management, congratulated, and left to cope. Stereotypes and misleading assumptions interfere with becoming an effective leader. *Psychology for Leaders* fills some of these gaps by describing critical ideas and skills that can help managers overcome obstacles and gain the rich, complex gratifications of leading successfully.

PART ONE

PSYCHOLOGY FOR SUCCESSFUL LEADING

> The most visible differences between the corporation of the future and its present-day counterpart will not be the products they make or the equipment they use—but who will be working, how they will be working, why they will be working, and what work will mean to them.
>
> Robert D. Haas, CEO, Levi Strauss

Leaders have to break out of old habits and stereotypes to build organizations that continually improve quality and reduce costs to prosper in the turbulent marketplace. Chapter 1 shows how leaders must be psychologically savvy to create motivating, measurable bottom lines that earn internal commitment. They have to translate visions and aspirations into new, concrete ways of working.

Learning is a common journey that binds leaders and employees together. To be credible and persuasive, leaders have to model the ongoing learning and self-development they expect from employees. Chapter 2 describes how people can develop their abilities to lead and work together by applying psychological ideas and reflecting on their experiences. Leading and learning psychology are both "we things" that are much better accomplished together than alone.

1 YOUR BOTTOM-LINE GOALS

A leader is a person who has the ability to get other people to do what they don't want to do, and like it.

President Harry S Truman

Leadership is the ability to decide what is to be done, and then to get others to want to do it.

President Dwight D. Eisenhower

In 1984, Arden C. Sims, president of Globe Metallurgical, confronted an often paralyzing problem: how to make a rust-belt, bureaucratic, high-cost, and low-quality company competitive in a marketplace where Japanese producers offered superior products and Brazilian and Argentinian producers offered cheaper ones.[1] Steel and aluminum customers were canceling orders and embarking on programs to reduce the number of their suppliers. The union resisted change and eventually called for a strike.

Through Sim's tenacious leadership, Globe used these difficulties to forge a lean low-cost, high-quality company. In 1988, Globe was the first small company to win the Baldridge Award for Quality and it also won the Shingo Prize for Manufacturing Excellence in 1989. Such awards have not slowed Globe's continuing pursuit of excellence.

Tough, but conventional cost-cutting proved inadequate in the mid-1980s. Backed into a corner, Sims began experimenting and, with the urging of Ford, GM, and other major customers, began in earnest to implement a quality, efficiency, and cost program. All plant employees had six hours of training in basic statistical process control including

11

control charts. It was not an option; either they accepted quality or there wasn't a place for them. Sims talked sternly to any supervisors whose control sheet was inadequate, but did not fire anyone. Workers also visited the plants of customers to gain an appreciation of how vital Globe's alloys were.

Rigid work rules held back real breakthroughs. The answer to Sims was to negotiate a different kind of contract, but it was not the U.S. Steelworkers Union answer. The parent company announced it wanted to sell Globe; the union thought that Sims would not risk a strike.

But Sims was convinced that the long-term success of Globe required a partnership with workers to reduce costs and jobs. In October 1988, the union went out on strike and Sims, 35 salaried workers, and 10 managers stepped into the plant to operate two of the five furnaces. Everyone was assigned a job—Sims, the president, was assigned to maintenance, the dirtiest job in the plant. They spent the next 60 hours in the plant and then moved to 12-hour shifts, 7 days a week.

Ironically, the year-long strike improved communication between those who managed and those who worked on the shop floor; they were all part of the same team. Each day of the strike, Sims filled a notebook with everyone's suggestions to improve operations. At dinner, they proposed how their jobs could be made simpler or even eliminated and made decisions on the spot. By the tenth month of the strike, Globe was making money and, more vitally, had discovered the power of teamwork to find more efficient ways of working and improving quality.

Their experience confirmed that it took everyone working together cooperatively—welders, crane operators, furnace operators, forklift drivers, stokers, furnace tappers, and tapper assistants. Soon they were organized into eight-person, cross-functional teams without any first-line supervisors. They discovered to their astonishment that they needed only 120 people to operate the plant, not the 350 workers that had been required before the strike.

The strike experience changed Paul Smith from cynical, disgruntled supervisor into the highly committed number-two furnace operator at Globe. He had blamed workers for their sloppiness and management for their cowardice in not backing him and other supervisors up. During the strike, he came to respect Sims and other managers, coming to believe that they were serious about quality and cost-reduction. He saw that Sims was "just a person, just like the rest of us. He's as common as the day is long. He doesn't lie and he doesn't expect to be lied to."

One unexpected outcome of the strike was that it broke the union. The experience made it impossible to go back to the old ways. The union remained inflexible and filed an unfair labor practices suit, which it eventually lost. Later the union agreed to return without conditions, but Sims had already hired 35 non-union workers and early in 1988 called back 30 ex-union workers.

Globe continued to build upon its new attitudes and practices. Sims led a leveraged buy-out to deepen the transformation. Without the security of a cash-rich parent and its restraints, he and others at Globe doubled their cost-consciousness and their commitment to building the organization.

A profit-sharing plan was introduced to make it clear that employees benefit from their efforts to improve plant efficiency. Information about budgets, salaries and wages, investments, and other expenses were shared with the workers. Sims held quarterly meetings with employees in groups of 10 to 20 to discuss all company matters and hear employee concerns. Management gave the employees a commitment to full employment at the plant. The employees initiate and form the budget so that they know what is expected if they are going to make a profit. With such teamwork, Globe averages nearly $4 million a year in quality-related cost savings.

More confident of its abilities, Globe has gone global. Its focus on specialized metals requires it to keep the furnaces operating at full capacity. A strategic alliance with the British firm, Materials & Methods, helped it capture 20 percent of the Western European market. Success in Japan has been slower but Globe has 7 percent of the market. Sims is convinced that it will eventually be the supplier of first choice in Japan. Growth in the rest of Asia has been faster where it is replacing Japanese firms as supplier.

The need to survive by reducing costs and improving quality drove Sims' leadership and the transformation of Globe. He did not set out to forge a corporate culture or develop a team organization but he ended up doing so to save and build the company. He applied basic psychological ideas. Through statistical process control, employees became more focused on their objectives and identified problems that interfered with quality. Sims and the employees opened up lines of communication and developed mutually respectful, honest relationships. Together they reduced layers of management to help the company become more flexible and feel more powerful to effect change. The employees formed teams to get the job done and to forge more effective ways of working. They adopted job security and profit-sharing policies to strengthen loyalty and teamwork. Through their ordeal, they had learned that to develop a real team behind quality and cost reduction they must confront problems and manage conflict.

Smith reflected, "I consider myself a fairly conservative manager. But over the last eight years, I've had to take some pretty big risks just to survive, and I've had to fight some pretty fierce battles. . . . I've found that one of the most important components of a successful transformation is to gain the respect of your workforce. I don't mean the workers have to like you, although that helps, but they have to understand that you will stand your ground when it comes to forcing through big changes. To initiate change, you have to be tenacious, and you need to show that you're not afraid of getting a little dirt under your fingernails."

THE IMPERATIVE FOR LEADERSHIP

Globe and other companies need credible, skilled leadership to prosper. Sims used competitive threats to his company's survival to break out of old ways of thinking and acting. He realized that for his company to survive, people had to work together in new ways but he had to be a strong leader if the workers were to feel empowered. No. 2 furnace operator, Paul Smith, put it this way, "Arden [Sims]. . . turned things around where everyone feels that if it wasn't for him, and the changes he introduced, we wouldn't be where we are today."

Coping with Change

Too many companies are not prepared to manage the turbulent changes and the intense feelings of today's work. Arden Sims observed, "I think a lot of senior managers have lost their resolve and their ability to face up to hard work. Change is never easy, and there are no special formulas, no quick fixes. You just have to roll up your sleeves and keep working at it without backing down."

Complaints about our organizations and despair over our leaders are loud and clear. Managers blame a complacent workforce; employees blame self-interested management. Through the 1980s, according to several polls, employees yearned for more openness and partnership with management but thought they got less honesty.[2]

Sixty percent to 75 percent of employees in many different kinds of organizations report that their immediate supervisor is the biggest source of stress in their jobs.[3] In the last ten years, 50 percent of all senior managers have failed.[4]

We have been caught off guard. We expected change to be beneficent and our work lives to be predictable. Feelings and relationships were for our lives outside work. Our literature portrays the tragedies and struggles of family and private life, seldom the rich drama of work. Stereotypes of the hard-charging businessperson and the reluctant employee dominate our images and thinking about organizational life.

Business is supposed to be rational and impersonal. The focus is on the end and what it takes to get the job done. Top management sets policies, managers make decisions and solve problems, and employees do their assigned tasks. People do their jobs to obtain the necessary money to have a life outside the business. These assumptions are too far removed from reality to work anymore.

Emotions and frustrations in today's work place are so great they cannot be denied. People feel burnout by the incessant crises and demands to get the job done. Some are too scared to speak out or even to have children for fear of jeopardizing their job. Many are less and less prepared to sacrifice and give their all to a company because their boss has asked them. Feeling pressured and anxious, they are searching for meaning and purpose in their work.

The disaffection of people poses great hazards because organizations need highly skilled, committed employees to deal with ongoing problems. To cut costs, organizations have reduced the layers of management that before supervised and cajoled employees. Today's employees must be able to operate complex technology, establish personal links with customers, and handle specialized information, often at a site away from colleagues and bosses. Without employees who have a conviction that their work is important and valued, organizations are vulnerable.

Need for New Ways of Working

Leaders like Globe's Arden Sims have a vision—though not necessarily a plan—for the organization and of how employees should work together. It is that vision that captures people's hearts and minds. Leaders inform and inspire so that people are convinced that they can find more productive, enhancing ways to collaborate. Leaders and followers channel their strong aspirations and intense feelings to build organizations that innovate and serve customers more effectively.

Managing in the sense of handling the requirements of the status quo and getting by in the short-term is insufficient. We need leaders who recognize the shortcomings of present ways of working and have the credibility and tenacity to create the spirited teamwork necessary so that people believe they are in charge of change, not pawns of irresistible forces.

But because we need leadership does not mean that we will get it. The very demands for leaders make becoming an effective leader seem difficult and foreboding with few realistic models to follow. "Charismatic" leaders who single-handedly turned around a company from the brink of bankruptcy are often celebrated, but these stories seem distant from the possibilities and demands for leading a hostile work group or an established company operating in a mature market.

Command-and-control management has left much fragmentation and mistrust in organizations. In many companies, divisions see each other as rivals rather than partners in creating value for customers. Employee grievances have been smoothed over but antagonism builds. Nearly everywhere people complain that their bosses are so arrogant and uncaring that they don't even listen. How can leaders bring us together when people distrust them and each other?

No wonder managers turn to quick fixes. They hope more meetings will make the organization more synergistic and pep talks about the importance of quality and some measurements of it will unite everyone behind quality improvement. By having people talk with customers, they will work together to improve customer service. After these brief interventions, people are told to get back to work and deal with new crises. Under pressure, they revert to traditional ways and hope that working harder and longer will be enough.

In some organizations, top management has boldly and radically restructured organizations. They have collapsed managerial levels, reduced the workforce, formed divisions focused on specific customers, and initiated self-directed work teams. Despite the enormous upheaval and costs of such changes, scant attention is given to creating a new way of working together and the leadership necessary for it.

New structures do not themselves create a new culture and way of working. Telling the fewer managers who are left after restructuring to facilitate, not lead, is not effective. Talking about teamwork and labeling people a team does not mean that people can operate in a nonhierarchical manner. It turns out to be much easier to condemn traditional managing and organizing and devise new organizational charts than to foster the leadership to build synergistic teams and organizations.

Outmoded beliefs and inadequate ideas about people and their relationships lie behind our failures. Valid psychological knowledge is critical for creating high involvement, high commitment organizations.

PSYCHOLOGY TO CREATE A BOTTOM LINE

Although often assumed to be simply a measure of financial performance, the bottom line of an organization has many components. Short-term profitability must be balanced with long-term effectiveness. Measures of product quality, customer satisfaction, reputation, and relationship with regulators may all be relevant for the bottom line. Many companies recognize that being ethical and contributing to the local community are vital goals.

Effective bottom lines must be created through considerable debate. Vital goals are not simply there, but the leader and employees must together envision them and develop the tools to measure progress. They must apply psychology if they are to have a meaningful bottom line. Discussion throughout the organization is needed to see how the different goals of the bottom line can complement each other, what priorities are needed in making trade-offs, and how the goals of the bottom line unite people and teams in a common endeavor.

Ambivalence Toward Psychology

Managers taking up the leadership challenge have realized that people are a company's greatest resource. It is through them that plans are devised and implemented, problems are identified and solved, and productivity and success are achieved. The work place must be characterized by mutual trust and mutual accountability. Key to the transformation of our organizations is to involve people and gain their commitment. Globe's Arden Sims began by changing the autocratic way of his predecessor. "I know for a fact that you can't run a company very effectively with one person making all the decisions."

In developing the people side of the organization, leaders are moving themselves and others away from the emphasis on technical and financial skills to the human relations ones. Yet many managers are skeptical about psychology. Theories of leadership often seem grand and abstract and reinforce the stereotype that psychology is removed from the real demands of work. Psychologists appear to have more abstract concerns of whole person, job satisfaction, stress reduction, and feelings of well-being; their ideas are not central for creating competitive advantage and meeting crises. Psychology seems irrelevant for the bottom line and the problems of our times.[5]

Psychologists have responded to these attitudes. They have shown that following validated employee selection procedures can save companies thousands of dollars compared to typical unstructured interview methods.[6] Research has demonstrated that failed coordination between people and groups cost organizations money and that these costs can be steep indeed.[7]

Applying psychology is not only entirely consistent with striving for bottom-line goals; it reasserts the value of a bottom-line focus. As we will see in future chapters, people want to achieve, feel the success of completing tasks, and be a part of something greater than themselves; they seek goals and feedback in reaching them successfully. They want information that confirms their competence and hard work. Indeed, job dissatisfaction pales compared to the despair of unemployment.[8] Losing one's job is often a catastrophic experience because of the basic needs that working fulfills. While some people have higher needs, the desire to feel the internal satisfaction of doing a task well and being valued by others are built into all of us.

The problem is that in many organizations the bottom line is not clear and measured. Many so-called hard-nosed, bottom-line managers have only the fuzziest notions about what their bottom line is. They are busy, pressed and running hard, but why and where to are unknown. They take refuge in the "hurry up" offense of the company and doing their many tasks but ignore issues of goals and purposes. But leaders simply working harder is not a solution for today.

Uniting Behind the Bottom Line

Even managers who have well-articulated purposes and goals are often woefully inadequate in helping employees develop their own complementary goals. They assume that employees should think and feel like they do; an after dinner speech should clarify any confusion and put everyone on the same wavelength. They assign tasks and give deadlines to keep employees busy but seldom have any discussion about an inspiring, uniting vision. Then these managers complain that workers do not care. We offer you a new understanding of leadership: Leaders help people care.

Though often advocated, it is unrealistic and undesirable that everyone should be committed to the identical goals and bottom line. Although it is useful for people to buy into overall company goals, what goals the marketing group strives for are not the same as the goals of the production department. What one production employee finds motivating and inspiring, another does not.

We must appreciate that individuals, teams, departments within an organization have their own special perspectives, interests, and capabilities. However, this diversity itself does not prevent effective bottom lines. In fact, leaders learn how to use this diversity to enhance the organization. What is critical is that the bottom line of groups and individuals be *cooperatively* aligned, not necessarily the same. To achieve a cooperative bottom line requires a great deal of discussion and reflection so that the goals of the company, its teams, and individuals are understood and mutually reinforcing.

Divisions, departments, and other groups must understand the various aspects of the organization's bottom line and determine what specific goals in their group will contribute most effectively. Texas Instruments calls the ongoing "give and take" between groups and executives as to their goals and the company's vision "catchball." Groups need to develop their bottom line in conjunction with the organization's goals or risk being seen as irrelevant. But a group's bottom line has to be responsive to its own capabilities and aspirations. What are the ways that the group is able and motivated to contribute to the organization's bottom line?

A group's goal cannot be assumed to be an individual's. The group may determine that zero defect quality products is its bottom line. An individual may decide that learning and applying quality control statistical methods should be foremost in her own bottom line. She may be committed to this development because it increases her income, promotion opportunities, or group support or all of these. Employees should see how their individual goals fit with the goals of the group and organization and, at the same time, promote their own needs, values, and aspirations.

Psychological research suggests that the goals for the organization, teams, and individuals should be specific enough to be measured and allow regular feedback.[9] Recognition and rewards for reaching bottom lines should be public and frequent, and, as will be discussed at length in Chapters 5 and 6, they should reinforce the cooperative, mutually reinforcing goals of the groups and individuals in the organization.

Leaders need not choose between being sensitive psychologists and hard-charging, bottom-line businesspeople. Rather considerable sensitivity and psychological sophistication are needed to create motivating bottom lines.

Psychology for Bottom-Line Leadership

Respond to Change

- Handle stress.
- Deal with intense feelings.
- Cope with burnout.
- Confront distrust.
- Make change a friend.
- Learn to take advantage of ongoing change.
- Motivate everyone to innovate.

Determine Our Direction

- Help individuals find value in organizational work.
- Gain employee internal commitment.
- Inspire a shared vision.
- Create more effective ways to serve customers.
- Align the goals of individuals and groups.
- Forge unity out of diversity.

Getting There

- Translate intentions into effective action.
- Move from alienation to trust.
- Build cooperative, synergistic team organizations.
- Develop mutual confidence and power.
- Communicate effectively.
- Debate and make business decisions.
- Manage conflict.
- Become self-directing.
- Improve continuously.

GETTING THERE: MORE THAN GOOD INTENTIONS

Why do so many of our organizations fail to meet our expectations as good places to work and meet customer expectations of quality service? Why don't they reach their bottom lines? The most common answer is the lack of motivation and good intentions. "If employees cared more about their work," businesspeople have argued, "our organizations would be more competitive." "If bosses were not so greedy," employees have argued, "they would be more able and motivated to contribute." The "other guys" just do not have good intentions to be productive and fair.

Good intentions and motivation themselves are seldom the culprits. Most bosses want their organizations to be enhancing, rewarding places to work. Most employees want to do high quality, first class jobs, not be embarrassed that they work for a company that delivers defective products to their neighbors and other customers. However, good intentions do not automatically translate into effective work. Bosses withhold information they consider confidential and thereby unintentionally create suspicion. Employees are annoyed that their suggestions to improve quality are not considered and resign themselves to lesser goals or possibly express their anger by letting defective products through to the marketplace. Although no one wants an organization to be fragmented and unproductive, it ends up that way.

The failures and successes of our organizations must be seen as jointly caused. The credit and blame are rarely attributable to just one person or group. Although people have good intentions and technical skills, they may end up working at cross-purposes and against each other. They must coordinate their abilities and energy as well as have good intentions.

To lead by building more synergistic ways of working, managers need to be psychologically savvy. It is not enough for them to want teamwork; they must have ideas, procedures, and skills to make it happen. Many managers are able to work with others honestly and productively, but leadership requires more. Leaders articulate a realistic vision and credibly take steps so that people throughout the group and organization feel like a team and are able and committed to working together.

Building a team organization requires leaders to be knowledgeable as well as inspiring. They should understand the nature of productive teamwork and feel a passion for creating it. They should know practical procedures for realizing the vision and have the psychological confidence and hardiness to persist. But leaders must also have the interpersonal skills to reach out and involve employees so that they too are convinced that together they can forge more spirited cooperation. Psychology is critical for creating the new way of working necessary to achieve today's bottom lines.

Psychology can help leaders address the fundamental issues of where are we going and how are we going to get there. Part Two explores how we can understand our hopes and aspirations to develop visions and careers that are meaningful for us. Leaders not only should know where they are going, but also help employees understand the company's direction and discover whether they want to go with it. Parts Three and Four address how people can best work together to realize their joint and personal aspirations. We turn in Chapter 2 to how to learn psychological ideas and skills that are the background for knowing our bottom lines and developing our mutual plans.

2 LEARNING PSYCHOLOGY

> To know that we know what we know and that we do not know
> what we do not know, that is true wisdom.
>
> Confucius

Ralph Strayer's leadership challenge was not the hit-you-in-the-face one that Arden Sims had confronted at Globe.[1] Strayer had developed the family sausage business, Johnsonville Foods, into an above average money maker with 20 percent growth with a reputation for quality and respect from the community. Yet he had a knot in his stomach. The company was vulnerable. Big producers could out market it; small producers could provide quicker, superior service. The biggest worry: workers did not seem to care.

Strayer's vision came quickly. He wanted employees who would fly like geese, each taking the responsibility to lead and drive the company forward. What he had was a herd of buffalo that, if the leader was gone, hunters could pick off one by one. Through starts and stops, Strayer came to realize that learning was the key to get from where the company was to where it could be.

By 1990, the bottom line of quality product, profit margins, productivity increases, and sales volume far exceeded anything that Strayer could have predicted in 1980. A critical turning point was the possibility of acquiring a major competitor in 1985. Strayer was initially reluctant and by himself would have rejected the acquisition. But the employees weighed the risks, the need to train new employees, and the possibility of losing the acquisition's only major contract. A full discussion convinced employees and Strayer that the risks could be managed; this kind of teamwork also made the expansion far exceed expectations.

But getting to this empowering teamwork required more than drive and intention. Telling people to be more responsible, even demanding that they be, was insufficient. Strayer had the fundamental leadership insight that change and learning should begin with him. How could he expect others to go where he had not been? "I had created the management style that kept people from assuming responsibility. . . . I had made the company, so I could fix it. . . . The fault was not someone else's, the fault was mine." Strayer had to analyze his own approach and look for ways to modify it.

He realized that he had fixated on the financial side of the business—margins, market share, and return on assets. People were dutiful tools to make the business grow. "Now the very things that had brought me success—my centralized control, my aggressive behavior, my authoritarian business practices—were creating the environment that made me so unhappy."

He began to experiment with the psychological side of running a business. But at first he used misguided ideas. He abdicated decision-making authority only to leave his managers feeling that now they had to guess how he would make decisions and do that. They felt that they were being asked to be his clones. The detailed strategic and tactical plans to make the company a world leader that Strayer busied himself with were largely irrelevant to the needs of a growing company.

After years of frustration, Strayer concluded that he would have to be a coach. He would help the employees be psychologists who could "see their own behavior, harness their own frustrations, and own their own problems." He would provide the opportunities and psychological support for employees to solve key issues.

Employees complained about overtime on weekends at one of the plants. Strayer asked them to solve the problem. Employees quickly discovered that the equipment was down over 30 percent of the time and these breakdowns had causes they could fix. Soon the machine was down less than 10 percent of the work week and the workers were enjoying their weekends.

Strayer had the insight that he could help managers and employees manage themselves by influencing the environment in which they worked. The first system to be revamped was quality. Managers were to stop tasting to test the product and employees were to begin tasting and be responsible for quality. Quickly they accepted this responsibility. One team explored the problem of leakage in the vacuum packed packages, created solutions, and worked with suppliers to implement them. Rejects of spoiled sausage fell from 5 percent to 0.5 percent.

Strayer saw how teams could empower employees to solve problems. Newly created teams up and down the line began tasting the product. They asked for information on costs and customer reactions. They responded to customer complaints directly. Rather than complain about co-workers, they were coached to develop performance standards, confront poor performers, help them learn, and, if needed, terminate them. Then workers asked for, and got, the responsibility to select and train new recruits.

The teams also pushed for structural change. The quality department worked with production to improve quality rather than to measure it. The personnel department became the learning and personal development team to help employees develop their own aspirations and plans. More than 65 percent of all employees are involved in formal education.

Promotion standards had to change. The message no longer could be: To move in the company, you need to become a manager and solve other people's problems. The need was for coordinators who could build team problem solving. For a while, Strayer de-emphasized technical skills. Later, the company developed a career path for technicians as well as coordinators.

Johnsonville shares profits on the basis of performance in a system designed, run, and modified by employees.[2] Peers determine whether employees have mastered a series of skills and get a raise. Bonuses are given for great performances and for teaching new ways of being productive. "Often we talk in terms of performers and enablers," coordinator Leah Fowler said. "We're all attempting to work a lot smarter."

Strayer has tried "for the last five years to eliminate my job by creating such a crowd of self-starting, problem-solving, responsibility-grabbing, independent thinkers that Johnsonville would run itself." Now employees are as or even more committed than he is to the company. He told the new chief operating officer to treat him as a paid consultant. But when he left him a note, "I want you [at a meeting] at 8:15," Strayer was angry that he was being told what to do after he had built and fixed the company. Then he laughed. "It's not always easy giving up control. . . . He wanted me there at 8:15? Well, good for him. I'd be there."

THE IMPERATIVE TO LEARN PSYCHOLOGY

Strayer and others at Johnsonville Sausage had come to realize that learning held the key to their success. No snappy slogan or slick technique would do. Indeed, they had to continue to learn and could not let success go to their heads and become their enemy. Strayer concluded, "Change is the real job of every business leader because change is about the present and the future, not about the past. There is no end to change." The company cannot rest on its laurels. Teams must be working on next year's budgets, new product ideas, today's production schedules, and yesterday's quality, cost, and yield. They must also be redesigning their systems and structures to be prepared for tomorrow.

Learning psychology has underlined the capacity of Strayer and Johnsonville to adapt and improve business. Strayer had to become more self-aware and experiment with new ways of working with employees. He needed to be psychologically hardy and robust for not every experiment was successful. He could not direct employees to work smarter but he could create a supportive environment in which employees became more self-confident, self-directed, and able to work together. Then they were prepared to tackle problems and engage in the continuous improvement needed to make Johnsonville a highly successful business.

Strayer had discovered that the "most important kind of learning teaches us to question our own actions and behavior in order to better understand the ways we perform, work and live. Helping human beings fulfill their potential is of course a moral responsibility, but it's also good business. Life is aspiration. Learning, striving people are happy people and good workers. They have initiative and imagination, and the companies they work for are rarely caught napping."

Getting Focused on Psychology

Leaders like Strayer must be intellectually prepared to grapple with sophisticated problems. They must have a courageous heart to challenge the status quo and persist to innovate. They must be genuine to expect that people will trust and follow them. They must demonstrate their own willingness to change if they are to ask people to change. To be credible, leaders must model the way.[3]

Unlike Strayer, many aspiring managers fail to appreciate that they need to become sophisticated users of psychology to meet these challenges. They remain fixated on their technical backgrounds. They draw upon that which is familiar and comfortable. They hope that they can apply the skills they are already good at to the challenges of leading.

An engineer recalled how he had to struggle to learn that he needed psychology to become an effective leader of people.[4] "When I first became a supervisor of a group of development engineers, I looked at management like an engineer would. I read all about performance reviews, and boy, was I ready to give performance reviews. I told them in detail all the things they did wrong, and all the things they did right. No one had ever given them that kind of feedback before. But I just about killed those engineers, and nearly crushed the morale of that organization. I was clearly not a skilled coacher of people. So I went out and got some help. I finally learned that just as you had to know the laws of physics to be a good engineer, I had to know the laws of psychology to be a good manager.

"This was a tremendous lesson for me: that you can't just translate the skills of one profession to another. When you're going into a new profession, you'd better learn as much as you can about it before you jump. Take as much time as you can learning the differences so that you don't use your own experience when it really doesn't apply."

Leaders have the opportunity to make a difference. But they must become psychologically sophisticated because the instrument for making this impact is themselves. They must lead in ways that build upon themselves as a unique person. They must respond to the unique values, aspirations, and needs of their colleagues and customers. Their leadership must help their group accomplish its mandates, serve its customers, and feel successful.

Though technical abilities have been traditionally emphasized, people skills are critical for leading. Closed-minded, self-centered, and impersonal managers do not gain the internal commitment of people to meet contemporary challenges. To be sensitive with people and help them be productive requires considerable psychological competence. Psychology can help you forge a leadership style that fits you and the people you want to inspire.

Need for Formal Psychological Knowledge

Yet many leaders try to develop themselves and their teams with little or no reference to formal psychology.[5] They build on ideas and values they learned living with their family and working in organizations. They model successful, inspiring leaders such as Arden Sims and Ralph Strayer. They found insightful people to clarify their thinking. But this trial-and-error learning was less risky in slower paced times. The fierce demands and rapid changes of today's work place have exposed the inadequacies of traditional ways of learning to lead.

People not only learn valuable lessons without explicit reference to psychology; they also learn ineffective ideas and reinforce biases.[6] Arden Sims and Ralph Strayer lamented the false starts and the time and energy wasted pursuing ideas that, in retrospect, had little chance of paying off. Nor can we simply do what previous leaders have done; our situations are different than theirs. Observing successful leaders does not mean that we have the same insights as they do nor does it mean that we necessarily know how to apply them.

The incredible pace of change puts leaders in new and complex situations in which traditional sign posts do not apply. One thing we know about the future is that it will not be just like the present and, increasingly, that it will be much different. Leaders need tested ideas so that they can expand their thinking, refine their skills, and confront their biases and limitations as they deal with emerging issues.

Now products must get to the marketplace quickly before the competition takes the market and goes after the next generation of products. No longer will the marketplace allow, in sequence, research and development to build a prototype, the marketing department to research its sales potential, and engineers to study its production. Companies must experiment with new ways of operating that enhance rather than disrupt the environment. Leaders must now help varied specialists work together in cross-functional teams in synergistic and efficient ways.

Dramatic changes in the work place require more adaptive, flexible leadership. With immigration and increasing entry in the workforce, employees of many companies in the United States and other countries are increasingly diverse in gender, ethnicity, and cultural and national backgrounds. Divisions, mistrust, and new sensitivities have mandated that leaders confront sexual harassment, abuse, and violence in the work place.

Employees in many companies are geographically dispersed so that they must coordinate through telephone, computer lines, and fax machines. They have few opportunities for informal interactions where they can feel part of the organization, find out the latest developments, and make spontaneous contributions.

Traditional forms of leading and organizing are increasingly out-dated and inappropriate. Learning to lead has become too vital and too complex to be left for serendipity and informal methods. A new partner-ship between theory and practice, between researcher and manager, is needed to meet our leadership challenges.

LEARNING WITH EXPERIENCE

But how can managers learn to be leaders? Experience is critical. No one is born knowing how to lead. But experience is not enough. Man-agers incorporate valid ideas into their action, think about their use, and learn from their experiences. (See Figure 2.1.)

Too often ideas and theories are thought to be in the world of books and classrooms where people learn to think and talk in new, in-teresting ways. Actions and strategies are in the world of organizations where people get things done. Theory is impractical and not very rele-vant to the world of action, which evolves from feelings and instincts.[7] But the wall between theory and practice must be torn down.

Parallels between Being a Leader and Researcher

Stereotypes portray the researcher and leader as having distinct inter-ests and orientations. But the worlds of action and research complement each other. For centuries, economic vitality and scientific progress have marched together. The ancient Egyptians, the Renaissance Dutch, and the modern Americans advanced science and business.

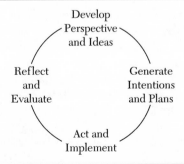

FIGURE 2.1.   Learning cycle.

Kurt Lewin: Psychologist and Leader

Kurt Lewin was a highly creative, original, tough-minded theorist with a profound interest in the philosophy and methods of science. He was also a tender-hearted psychologist deeply involved in developing knowledge to solve critical social issues.[8] He also credibly applied his psychological insights into developing teams and organizations that have had an enduring impact on psychology and organizational change. He was a visionary scientist and an inspiring leader who opened up new areas for psychological study.

In 1943, he stirred psychologists with his bold picture of what the future could be. "Although the scientific investigations of group work are but a few years old, I don't hesitate to predict that group work—that is, the handling of human beings not as isolated individuals, but in the social setting of groups—will soon be one of the most important theoretical and practical fields. . . . There is no hope for creating a better world without a deeper scientific insight into the function of leadership and culture, and of other essentials of group life."

To fulfill this mission, the development of psychology required the close cooperation of theorist and practitioner. This "can be accomplished . . . if the theorist does not look toward applied problems with highbrow aversion or with a fear of social problems, and if the applied psychologist realizes that there is nothing so practical as a good theory." Practitioners would keep theorists confronting social reality; theorists could provide practitioners with a deeper understanding of social issues.

Like other good leaders, Lewin led by example. He went where others had not dared to go. He developed ways to study groups and leadership, areas that psychologists had previously considered too abstract for careful experimental study. His studies showing how group discussion and decisions could actually help people use less popular cuts of meats to support the allied effort in World War II also advanced knowledge on how groups were effective ways to change the attitudes and behavior of individuals.[9] He conducted studies demonstrating the value of democratic leadership as an alternative to laissez faire and autocratic leaders.[10] In testing these ideas, Lewin and his colleagues had to train people and develop a more complete and detailed understanding of democratic leadership.

His passion had deep personal and social roots.[11] Born a Jew in Germany in 1890, he knew racism first hand. Repulsed by the German professors' practice of demanding intellectual servitude and their emphasis on rank, hierarchy, and aloofness, he was very open to students and colleagues regardless of their status. Pushed away from his beloved

(Continued)

(Continued)

homeland by the Nazi movement, he quickly embraced the language, customs, and aspirations of his adopted America. He was able to sponsor his brother and other Jewish refugees but his mother refused to believe that she was in danger. After the war, he discovered that his mother had been transported from The Netherlands and killed in a Nazi camp. He then redoubled his commitment to know the nature of prejudice and outgroup aggression and how to prevent, control, and defeat them.

His achievements and imagination drew students and young scholars to him. Informal discussions often lasted well into the night; there was an excitement that a new insight might emerge at any time. In 1945, Morton Deutsch was so caught by Lewin's enthusiasm, charm, and ideas that he knew after a first interview that he would become Lewin's student. Lewin treated Deutsch as a serious professional, engaged in penetrating discussions of prejudice and other issues, asked Deutsch to complete important tasks, and gave him the freedom to to do his work as he saw fit.

Although Lewin died before Deutsch completed his graduate work, Deutsch concluded after nearly 50 years of significant contributions to social psychology, "I feel fortunate to have been one of Lewin's students, and I hope that, had he lived to the present, he would have been happy that I was."[12] Lewin knew how to inspire and empower long before those terms became popular.

As a practical leader, Lewin saw the potential of organized effort. He worked hard to develop the support for the Research Center for Group Dynamics, which he led at Massachusetts Institute of Technology. He also founded and co-chaired the Commission on Community Interrelations to use knowledge to reduce prejudice. He recruited an extraordinary mix of mature students and young faculty members who were open to each other and who had opposing viewpoints. Lewin relished the give and take of controversy. He often would show how opposing ideas could be integrated and how research and application complemented each other.

Morton Deutsch wrote that Lewin "was a creative scientist who enriched our understanding of individual and social life by his concepts and research. He was a . . . scientific leader who enthused and inspired his many students to do important work of their own. And he was a socially concerned, responsible human being who constantly sought to apply his ideas to make the world a more humane habitat for all of us."[13] Although he died in 1947, less than two years after the founding of the Center for Group Dynamics, he had established an institution that has strongly shaped the development of social psychology and its contribution to our social life.

To be effective, leaders and researchers both need the attitudes and practices of open-minded experimenting. Leaders must understand ideas well enough to use them; researchers must test their ideas in actual situations. Leaders are interested in results, especially ones that can be "measured"; researchers strive for the careful documentation of effects of their experiments. Leaders and researchers are committed to using these results to refine their ideas and interventions.

Robert Frey had to become an experimenter to make the Cincinnati tube and can manufacturing company he had bought ten years ago succeed.[14] Dismayed at how people worked, he developed and tested various hypotheses. Knowing that something was wrong was the easy part. Product lines were outdated, profits were marginal, labor costs were out of control, job definitions were rigid, and union relations were poor. But what, he wondered, caused these frustrating results and what could he do to change them?

An engineer by training, he did time and motion studies. He ordered new machinery without helping employees learn how to use it properly. He imposed wage cuts and the union went out on strike. He did improve the product offerings. He admitted, "Mostly, however, I made mistakes."

He began to realize that "What the company needed was an atmosphere of teamwork and participation, whereas the atmosphere we had was adversarial and acrimonious." He read books, examined corporate profit-sharing plans, and announced that "I do not choose to own a company that has an adversarial relationship with its employees." Yet he felt he and his employees were in a bad marriage with no possibility of divorce.

He learned through the experience of working on the shop floor during the strike how difficult employee jobs were. His employees told him he was not listening so he took a course on how to listen. He joined his employees on courses on improving quality. With employees, he developed a corporate profit sharing plan with the possibility of big payouts. Employees and Frey gradually came to trust each other, work together, and care about each other and the plant.

Profits were slow to come but when they rose the effect was electric. In 1989, the bonus averaged 36 percent of the annual income of employees. Employees and Frey knew they had turned the corner, but they continue to debate issues and experiment with new ways. His employees want him to be less involved. He wants them to buy him out to insure the continuation of the company into the next generation. He and his employees have learned that a business requires ongoing examination of the present and experimenting for the future.

Leaders and researchers have different emphasis. Researchers have more precise ways of measuring the effects of their interventions. They often withdraw from the experiment in order to obtain unbiased findings that apply to many situations. Leaders like Frey are usually the source of the actions, highly involved and committed to making their impact effective in their specific situation. However, both researchers and leaders want powerful, elegant ideas that simplify complex reality and identify actions that make a difference.

Ideas to Learn from Experience

In a study on how managers learn, chief executive officers reported that practical experiences were critical for their success.[15] Rising to the challenge of turning around a weak operation, starting from scratch, moving from line to a staff position, and heading a task force compelled them to develop and learn. Through the fire of this real test, they drew upon their inner resources, gained insight, and experimented with new ways of coping. Twenty years later they vividly recalled learning valuable lessons, refining their abilities, and solidifying their self-confidence. Yet people have experiences, even challenging tests, but learn little from them. Many others learn without dramatic opportunities to prove themselves leaders. Every job has opportunities for leadership too often not taken.[16]

Ideas complement experience. Leaders must challenge outworn ideas such as competition between companies in the marketplace requires competition between employees in the work place. They need valid models for how to lead and build successful organizations; they must put their values and ideas to work in credible, effective ways.

Ideas are needed to analyze situations, determine what should be done, create plans, and inspire persistent action. With such a framework, people can use their experiences to get feedback on the usefulness of their decisions and actions. Feedback can confirm or disconfirm the ideas they used to guide their actions. Experience itself does not teach; using ideas to make use of opportunities and to reflect on experience does.

For example, you will later learn about cooperation theory as a way of understanding the nature of productive teamwork. That idea can spur you to experiment and reduce the gap between how people in your team do work together and how they could potentially do so. But you need a great deal of planning to apply the idea sensitively and appropriately. The procedures have to fit the people as well as the problem.

Learning should be ongoing and continuous. Reading and discussing need to be supplemented with trying to apply the idea to gain a fuller understanding about cooperative work. Then leaders are more knowledgeable and prepared to use it more skillfully. Leading and applying ideas like cooperation are two sides of the same coin.

TEAMS FOR LEARNING

Learning to lead through understanding and applying ideas and reflecting on experience to develop confidence and skill are themselves highly challenging. Becoming a leader is so complex and demanding that it calls out for teamwork. Research has documented that people understand ideas and their uses and learn from their experiences much more thoroughly through the rich exchange, discussion, and debate of joint learning.

Mentors and colleagues model important values and effective procedures and provide the emotional support to incorporate new ideas. Several people can use their various perspectives to create plans appropriate and effective for a given situation. There is a great deal of ingenuity needed to apply leadership ideas to fit the personalities and circumstances of situations. Individuals have blind spots to own up to shortcomings. Biases can exaggerate our successes and our failures. It is easier to accept negative feedback if other people help us use it to improve our abilities for the future.

Spirited teamwork is both the goal of leading and the means to learn to lead. To become a leader, managers debate ideas and explore issues with trusted colleagues; they gather the support to take courageous risks; they get feedback and suggestions from employees. The method of learning to lead reinforces the leader's message of spirited teamwork.

Cooperative Learning Research

David Johnson, Roger Johnson, and other researchers have documented the value of cooperative goals and interaction for learning.[17]

In a statistical review of over 500 studies, cooperative learning was found superior to people working competitively and independently across a wide range of learning objectives.[18] This finding applied to adults as well as to children.

Cooperative goals facilitate open discussion and other interactions that help people understand such abstract, powerful ideas as cooperation. They discuss and debate issues to clarify confusions; they critique, challenge, and probe into ideas; they connect present with past learning. In cooperative learning, people have been found to use higher level thinking, ask more questions, debate different positions, elaborate their views, and engage in problem solving, all of which helps them understand and evaluate the strengths and limitations of ideas.[19] People learn by having ideas explained and by explaining ideas. There is a richness to the exchange when people learn together that is not possible when they learn competitively or by themselves.

Personal Change

Learning together is especially useful for the personal and emotional demands of changing the way that we lead and work with other people. We tend to adhere rigidly to our ideas about relationships and to our beliefs about how successfully we work with others.[20] Many leaders have highly inflated, narcissistic views of their abilities and impact on employees.[21] New ideas and feedback challenge our habits, ask us to think about our relationships and ourselves in new ways, and open up possibilities of more effective behavior. Cooperative learning encourages the support, feedback, and problem solving needed for personal change.

Personal change requires applying ideas and feedback. Colleagues can provide the emotional and problem-solving support needed to translate psychological ideas into personal change. Through discussion with peers and employees, leaders are able to identify concrete new ways to lead that fit them and their situation. Studying and thinking alone are much less productive for developing an effective leadership style.

Forming Learning Teams

You can informally discuss the ideas described in future chapters with colleagues and friends to deepen your understanding and decide how to use them. A more thorough approach is to establish a learning team with the explicit mandate to help each other become more effective leaders.

In a learning team, two to six managers meet regularly to talk about their efforts to apply psychological ideas and build their competence and confidence in leading. They provide assistance, serve as a support group for sharing problems and letting off steam, allow more experienced leaders to serve as mentors and assistants, and foster shared camaraderie and success. Learning teams are safe places where members like to be, experience support, caring and laughter, and reinforce their determination to become effective leaders.

Managers use their learning teams to share information, celebrate successes, and solve problems. Together they plan, design, and evaluate their efforts at developing teamwork. They visit each other's offices and teams and provide feedback.

The teams foster professional discussions in which managers talk directly and honestly about the challenges, frustrations, and opportunities of leadership. They talk in increasingly concrete and precise terms about the nature of leadership and how it can be achieved. They use their shared, precise language to describe leadership and integrate it with other ideas and approaches. Through discussing, explaining and teaching, they deepen their understanding and skills in leadership and teamwork.

Managers together plan programs and activities to begin and strengthen their leadership and teams. They decide how to create shared vision and programs to improve communication and conflict management. They share the burden and excitement, and learn from others' experiences. As they put psychological ideas in place, they clarify their understanding of teamwork and get the encouragement needed to experiment with plans that are appropriate for their people and situation. Discussions about the effectiveness of previous attempts suggest how they can modify their plans for future action.

Managers observe and give each other feedback. Most managers are unsure of their impact on employees, and believe that employees are reluctant to be direct and honest. Managers can visit each other's teams and give an outside, informed perspective on group dynamics and leadership. Reciprocal observation and feedback emphasize that everyone is helping each other learn. Managers need to be respectful and, when pointing out shortcomings and problems, recognize that everyone has strengths and weaknesses and good and bad days.

THE LEARNING LEADER

Traditionally, leaders were expected to project themselves as competent and in charge. They communicated that they are strong, decisive people who can make tough choices and take the heat. They get things done.

These images are increasingly dysfunctional because organizations must adapt and continually innovate. It was not enough that Arden Sims and Ralph Strayer wanted to get the job done; they needed people throughout the organization to improve quality and reduce costs effectively. Moreover, the advantages of developing new products, improving marketing, and using technology to reduce costs are increasingly fragile and short-lived, for competitors soon develop new products and implement new technologies. What is needed is an organization where people are continually striving to improve quality and meet the demands of stakeholders.[22]

Continuous improvement is more than a slogan: it is necessary for organizational survival and success. For organizations to learn and remain viable requires full, committed effort throughout the work force. Leaders must work with people so that they *want* to do the things that must be done.[23]

Leaders model effective judgment and persistent effort to inspire employees. But leaders must also model open-minded learning. Leaders build their credibility, not on demonstrating their superior power and competence, but on their exploring emerging ideas, experimenting with new ways of behaving, and working for ongoing improvement in themselves, in their employees, and in their organizations.

Learning to use psychology doubly reinforces leadership. Leaders become more sensitive and skillful in working with other people. Simultaneously, they demonstrate their credibility and model the way for employees to develop themselves.

Learning binds leaders and employees together. To lead today is to learn and grow. The pertinent issue is not whether leaders are made or born, but how leaders can continually develop themselves as they ask others to learn and extend themselves.

Employees too must learn. The managers and workers at Johnsonville did not change from pawns of Strayer's plans to empowered, self-managing people overnight. Strayer had to coach his managers to become facilitators who in turned coached others to solve problems and learn.

Learning is a common journey with no end destination. Strayer reflected, "As I gained one insight and mastered one situation, another situation arose that required new insight and more learning. As I approached one goal, a new, more important, but more distant goal always began to take shape."

Applying psychology, like leadership, is something too complex and precious for one person to do alone. Leadership is a "we" thing that requires both leader and employee. So too does using psychology. You will be much more effective if you involve your employees, colleagues, and friends in helping you develop your psychology skills and strengthen your leadership competence. Learning unites leaders and followers in a common journey of self-discovery and team development.

PART TWO

FORGING A
COMMON DIRECTION

We may have come over on different ships, but we're all in the same
boat now.

Whitney Young, Jr.

Employees, as well as leaders, must want to do what needs to be done if
organizations are going to meet today's challenges. Fortunately, it is possible to develop organizations that deserve such loyalty, but these high
involvement organizations require creative leadership. Chapter 3 shows
that the core of effective leadership is developing relationships that are
personally enhancing and organizationally productive. Leaders can find
building these relationships and the striving to be successful leaders
personally rewarding.

Chapter 4 describes how employees can meet needs to achieve, to
be part of a larger effort, and to have an impact as they work with others to accomplish organizational goals. Through constructive relationships, they develop self-confidence, build social support, and accomplish
tasks they could not do alone. Chapter 5 details how a shared vision can
bring individuals with diverse styles, perspectives, and goals together so
that they are convinced that together they can realize the potential
value of work in organizations, serve their customers, and become more
secure in their jobs and themselves.

3 BECOMING COMMITTED TO LEADING

You can't pick cherries with your back to the tree.

J. Pierpont Morgan

For nearly three decades, Mary Tjosvold has been fully involved in becoming a leader. She has changed a great deal in this journey, but she also had returned to re-occurring themes and basic lessons.

Teaching in suburban Chicago and then inner city Minneapolis, she learned that to be successful required her to motivate and provide structure so that the students learned. It was not enough for her to work hard and do; she had to involve the students. Junior high students, whether from rich or struggling families, are preoccupied with questions of who they are and whether they are accepted. She had to be a cheerleader and friend as well as a guide.

Confronted with the reality of discrimination against women in the workplace and her Native American students, Mary became an activist for educational change. She developed new math curriculum, organized protests of the continued gender, racial, and other biases in education, and searched for alternative education. Here too she had to involve and include, not just other activists but also white male administrators and board members who had the power to make real changes. From her experience and Dean Tjosvold's dissertation, she learned that, if she was to achieve change, she could not affront the social face of people in power by insults and challenges to their appearance of competence. People who fear that they may lose face by appearing weak and ineffective become intransigent and counterattack.

41

Realizing that she did not fit nicely into an established school, she returned to graduate school for a doctorate in educational administration. She took up our mother's vision of using our grandmother's land to build residential services for elderly and handicapped persons where they could flourish and learn. Our grandmother was a nurse for whom taking care of people was a way of life. During the Depression, no hungry person was ever turned away, even when the neighbors protested. In her seventies, she nursed people in their eighties.

To realize our mother's vision took a great deal of psychological determination and flexibility: endless meetings with government officials, bank and mortgage lenders, the pursuit of many leads only a few of which moved the project forward. She and our mother had to negotiate and modify to gain a certificate of need, government approval, and funding. They invested years of work without an assurance that anything would happen. Their entrepreneurial commitment required a belief in themselves and others, risk-taking, and a long-term perspective.

After the convalescent center for elderly and a residence for adults who are developmentally disabled were built came apartments for families, a home for children who are developmentally disabled, apartments for elderly, group homes for adults who are developmentally disabled, and homes for those stricken with Alzheimer's disease. Mary was a professional who had to learn how to manage. As the company expanded, she confronted the challenge to learn to be a leader.

As entrepreneurial developer, she had become used to doing many tasks herself to keep the project going. It was natural to be highly involved in the all aspects of the business and providing services to the clients. Mary spent a great deal of time with clients because she found the work highly rewarding and wanted to model the way for employees. But she was frustrated with the many demands, too. Despite her best efforts, she could not be everywhere at once and do it all.

Especially as the businesses grew and expanded geographically, it was clear that she could not be at the center or driving force of all important activities. There were too many good ideas and projects for her to drive all of them. Everyone, she realized, had to be involved to ensure quality and be a client-centered organization. She would have to develop the organization.

She would have a more effective impact providing the corporate culture, education, and aids that would help others serve clients and conduct business. Her work was to clarify the vision, set parameters, and get people involved in strategic planning. She led the development of written statements of the organization's vision, missions, values, goals, and code of ethics. She invested a great deal in moving from a complex hierarchical structure to an enhancing culture and a team-based structure.

Becoming a leader entails many ups and downs, steps forward, sideways, and backwards. A recurring theme for Mary is the need to keep learning. Owning and operating a business require deep understanding of the core activities, knowledge about business, psychological sensitivity with people, and the capacity to develop an organization. These are not lessons learned at one time, but learned continuously. She has learned much through reflecting on her successes and mistakes, discussions with entrepreneurial and managerial friends, and a three-year Harvard Business School program for owners and presidents of small business. Leaders also help employees learn for they too must keep continually updating their abilities. Leading, learning, and teaching all go together.

Another recurring lesson for Mary can be simply put: leaders can only be successful with others. You cannot be an effective teacher, activist, entrepreneur, or leader by yourself. *Leaders work with and through others.* She has learned in the words of Virginia Woolf, "One of the signs of passing youth is the birth of a sense of fellowship with other human beings as we take our place among them." Remembering your interdependence and strengthening the abilities to accomplish things together are not simple but are part of the rich, complex gratifications of becoming a leader.

ACCEPTING THE CHALLENGE TO BECOME A LEADER

To be a leader requires the heart as well as the head. Leaders need to be passionate and persistent; simply going through the motions won't do nor will just working hard. Followers need leaders that they can trust to be committed, honest, and determined. Leading is so demanding that leaders must work persistently if they are going to make a difference. Leading is much more than a job to do.

Leading is not for everyone. Even those who choose to be a leader need to base their commitment on a realistic assessment of what life is like for leaders and what they must do to be successful. Many a would-be leader has been misled by stereotypes of leadership, leaving both them and their followers frustrated and disillusioned. Accepting the challenge to lead should be a rational conviction, not a whimsical hope or desire for more status and money.

Leaders want the challenge to fit them. To the extent they meet their needs and promote their values, they will be more motivated, intense, and fulfilled. Before you commit yourself to leading, you should know about the demands on managers and how leading can be personally rewarding so that you can determine whether you are the kind of person who will find leadership fulfilling.

Yet it is not simply finding a fit between your personality and the leader's role. Leading offers potentials for people to find new activities and responsibilities satisfying. Leaders develop as people so that they become more in touch with needs to impact and assist others and enhance their values of being an important part of a team that serves customers well.

Researchers have detailed the daily activities of what it is like to manage, have defined and described the leader's role, and identified the needs and goals that leaders can achieve. You can use this knowledge to decide whether you want to take the path toward leadership and how you can grow into and grow from leading.

THE DAY-TO-DAY OF MANAGING

The traditional portrait of managers and executives is that they are bosses who oversee and take the long-term view, grapple with the complexities of problems, and make decisions. They are engaged in dispassionate analysis, thoughtful discussions, and future forecasts. Leaders use their superior authority and power to implement their decisions and keep the organization on a prosperous path. If need be, they issue commands and demand compliance but prefer that employees willingly accept their requests and at times ask employees for suggestions. It is lonely at the top, but leaders have the rich rewards of being in charge and in control and making more money.

These traditional views have some truth behind them but are a long way from the reality of the daily life of most leaders. Forty years of studies observing how supervisors, managers, and executives actually spend their time portray leaders as very much enmeshed in the intensely interpersonal, verbal world of organizations.[1] Managers oversee, encourage, plead, and cajole employees to complete and coordinate tasks. They assign jobs, give pep talks, enforce deadlines, knock down barriers, discuss problems, and provide assistance. They continually interact and work with employees, colleagues, superiors, suppliers, and customers. Managing is a psychologically rich and demanding profession.

Studies show that supervisors interact with 25 to 50 people a day.[2] Managers typically have fewer interactions but work with more people outside the organization. Managers communicate orally, usually face to face, about 75 percent of their office time. They may be alone for one-third of the day, but usually for less than half an hour at a time. Although they are continually talking, listening, and exchanging information, they give few orders and make few decisions.[3]

The life of the executive is not the common picture of serenity in an oak panelled office. Executives dash about, doing many things at once. Business is meetings, meetings, and more meetings. Studies have documented that executives spend a lot of time in meetings, many of them spontaneous. One study found that executives had four scheduled meetings and four unscheduled meetings a day.[4]

Despite loud complaints about meetings and interruptions, managers seem to like their interpersonal world. They overestimate their time alone and underestimate their time with others.[5] They find interactions stimulating, being alone boring. When not being interrupted, many managers find people to interrupt rather than experience the feelings of being isolated and alone in their office. They find the excitement of give-and-take more enjoyable and productive than the quiet, slow-pace of independent deliberation. A few years ago, an MBA student got approval of the top executives to participate in his study, but they wanted him to ask the questions face-to-face even though completing the written questionnaire would have been much quicker.

Past research on managerial work life are probably conservative estimates of the life of most managers today. Each year the world of managers is becoming ever more interpersonal, fragmented, and demanding. To help their organizations respond to the competitive marketplace, high customer expectations for quality and service, government regulations, and employee pressures for more access and openness, managers are working long, intense days. They are working with employees to find new ways to reduce costs and improve quality. As they ask employees to give more to the organization and its customers, many managers feel obligated to attend more to the needs of employees.

Studies of managerial life, like much useful research, help us face reality obscured by outworn images. Organizations are not machines built and kept going by a few leaders on top making decisions and pulling strings. Rather organizations are filled with interactions, of people debating positions, digging into issues, coping with crises, and experimenting with possible solutions.

Managers are not architects independent and above the daily activities of their organizations, but are builders and workers within them. They are at the center of their group, not so much on top looking down. They are important hubs as they work with and through other people. Managers are at the heart of the continual give-and-take we call an organization.

These studies have also been thought to mean that leaders avoid in-depth analysis and thoughtful planning. Undoubtedly in many crisis-prone or complacent organizations, there is little planning for the long-term. But because managers are not alone for extended periods does not mean they do not plan. Leaders must plan for the future, but they must do so with other people.

Suggested Activity

Keep a diary of your work life. (See page 47.) Make a daily diary sheet of the hours you work in one column, the issues you deal with in a second, and the people you are working with in a third column. At the end of the week, you should have a good view of what you are working on and with whom.

Count the number of scheduled and unscheduled meetings. Total the amount of time you spend alone and with others. Are you surprised by your findings? Would you characterize your work as independent or interpersonal? as planned or unplanned? fragmented or not? Do you work most on developing the organization and its systems, getting tasks done, or managing crises?

Many managers are so task oriented that they do not work on the organization, its relationships, and systems. Are you one of these managers?

A Diary of Your Work Life

Time	Issues	People Involved
7:00 AM		
8:00		
9:00		
10:00		
11:00		
12:00 PM		
1:00		
2:00		
3:00		
4:00		
5:00		
6:00		
7:00		

Reflections:

CONFRONTING LEADERSHIP

Leaders do not just get through the day but are committed to success. They have to be more than managers who involve themselves in ongoing daily dialogues of the organization and keep the organization running by attending meetings, fixing deadlines, and overseeing tasks. They do not just handle the status quo, but create a new future.

Though not in complete control of their own destiny much less the entire organization, leaders develop a team that anticipates changes and believes that it can adapt and improve its abilities. They re-invent their organizations and find new ways for people to work together necessary for success today. They take us on a journey where we have not gone before.[6]

This section examines definitions of leadership, leadership traits, and employee views of leaders to focus on what makes a manager a leader. What do leaders do that makes them effective and have an enduring impact?

Defining Leadership

Leadership has traditionally been seen in terms of influence and moving a group toward its goals. Roger Stogdill, a pioneer in leadership research, defined leadership as "the process of influencing the activities of an organized group in its effort toward goal setting and goal achievement."[7] Leadership involves actions that engage group members to direct and coordinate their work.

Leaders are especially potent and constructive. They have more power and have more influence than group members. Leaders use power and persuasion to have an impact on group success.

In his comprehensive review and analysis of leadership, Bernard Bass defines leadership as interaction between two or more group members that structures or restructures the situation and alters the perceptions and expectations of members.[8] Leaders are agents of change. They modify the motivation and competence of group members so that the group is more able to reach future goals.

Leader Traits: Research Findings

The often asked question is: What is it about leaders that gives them this constructive power to strengthen employees and make their groups more effective? How do they differ as people from those managers without such a constructive impact? What makes them different from followers? These straightforward questions have not resulted in many straightforward answers.

Studies indicate that leaders tend to have a wide range of desirable characteristics.[9] They are intelligent, self-confident with strong sense of themselves, hardy, persistent, controlled, verbal, diplomatic, and popular. They are conscientious and seek responsibility, are venturesome in problem solving, exercise initiative in social situations, accept responsibility, pursue goals vigorously and persistently, tolerate frustrations, and know how to get things done.

But none of these traits themselves seems to be particularly vital. Even when many measures are combined in sophisticated assessment center techniques, characteristics only account for less than 20 percent of the variance in promotion rates.[10] Personal characteristics affect who becomes an effective leader but are far from sufficient. People with "leadership" traits are leaders in some situations, but not in others. Less successful managers and followers often also have these traits.

The definition of effective leadership as a constructive impact so that a group can be more successful in the future suggests that critical leadership traits are interpersonal. It is not so much that leaders are intelligent or even that they are hardy, but that they can influence groups to work more persistently and effectively. Indeed, managers can use their intelligence to appear arrogant and undermine motivation and can use their persistence to get in the way of group members' doing their tasks.

People who were able to perceive the needs and goals of group members and adjust their behavior accordingly tended to be leaders in various settings.[11] Leaders mature from a concern for personal goals and agendas to a commitment to common values and obligations for respect, quality, and fairness. Leadership involves influencing and relationships; success requires interpersonal competence.

Leader Characteristics: Employee Views

Leaders are people of action; they use their abilities to have a constructive impact. It is not just their abilities and traits that make them a leader but how these are demonstrated and conveyed to employees. Followers are not passive recipients but continually assess and react to their leaders.

Researchers Jim Kouzes and Barry Posner asked constituents to identify the characteristics of their effective leaders.[12] They began by asking 1,500 managers what values, traits, and characteristics they most look for and admire in their superiors. Eight hundred senior public sector administrators gave similar ratings. Fifteen thousand managers have responded to a survey based on the results from these first studies.

The characteristics rated by over half of these managers were honesty, forward looking, inspiring, and competence. Honesty is a basic condition for leadership, with over 80 percent of the managers citing it. People want to be told the truth if they are going to follow a leader. Faith in a leader is built upon the leader's ability to face reality and openly discuss the situation and prospects. Leaders and followers should venture together with their eyes open.

Honesty is a foundation for credibility and trustworthiness. Leaders talk about what they want to do and then do it. They express their ideas, hopes and fears, and act consistently with their intentions. Ethical standards are a fundamental basis of leadership.

Managers also thought their leaders should be forward looking. The problems of the past and the challenges of the present must be faced, but leaders also envisage how the team and organization can change to be more effective in the future. Organizations that try to stand pat quickly become obsolete and threatened. Leaders are not standing in place and keeping things moving, but are pointing to the future.

Over half the managers surveyed also thought leaders must be inspiring. More than knowing where they are going, leaders, through their commitment and enthusiasm, convince people that this direction is valuable, perhaps even noble. Employees are looking for meaning and purpose. If their leader does not believe, why should they?

Leaders should be competent; followers want to believe that their leaders know what they are doing. People do not want to invest themselves in fruitless activities and directions. They want a journey that they can move toward the destination and leaders who can help them get there.

Leaders use their abilities and character to have a constructive impact so that their team and organization is more effective for the future. Undoubtedly being resourceful, committed, and hardy are useful but these abilities have to be put to work for leaders and their followers must act and achieve. For leadership, like beauty, is in the eye of the beholder. The next section argues that it is the relationship between leader and followers, more directly than the leader's characteristics or strategies, that result in a constructive impact.

LEADERSHIP AS RELATIONSHIP

The straightforward question of the actions leaders use to empower employees, like the question of leader abilities, has resulted in rather general findings.[13] Often leaders structure an effective division of work, encourage employees to participate in making decisions, and use problem solving to negotiate conflict, but these and other strategies have not been found critical. Styles that characterize leaders' actions in broad terms do not consistently predict effective outcomes.[14] Rather leaders seem adaptable and use a wide range of strategies appropriate for people and fitting for the situation. But documenting when specific leadership actions lead to success is difficult.[15]

What has been found essential is the nature of the relationship between leader and follower.[16] Through productive, cooperative relationships leaders influence employees and have a constructive impact.[17] When employees trust their leaders are on their side and working for their interests as well as their own, they are open to being influenced and feel more empowered and motivated.

In productive relationships, followers believe that their leaders are honest, competent, forward-looking and inspiring. When employees suspect that their leaders are seeking selfish gain at their expense, they are on guard and demoralized. They doubt that their leaders are truly honest, view their competence and vision critically, and look for opportunities elsewhere rather than be inspired.

Leaders need responsive, committed partners. One who walks steadfastly down the road alone is not a leader. Leadership is done by leaders and followers together. The reasons for success or failure must be found in their relationships, in how they have worked together to accomplish their purposes.

Leadership involves the leader empowering and assisting employees as they empower her. But leadership also involves relationships among employees. How they relate to each other very much affects their willingness to be led and their effectiveness. Key to successful leadership is to structure and develop relationships among followers so that they empower each other. Leadership today is too complex and challenging to be left to one person; it is only successful when done together.

Leaders are the nurturers and stewards of an organization's relationships. They are the builders of the productive relationships necessary to a flexible, vibrant organization that takes advantage of change. Rather than act as managers of the status quo, they lead others to feel directed, united and empowered to accomplish their common vision.[18]

Managers have traditionally emphasized getting the job done, developing new products, improving marketing, and reducing costs. But the advantages of new products and cost reduction are increasingly fragile and short-lived. Soon competitors develop new products, create technologies to reduce costs and improve quality, and enter profitable markets.

Quality team relationships are a more enduring competitive advantage. They are an organization's lifeblood through which information flows, communication occurs, and problems are identified and solved. Spirited teamwork develops new products, reduces costs, improves quality, finds new customers, values diversity, and sets ethical standards. Organizations learn and adapt when individuals, groups, and divisions work together effectively. Leaders realize that by strengthening relationships they have a continuing impact.

Yet the leadership-as-relationship-building idea does not imply that leading is a simple quick-fix. Forming productive work relationships

---

Moving from Engineer to Leader

An engineer put his fundamental leadership lesson this way:[19]

"To succeed as a manager, I had to abandon the nitty-gritty details of engineering. I gradually realized that you can be competent without trying to know more than your people about what they do.

"I also learned that when managing your peers and friends, you have to consider their feelings. You have to realize you can't make everybody happy, and you can't always win. At least some of them will believe they should really be in your position. But most people do want leadership, and they will respond to someone who knows where he's going. I learned an important lesson then: that leadership contributes just as much as engineering to the success of an organization."

under the stresses and pressures of contemporary organizations is not a one or two step affair. Developing the leader relationship is an ongoing journey that requires much from both leader and followers. But it pays off in mutual respect and trust, self-confidence and achievement.

Developing the relationship between leader and follower is, as with other relationships, both simple and complex. It is simple in that it rests on a belief that the leader and follower are on the same side, that they can be successful together, their goals are cooperative. They must also be able to discuss their differences and negotiate agreements. Developing the leader relationship is complex because cooperative goals must be continually reinforced by a common vision, rewards, tasks, attitudes, and values, and because negotiation requires self-awareness, empathy, creativity, and compromise. Leader relationships must also be developed under the pressures for time and productivity of contemporary organizational life.

FINDING VALUE IN LEADING

Leaders are at the center of the give-and-take of organizations and live within an intensely interpersonal world. To be successful, they must use their abilities to establish credibility and develop productive, cooperative relationships. Then they can have a long-term constructive impact on employee motivation and competence.

But before taking up leadership, people legitimately want to know what leading would do for them. When they find leadership rewarding and meaningful, they can be more committed and effective leaders. Leaders can fulfilled important basic human needs as well as take satisfaction from contributing and being part of a joint effort.

Vital Human Needs

Leaders and employees can find organizational work very fulfilling, over and above any material benefit, and help them meet the basic aspiration of having a constructive impact on people and developing their talents.[20] Leadership is particularly valuable for satisfying the basic needs for power, that is, to have an impact and influence other people.[21] The speeches of successful Presidents Franklin D. Roosevelt and John F. Kennedy have many images and references to having an impact.

The Power Speeches of FDR and JFK

U.S. Presidents Franklin D. Roosevelt and John F. Kennedy had a profound impact on generations of Americans. Through their speeches and actions, they helped Americans believe that they could make a difference, often quoted lines from some of their speeches include:

Franklin D. Roosevelt

- Let me assert my firm belief that the only thing we have to fear is fear itself.
- The only limit to our realization of tomorrow will be our doubts of today.
- Happiness lies in the job of achievement and the thrill of creative effort.
- These unhappy times call for the building of plans . . . that build from the bottom up not from the top down, that put their faith once more in the forgotten man at the bottom of the economic pyramid.
- We, and all others who believe in freedom as deeply as we do, would rather die on our feet than live on our knees.
- Remember, remember always, that all of us, and you and I especially, are descended from immigrants and revolutionists.
- We have always held to the hope, the belief, the conviction that there is a better life, a better world, beyond the horizon.
- If civilization is to survive, we must cultivate the science of human relationships—the ability of all people, of all kinds, to live together, in the same world at peace.

John F. Kennedy

- For of those to whom much is given, much is required.
- Let us never negotiate out of fear but let us never fear to negotiate.
- For without belittling the courage with which men have died, we should not forget those acts of courage with which men have lived.
- The energy, the faith, the devotion which we bring to this endeavor will light our country and all who serve it, and the glow from that fire can truly light the world.
- Those who make peaceful revolution impossible will make violent revolution inevitable.
- And so, my fellow Americans, ask not what your country can do for you, ask what you can do for your country.

In addition, the demands and constraints of being an effective leader channel power needs constructively. Successful leaders do not express their power needs willy-nilly but are inhibited and self-controlled. Successful leaders meet their power needs by the sensitive, skillful influence of others to get things done.

Power needs, unchecked by the commitment to work cooperatively with employees, frustrate leadership. High power managers focused only on themselves have been found to use aggressive dominance and anger to exert their superiority and control. These ways of expressing power needs are destructive for the manager, employees, and organization.

Joint Success

Images of leaders gaining respect from dominating and standing over and above others are increasingly obstructive, but they continue to be prevalent. In the 1980s, employees wanted respect and honesty even more than financial gain and security, but thought they got less.[22] In opinion polls, only a minority of Americans consider corporate executives honest.[23] With strong complaints that their bosses often avoid confronting problems or act as tyrants, employees want leaders to be credible and trustworthy.[24]

Although leading cannot be egocentric, leading need not, indeed, should not, be a selfless act of altruism. People have to find value in leading if they are to work hard enough to overcome obstacles and develop themselves as leaders. As we have seen, leading offers the potential to

---

Do You Want to Lead?

Daily Life	Needs, Aspirations to Be Effective
Intensely interpersonal	Power needs
Fragmented	Have positive impact
Plan together	Joint success
Center of action	Establish relationships
Handle crises	Future oriented

meet vital human power needs, but these must be expressed in mature, social ways.

What is critical is that leaders focus on mutual benefit and mutual gain. Not pretending to be selfless, they search for how their needs and goals overlap with followers. They seek and emphasize cooperative goals and tasks where by working to be successful themselves they help followers also succeed. If the leader swims, followers swim; if the leader sinks, the followers sink. They are in this together.

Leaders must learn how they and followers benefit from joint success. Then people can meet their power needs by influencing and coordinating people so that together the team is successful. Leaders achieve by empowering followers to meet challenging tasks that they or any individual could not do alone. They feel respected as people by developing a highly productive team.

Leaders feel part of something larger and more significant than themselves. They see their organization as a whole and work for mutual success. Yet they feel they are a special, vital part of this joint enterprise. Rather than submerge their individuality, they see how to meet their needs and express and develop themselves through teamwork.

Leadership is often equated with control. Leaders use their superior authority and power to tell and direct employees. However, the attempt at unilateral control often results in the lack of control as employees resent and resist.[25] Effective leaders are open to employee ideas and suggestions so that employees are open to theirs. Together leaders and employees dig into issues and create solutions worthy of their commitment. Reuben Mark, CEO of Colgate-Palmolive, commented on power, "The more you have, the less you should use. You consolidate and build your power by empowering others."

BECOMING A LEADER

The major question remains: Do you want to be a leader? The evidence reviewed in this chapter indicates that you are suited and prepared to lead if you can flourish in the highly interpersonal, verbal world of leading. Leaders are able to find fulfillment through having a constructive impact on their team. They work hard to influence and develop relationships that empower employees to achieve and succeed. However, trying to dominate and lord over others, seeking to achieve through their own efforts, and trying to earn respect by smoothing over conflicts are incompatible with successful leadership. Leading is not just doing your own thing, controlling others, or simply getting along.

Yet, the issue is not the kind of person you are now. The critical issue is the kind of person you want to become. Leaders take teams on a journey of continuous improvement, but leaders are also on a journey of ongoing personal and professional development. No one is simply born knowing how to lead.

By committing yourself to becoming a leader, you are committing yourself to be more aware of how you are interdependent with other people and to see yourself as a part of a larger effort. You will need to learn to find fulfillment in working with others to succeed. You will develop the often demanding skills and values of managing conflict and working together productively.

Becoming a leader has great potential for self-development and enhancement. But it is not easy. Future chapters outline major approaches and competencies you will want to develop. You will need to do more than read these chapters. You will have to be honest with yourself and consider changing some of your basic orientations. You will have to take risks and experiment to find approaches and a style that fit you and your team.

You should not expect to transform yourself immediately into the leader you want to be. Perfectionistic, quick-fix expectations create unrealistic pressure and very much get in the way of leader development. But you can commit yourself to learning, not just over the next few weeks, but over months and years.

4 BUILDING EMPLOYEE COMMITMENT

> Large-scale success today is spelled "Teamwork." The successful
> teamworker doesn't wear a chip on his shoulder; he is not con-
> stantly on the alert least his "dignity" be insulted . . . and the
> business of each and all is to gear [the organization] up effi-
> ciently, to leave nothing undone to bring about the fullest and
> best results. And if the whole prospers, he, as an active, effec-
> tive, progressive part of it, will prosper with it.
>
> B. C. Forbes

"You can't do it alone," was Don Bennett's immediate answer.[1] Don, a
successful Seattle businessman, had been asked what his most important lesson from his five-day climb up the 14,410 foot Mount Rainer on
one leg and two crutches.

Don's daughter was with him for the five-hour trek across a particularly difficult ice field. With each new hop, she told him, "You can do
it, Dad. You're the best dad in the world. You can do it, Dad." No way
was Don going to quit his climb to the top with his daughter's love and
encouragement in his ear.

Successful teams and organizations have leaders and employees
pulling for each other. When they cheer each other on, they are amazed
at the obstacles they can overcome and the extraordinary things they can
accomplish. Arden Sims and Ralph Strayer enlisted employees' help
and earned their commitment to lead the transformations of Globe and
Johnsonville. The mountaineer Will Unsoeld advised mountain climbers,
"Take care of each other. Share your energies with the group. No one
must feel above, cut off, for that is when you do not make it."

59

Leaders realize that followers must be motivated and determined. Employees cannot just go through the motions but, like leaders, must be committed. To deliver value to customers and exploit state of the art technology requires that employees work diligently without costly, cumbersome supervision. Today's employees want challenge and purpose before they will commit to their organization.

This chapter shows how working in organizations is potentially very rich, rewarding, and motivating. Employees can feel fulfilled by superior achievement, see themselves as part of a larger effort, feel supported, and strengthen their self-esteem. However, to realize this potential, employees must develop constructive work relationships in which they know and value each other as individuals.

THE HIGH-COMMITMENT ORGANIZATION

An old belief is that most work in organizations is dull and dehumanizing. Bureaucracy suppresses individual creativity for it requires the conformity of the "organization man" to be productive. There is a tradeoff between efficiency and people; the requirements of organizations are incompatible with the needs of people; organizational effectiveness works against self-actualization. Organizations were thought to need rigid conformity and clockwork harmony; people were thought to need self-expression and leisure.

Today's organizations require the full involvement of all employees. To improve products and services, people must work to generate new ideas, even though any payoff in terms of recognition or rewards may be in the future. If focused only on their own jobs, individuals neglect to do the extra tasks organizations require.[2]

Organizations need employees to be "good citizens" who do more than what is prescribed in job descriptions and stipulated in union contracts.[3] Staying late to deal with a crisis, assisting an overloaded colleague, and listening to a distressed employee all contribute to a successful organization. Employees must care about the company and each other.[4]

The reality is, in the words of Konosuke Matsushita, Executive Director, Matsushita Electric, that "the core of management is precisely the act of mobilizing and pulling together the intellectual resources of all employees . . . only by drawing on the combined brainpower of all its employees can a firm face up to the turbulence and constraints of today's environment." The traditional thrust of "getting ideas out of the heads of the bosses into the hands of labor" is no longer viable.

Employees, surveys suggest, want to be committed. Although they still value traditional economic benefits of job security, opportunities to make as much money as they can, and good retirement programs, they want more: Work must be intrinsically meaningful. In one survey, 88 percent of U.S. employees said it was personally important to them to "work hard and to do their best on the job." In another survey, the majority of respondents agreed with the statement, "I have an inner need to do the very best job I can, regardless of pay." Only one out of four thought a job was an economic necessity or simply an economic transaction.[5] Employees want their companies to be successful, to give them well-paying jobs, and their work to be meaningful and rewarding.

Understanding the imperative for internal commitment is much easier than creating a high-commitment organization.[6] The traditional way to build loyalty by offering job security and regular promotions is becoming impractical for more and more companies.

Leaders are experimenting with new ways of working that are good for people as well as for productivity and innovation. Arden Sims and Ralph Strayer are exposing the myths about people and organizations that get in the way of this experimenting. Rather than emulate machines, organizations require individual diversity and spirited teamwork. People meet fundamental psychological achievement and social needs by working together to get things done. But to realize this potential requires psychologically savvy management so that employees believe that they will feel fulfilled through their work.

FINDING VALUE IN ORGANIZATIONAL WORK

In organizations like Johnsonville Foods in 1980, employees shifted along, waiting until the end of the day to come alive. A decade later, Johnsonville employees find their work fulfilling and meaningful and believe they are getting a fair return for their work. They have the more-for-more solution: they give more to their jobs and they get more. This change did not come easily, but it was essential to the continued well-being of the company.

Employees who see see how their personal needs and values can be met on the job find value in work. Money is not the only significant motivator, for employees bring very strong needs to feel accepted, to be

Leadership Motive Profile

It is tempting to conclude that effective leaders are high on achievement, affiliation, and power motives. They develop relationships so that they can have an impact so that their group achieves. However, results indicated that many effective leaders are high on power, but low on achievement and affiliation.[7]

People with high achievement needs are not necessarily effective leaders. Remember they want to do things better themselves. In a study at AT&T, individuals highly motivated by the need for achievement were promoted as long as the basis was for their own individual work and effort, not for empowering others.[8] They progressed rapidly but got stuck at AT&T's management three level. Working hard and successfully to do things by oneself and for oneself is insufficient to be promoted into managerial positions responsible for motivating and assisting others.

Having strong affiliation needs can also interfere with leading. Affiliated-oriented people are not so much interested in establishing productive, give-and-take relationships as in maintaining harmony and the relationship at any price. They help individuals achieve their personal agendas even at the expense of the team and make exceptions others see as unfair. Rather than use conflicts to solve problems and urge people to become more effective, they want to get along and not cause upsetting waves.

High power needs, on the other hand, predict success as a manager, especially when combined with low affiliation needs and the ability to channel and control power needs. Managers with high power needs did not plateau early at AT&T but continued to be promoted into management level four and beyond. These managers are interested in influencing other people; they do not try to do it all themselves or hide in their offices. Like Arden Smith at Globe, they are not overly concerned about being liked; they are able to confront conflict and make tough decisions and insist on the same high standards for everyone. At the same time, they control how they express their power needs and channel them into mutual goal accomplishment.

High power needs managers find leading personally valuable and help employees become committed. They relish the give-and-take of managerial life and enjoy the self-control that working in organizations demands. They also want employees to develop self-discipline and at the same time show real caring for their employees.

McClelland, David Winter, and their associates used images in their speeches to measure the achievement, power, and affiliation needs of twentieth-century U.S. presidents.[9] The three presidents whose

(Continued)

(Continued)
achievement scores were higher than power or affiliation needs and whose power needs were not greater than affiliation were Herbert Hoover, Richard Nixon, and Jimmy Carter, all of whom ran into difficulties getting things done. Like other high achievement people, they worked hard and came to good solutions, but were less effective in managing others and getting their good ideas implemented. In Nixon's case, he was prepared to work dishonestly to get his ideas implemented.

President Gerald Ford had the highest affiliation score of any president, but his power and achievement scores were below average. Like other affiliation persons, he was sensitive to the needs of others. He worked hard to try to put the country back together again after the Vietnam War and Watergate. In a defining moment of his presidency, he announced that "The man has suffered enough," and pardoned Richard Nixon. Although Nixon had suffered, many Americans thought that many who had worked for Nixon had also suffered but still went to prison for similar activities. Ford had made an exception to the rule in response to the particular needs of an individual. He lost the next election in part because people suspected his motives and thought the pardoned obstructed justice and the public's right to know the scandals of the Nixon presidency.

Effective leaders are often high on power, but not on achievement and affiliation. Yet, it is not just having these needs that makes one a successful leader. As with employees, leaders must find constructive ways of meeting their needs.

a part of something larger, to feel competent, and to achieve goals. To the extent that employees recognize their needs, understand how their working with the leader can meet them, and are confident that together they can be successful, they are committed and productive.

Leaders create organizations where people see how their personal interests and aspirations can be met through their organizational work. These organizations develop self-esteem and social support, vital to psychological health and well-being. Fortunately, these personally enhancing organizations also promote productivity.

Need Fulfillment

For forty years, David McClelland has persistently and creatively investigated how needs are developed and expressed.[10] He has found three types of motives particularly useful for understanding human behavior: achievement, affiliation, and power.

The need for achievement is the desire to do well compared to standards of excellence. People with high achievement needs want to do things better, not because they will be rewarded or praised, but because of the internal satisfaction of becoming more effective and efficient. They like the feeling of getting a job done. They state that their desire is to do well and use extraordinary efforts to win a contest, fix a machine, invent something, or achieve other goals. They are especially motivated by challenging, yet doable tasks where they can demonstrate their ability.[11] Simple tasks are less motivating because doing them well is easy; very difficult tasks are less motivating because of the high chances of failure.

Needs for affiliation involve the desire to be with other people. People with strong affiliation needs are especially concerned with establishing, maintaining, and restoring positive, emotional relationships with people. They worry about rejection, loneliness, and separation; they seek forgiveness and will change their ways to preserve a relationship. They spend a great deal of time talking and being with other people; they are sensitive to faces and successful in maintaining interpersonal networks.

As described in Chapter 3, the need for power revolves around the desire to have an impact, and to control and influence other people. People with high power needs are interested in expressing power, think about having a strong emotional impact on others, and are concerned about their reputation and position. Power can be expressed in various ways. Some individuals may seek to dominate others aggressively, enter professions and managerial positions that require influencing others, accumulate things and titles for prestige, and act to be recognized by others.[12]

Although research has shown that people differ in the strength of their achievement, affiliation, and power needs, the more fundamental finding is that everyone has these needs. Some people, for example, have more intense achievement needs than others, in part, because of how much their parents encouraged and structured striving to complete tasks. However, wanting to do well compared to standards of excellence is a shared aspiration. It is not just a few leaders with prestigious jobs who have achievement, affiliation, and power needs that can be fulfilled through organizational work—everyone has these needs.

People feel internal pride and achievement when their team completes challenging tasks they could not do alone. They feel part of a larger effort and accepted as valuable colleagues in their mutual work. Through the give-and-take of team effort where they are influenced as well as influence, they meet power needs to have an impact.

Yet in too many organizations, employees feel embittered because their central human needs have been ignored and frustrated. They become hostile and testy, unresponsive to calls that they should care more about a company that seems to care so little for them. They may accommodate by seeking to satisfy their needs with meaningful activity outside their job or by trying to deny the force of their needs.

Self-Esteem

Self-esteem or judging oneself as a worthwhile person very much contributes to personal competence.[13] People who value themselves make more favorable impressions on job recruiters and get more job offers; they also more effectively cope with job loss.[14] Low self-esteem leads to emotional problems, poor achievement, awkward social relations, susceptibility to influence, and rejection of others.[15] A strong, positive, integrated self-image is vital for well being.[16] Feeling confident in one's ability helps people solve problems, correct injustices, and perform effectively.[17]

Working successfully with other people builds positive self-attitudes. People develop their own sense of self and self-esteem by considering how others see and treat them. They see themselves through the mirror of other's eyes; if others tell them they are open-minded, people tend to see themselves as open-minded. When others value and think highly of them, they find it easier to value and think highly of themselves.[18] Our innermost thoughts about ourselves depend upon others. Organizations provide rich possibilities for feedback and confirmation.

Social Support

Through work in organizations, people can feel connected to others, have meaningful relationships, rely on others, turn to others for assistance, and be with friends. This support helps people be productive and achieve, avoid distressing feelings of isolation, live longer, recover from illness and injury faster, and experience less threatening illnesses.[19]

Social support provides the care and information necessary to cope with stress, maintain a sense of well being and self-esteem, and flourish physically and psychologically.[20] Social support is a proven aid for dealing with the stresses of modern life.

Forming personal relationships with managers and more experienced peers through formal and informal mentoring programs can help new employees adjust to the organization.[21] Feeling cared for and emotionally valued encourages conscientious work, willingness to be good citizens, and contributions to innovations.[22]

Feeling connected with supportive others offers opportunities to demonstrate one's own compassion and capability.[23] As Leo Tolstoy, the novelist, wrote, "We do not love people so much for the good they have done us, as for the good we have done them." Helping others results in a sense of responsibility and involvement.

Isolation runs counter to our nature. Loneliness is one of the most painful human experiences. Feeling estranged undermines psychological well being and the quality of life; it even shortens life itself.[24] Distrusting others creates resentment, vindictiveness, and a lack of compassion.[25] A focus just on the job and making money undermines psychological well-being.[26]

Sadly, the number of people experiencing clinical depression is growing rapidly in the United States; there has been a tenfold increase in the rate of depression in the last two generations.[27] The breakdown of relationships in families, communities, and organizations has created unprecedented feelings of loneliness, hopelessness, and self-rejection.

Working with others promotes psychological well being—though, like most good things, it can be overdone! The lack of work is psychologically unhealthy, distressful, and dangerous.[28] People are frustrated as basic needs are unmet. They lose support and positive feedback vital to maintaining a strong sense of oneself as a valuable person. They feel the pain of isolation. Not having work can be the most demoralizing of all experiences, driving people to depression and despair.

RELATIONSHIPS FOR HIGH COMMITMENT

How can the potential of organizational work for individual development and well being be realized? Experience and work itself is not enough to develop self-confidence and competence.[29] Constructive relationships between leader and employee and among employees are critical. Through these relationships, people feel social support and receive self confirmation that builds self-esteem. Relationships also allow, research has documented, people to achieve and get challenging tasks done.[30] It is through people working together that organizations reengineer processes, solve problems, and serve customers.[31]

Many managers and employees have realized that relationships are vital and that it takes a team to get today's important jobs done. Unfortunately, they have only vague notions about the kind of relationship that should be created or how to do it. What are the characteristics of relationships that people find enhancing? Our discussion on the value of work suggests that, in addition to being productive, people should know each other as individual persons, value their diversity, and be mutually respectful.

Productive Teams

People want to achieve and accomplish challenging tasks for the internal satisfaction of doing a job well. Relations on the job need to be structured so that people share information and resources and encourage each other to work effectively. As a practical matter, individuals find it very difficult to be productive without the advice, knowledge, and support of others.

People working together satisfy their power needs to influence and have an impact on each other. Productive teams give each other feedback and support that builds self-esteem.

Demands for work and striving to get the job done, in turn, build effective, supportive relationships. People under pressure to produce recognize clearly that they need each other to be successful. They use their tasks as common goals that unite them in a common effort.

Today's employees also realize that productivity is the key to job security. No union nor compassionate boss can make the credible promise of life-long job tenure. Robert Hubble, a production worker at Corning, Inc., in Blacksburg, Virginia, put it this way: "Everybody is willing to work long hours. We want to be multiskilled and learn how we can make the product better so we can be the best in quality and service to the customer. And if we do all that, this plant will be around a long time."[32]

Unproductive relationships can be very debilitating. If others obstruct their work, employees like Paul Smith at Globe, are left frustrated; they blame other employees and hold managers accountable for allowing such ineffectiveness. Rather than satisfying themselves in the give-and-take of work, they plot how they can use power to show their dominance and superiority over co-workers.

When there are too many people and resources and low standards for excellence, people assume they can just meander through the day doing their own thing. As head of IBM, Tom Watson argued prophetically, "A company can get itself into much more trouble in good times than in bad times."

Know Each Other

Business lore is that "it is not what you know but who you know that counts." The most resourceful person will be overlooked if others do not know her and trust that she will use her resources for mutual benefit. It is not enough to know a colleague is technically proficient; he must also communicate that he is willing and able to apply his competence with others. Employees must know their leader before they will follow; but it has to be two-way. Effective leaders get to know their employees and help them know each other.

Personal relationships are particularly important when working across organizational, cultural, and national boundaries. To do business with the Japanese, for example, North Americans and Europeans are told to expect to invest much time and energy in developing personal relationships and trust. Stereotypes, unspoken assumptions and expectations, and the practical difficulties of communicating and coordinating make working across major boundaries particularly challenging. Without personal bonds, suspicions can make managing the inevitable conflicts painful and unproductive.

Many Hong Kong businesspeople have moved their families to Vancouver and other western cities but commute to Hong Kong to do business. One confided to us that, as he did not know local Vancouver people, he was reluctant to extend the credit and trust needed to do business. He could be more effective by flying back to Hong Kong and keeping his business network there. To do business in Vancouver would be like beginning all over again for he would have to develop a new set of business partners.

A Swedish management consultant told us that his company could not reach its aspirations to be pan-European. As Europe moved toward one market, the idea was that the company should be in a position to help its clients take advantage of a "Europe Without Borders." The trouble was that the management company itself had strong psychological borders. He had tried to develop common projects with consultants in other countries. However, he soon learned that such cross-country projects were frustrating and often high risk. Consultants in another country would agree to a project but not get around to doing it. They would say "yes" on the phone, but after they hung up the project took low priority. He concluded that he should only call when he knew the consultant personally; otherwise he could not count on his foreign colleague to follow through.

Personal relationships make work rewarding and enhancing. Businesspeople fill their retirement speeches with gratitude for the opportunity to get to know diverse people and appreciate what makes them special and unique. Feedback that is specific and personal increases self-awareness and builds self-esteem. Otherwise, positive feedback is dismissed as flattery and manipulation. Social support is credible when given to a person as an individual, not an automatic response to everyone.

The popular caricature of business is that relationships are impersonal and task-oriented. But people who work together, especially under pressure to produce with high risks, want to know each other as individuals. Teamwork is not something between interchangeable parts, but between diverse people who know and value each other as individuals and have developed ways to coordinate suitable to them. Relationships cannot be engineered and teamwork imposed; employees themselves must come to feel personally bonded. (See Figure 4.1.)

Relationships	Value
Productive	Achieve, affiliate, and power needs
Personal	Self-confidence
Diverse	Social support
Respectful	Serving part of a larger effort

FIGURE 4.1.   Finding value through work relationships.

Value Diversity

Persons who consider each other unique and support each other's individuality form valuable relationships. Diversity, not uniformity, is our basic condition. People see and react to the world from their own perspective. No one sees the world or thinks exactly as another person does.

In addition to racial, ethnic, and religious background, people have diverse styles of working. They differ in judging; some people are quick to evaluate whereas others like to gather information before making conclusions. When confronted with a problem, some people swing quickly into rational problem solving whereas others want to experience and express their feelings.

Today's organizations are particularly diverse as people become more specialized. They have their own professional standpoint, standards, and attitudes. Geographical dispersion and international agreements mean that people from different regions and nations must work together. The U.S. work place is becoming increasingly diversified because of immigration and differential birth rates. Skilled people from developing countries are migrating to Europe, North America, and other high wage locations.

Valuing diversity stimulates self-esteem and personal development. Feedback and support are given to individuals as they are, not as to how they conform to a common image.

Valuing diversity not only recognizes the reality of our complex differences, it also promotes productivity. Teams are potentially powerful task accomplishers because they bring together the diverse perspectives and skills needed to get the job done. To work together, employees must know and appreciate each other and manage their conflicts. Valuing diversity within an organization helps employees develop the abilities and attitudes needed to serve diverse customers and work with suppliers and marketing agents.[33]

Mutual Respect

Mutual respect is not only a moral imperative, it makes the most practical business sense. People who respect each other dig into their work, help each other strive, and innovate. They build a relationship in which they confirm and support each other. Mutual respect is a foundation of effective relationships which in turn is the basis for a successful organization.

People who feel embarrassed and insulted feel a loss of social face.[34] To re-establish their face, they reject the influence of others and refuse to compromise, though such intransigence is costly to everyone.[35] They re-assert that they are competent, strong people by being tough and closed-minded. They devalue those held accountable for the lost of face and feel competitive toward them.

Managing by Walking Around: Symbol and Practice

In some outstanding companies, leaders manage by walking around (MBWA).[36] They do not hide in their offices but search out people and try to catch someone doing something right. Walking around reinforces the leader's talk about the value of personal relationships and working together and encourages supervisors and employees to know each other.

In short visits with employees, leaders observe, provide immediate and relevant praise and compliments. They avoid repeating generalizations, but give specific, timely feedback that shows the leader knows and cares. Leaders realize that surveys have repeatedly shown that the lack of praise and recognition is high on the grievance list of many employees.

Managing by walking around builds trust with employees, helps them feel a sense of self-efficacy, and increases commitment for performing well. Leaders recognize the individual contributions necessary for the team to be successful. Each experience should build the expectations that the employee will feel valued and empowered in the next visit.

There is tremendous power in regular, positive recognition. Leaders search out exhausted, disenchanted employees to boost their confidence and ability to build upon success. Leaders should be masters at the honesty and hoopla of powerful, positive feedback to employees.

Although the emphasis is on positive feedback because it is empowering and invigorating, leaders also spot shortcomings and sometimes deal with problems, especially those brought up by employees. Generally, leaders want to avoid surprising an employee but arrange a time to discuss the problem when the employee is prepared.

A leader's door may seem always open to him, but many employees see a closed door in the eyes of the boss's secretary and are afraid of interfering with the leader's work. MBWA reaches out to employees and is a symbol that the leader wants employees to reach out to each other.

Leaders and employees want to create personal relationships oriented to being productive. They value their diversity and respect each other. Yet to invest substantially in their relationships, leaders and employees must know what lies behind these valuable relationships and how they can create them. Future chapters detail how to develop a shared vision and cooperative goals and the skills to communicate and express feelings that make work relationships effective.

COMMITMENT IN AN AGE OF CHANGE

To adapt to intense competition in the marketplace and rapid changes in technology, organizations require employees to be internally committed. But in responding to change, organizations have had to restructure and move people into new work groups, lay off long-service employees, and demand more from the employees who stay. The resulting divisions and suspicions mean that more than ever leaders need to work directly and diligently to know their employees and have them build personal, enhancing relationships.

Committed employees take the long-term view, suffer through frustrations, and master hurdles to help their companies adapt. Fortunately, the organization's requirement for change and continuous improvement can overlap and reinforce the needs of people to achieve, feel the support and power of being part of a larger team effort, and enhance their self-esteem. The tension between people and organizations can be resolved in a "win-win" way when leaders and employees know and value each other as individuals.

Leaders have a powerful impact on developing the needed commitment by fostering personal relationships where people take the time and interest to know each other. Leaders espouse the value of relationships and set the example. They walk around and see employees in action and talk with and interview them in depth to understand their perspectives. Leaders model the way for employees by appreciating people's styles and respecting them as unique persons.

5 DEVELOPING A SHARED VISION AND PURPOSE

Successful companies have a consensus from top to bottom on a set of overall goals. The most brilliant management strategy will fail if that consensus is missing.

John Young, President, Hewlett-Packard

How can the unity and relationships necessary for leaders and employees to meet vital needs and fulfill basic aspirations through organizational work be built? How can they avoid working at cross-purposes that undercut commitment and create alienation? How can their diversity be channelled for mutual benefit?

A shared vision is the critical first step to high commitment, high performance organizations. This vision inspires and directs people so that they work together successfully and feel fulfilled and purposeful. Shared visions not only tie individual employees together but also bind them with the people they serve. Employees realize that their efforts are paying off and giving value to customers. They are improving the quality of life and the effectiveness of other people. Customer satisfaction provides employees with the security that they will continue to enjoy the customer support necessary for any team and organization to survive.

Because of a breakdown in communities and families, people are now especially eager to find purpose and meaning from their work. They want to believe that they are part of something larger than themselves, that they are creating value and moving forward. Employees will

73

give their loyalty and energy to organizations able to build an inspiring, shared vision.

AN INSPIRING VISION

Unfortunately, too often our work places are filled with activity and crises but little direction. Stereotypes get in the way of constructing effective visions. As J.C. Penney demonstrated decades ago, visions must be rational as well as emotional, serve the self as well as others, and be focused on the business and people.

The Penney Vision

The Penney Idea, formulated in 1913, continues to inspire J.C. Penney people:[1]

1. To serve the public, as nearly as we can, to its complete satisfaction.
2. To expect a fair remuneration for the service we render and not all the profit the traffic will bear.
3. To do all in our power to pack the customer's dollar full of value, quality, and satisfaction.
4. To continue to train ourselves and our associates so that the service we give will be more and more intelligently performed.
5. To improve constantly the human factor in our business.
6. To reward men and women in our organization through participation in what the business produces.
7. To test our every policy, method, and act in this wise: Does it square with what is right and just?

Although the language may be a little old-fashioned, the message is contemporary. The Penney Idea focuses the company and its teams on the challenge of competitive advantage by creating value for customers so that the company can remain prosperous.[2] It recognizes the need for continuous development in the skills of people and in how they work together to improve service. The vision also speaks to the values and needs of employees. Men and women are to share in the rewards of a successful company, strengthen their abilities, and be treated fairly.

The Penney Idea must be translated into action. It is not enough to be recited at company functions or displayed in employee lunch rooms. Ongoing teams that involve associates are an integral part of the company and consistent with its vision of productive partnership. Teams have shared responsibility for operating results: the company recognizes that no one person can make the company successful. After senior management identifies issues, ad hoc teams are used to bring pertinent viewpoints and information to bear before a decision is made. The company uses compensation to support these teams. All managers have a sizeable portion of their income based on how well their teams perform. Many of the 70,000 sales associates are rewarded on the performance and improvement of their teams.

Teamwork extends beyond organizational boundaries to those that Penney's Terry Palmer, a senior project manager said, "I expect support from service people, from upper management, from shipping, the whole cycle [of the supplier]. Everyone should be trying to make J.C. Penney better and get more of our business. That needs to come across to us."

Emotional and Rational

Visions should inspire. They portray an uplifting and ennobling future that provides energy and directs people to action. A vision is a forward-looking ideal that stretches people's imagination and abilities. It lifts people away from the humdrum of a daily routine where they can feel purpose and meaning.

To motivate, people themselves must be convinced that the vision has value. The vision has personal meaning. They know that the vision will promote their own values and needs. They want the company recognition and monetary rewards that they will earn if their new product is successful in the marketplace. They want to feel proud and enhance their self-image by being part of a team that respects and appreciates people's racial diversity and personal individuality.

At the Ritz-Carlton Hotel, a 1992 Malcolm Baldridge Award winner, all employees have a card as part of their uniform with the vision statement: "We are Ladies and Gentlemen Serving Ladies and

Gentlemen."[3] They also have 20 prescriptions to implement this vision. For example, they are reminded that "any employee who receives a complaint 'owns' the complaint" and should make sure that it is dealt with.

A motivating vision challenges. Team members stretch their abilities to become more effective. They break out of the routine of the known to seek the excitement of furthering and demonstrating their competence. The accounting group challenges themselves, "We can, if we pull together, do what it takes to provide timely, useful information managers need to make decisions in our highly demanding marketplace."

To inspire though, visions must first be rational and realistic. People are not going to be excited about ideas and plans that have no pay off. They must believe that the company has the strengths, abilities, and wherewithal to move toward realizing their vision. There must be a good chance for success.

The vision must "fit" the company's environment in that it takes advantage of opportunities and wards off threats.[4] It must be realistic in that it recognizes how competitors and legal restrictions may try to create barriers. Employees believe that they can create enduring value for customers who in turn will support them.

The organization framework should be based on sound psychological and management ideas developed through empirical research. Employees, for example, want to know whether the leader's emphasis on teams is sound. Have other companies experimented successfully with these ideas? Did they work? What modifications have other groups tried? Articles summarizing supporting research, studies documenting the value of teams, examples from other organizations, and expert testimony lend credibility to a team organization.

Getting people to consider ideas and research seriously requires overcoming obstacles. Finding useful and appropriate articles and books is difficult especially when there are so many available. Fortunately, business people do not have to rely on reading articles from research journals but can turn to magazines and books that summarize research studies and suggest their major implications. Few managers and employees are prepared to read technical management research reports.

Passing around articles should be complemented with team discussions where people debate the readings and decide how to use them. Without these opportunities, people doubt that they will learn the ideas thoroughly or use them to change the organization. In our family business, leaders from various units take turns hosting discussions on assigned chapters and articles on leadership and teamwork. They critique and ask questions about the reading and help each other understand it. They discuss how they can use the ideas to improve their leadership and their teams. They make recommendations to the rest of the organization about how the ideas should be incorporated into the management of the business.

Serve Others and Yourself

The vision must break out of the stereotype that there is a tradeoff between what helps others and what helps the self. Employees believe that the vision binds them together with each other and that they need to work together to achieve their own goals. But the vision also binds them with their customers, with the people that receive the value the team creates.

An engaging vision has social significance. Team members believe that people they care about will appreciate their efforts. For example, they work hard to develop international marketing opportunities because their coworkers in the company will feel more secure and productive with more orders. Employees at a food company are proud to be part of an effort to bring highly nutritional, affordable food to infants in developing countries. The work team takes pride in the fact that their state's governor regularly buys its products.

Serving people is an obligation and privilege. To be successful, teachers need students to learn and grow. Professionals are effective when clients are protected and enhanced. Computer support departments accomplish their mandate when other departments use technology wisely. Leaders require inspired, empowered followers to get extraordinary things done. Companies need satisfied customers for the financial and emotional support necessary to survive and prosper. We feel most successful and fulfilled when our work results in service to others.

Serving others well challenges us to be sensitive people who reach out and create value. It requires us to develop the management competence and the marketing savvy needed for a successful organization. We must be compassionate, skilled, and determined.

For an organization, serving customers is a "moment of truth," an opportunity to demonstrate its credibility and ability.[5] Delivering value to customers earns the organization respect and repeat business and binds employees together in a meaningful common mission. Serving customers is the essence of a shared vision and the ultimate "bottom line."

Companies that fail to deliver value to customers wither. Customers walk away and turn to alternatives. Disenchanted employees lose their common direction and confidence. Studies document that quality service is a valuable, profitable competitive advantage and that low quality service is a serious disadvantage.[6] Better than average service and product quality companies were able to charge 9 to 10 percent more for their products, had a return on sales of 12 percent compared to 1 percent, and their market share grew by 6 percent compared to a decline of 2 percent for below average companies.

Serving other people is a foundation for our own personal well-being. We cannot be successful alone. We cannot develop our individuality, feel confident in ourselves, and pursue our goals by ourselves. Much less can we feel fulfilled by pitting ourselves against each other. Organizations that serve people are the irreplaceable building blocks of a strong society that sustains the psychological and economic health of its people.

BUSINESS MISSION AND ORGANIZATION FRAMEWORK

A company vision should define both its business mission and its organization culture. A business mission should fit the company so that the company is responsive to its strengths and faces its threats. However, a strategy, regardless of how elegant, requires organizational effort to be realized. A viable business strategy in turn unites and empowers people to work together. When the business strategy and organization framework are in sync, then the company vision inspires.

There is no blueprint for how a company should be structured.[7] Each firm must develop its own organization framework that fits its personality and situation. As we will see in Chapter 13, leaders and employees can use psychological knowledge to understand major characteristics of their organizations and create the particular design, procedures, norms, and styles that facilitate their work.

General and Concrete

Employees want to know the overall vision and mission of their teams and organizations so that they understand the direction and appreciate the meaning of their work. The work of an individual takes on value as it fits with the overall purpose of the organization. For example, janitors at a center for refugee children know that they are an important part of the center's mission to help refugee children make it in their adopted country. They are not just cleaning floors and picking up, but creating an environment needed to help children create a meaningful life in a new land.

Yet the vision should be linked with concrete objectives and plans. Specific as well as challenging goals are highly motivating.[8] Specific goals lead to practical action plans and make charting progress more concrete. The janitors at the center work with teachers to develop a checklist for how to make each classroom organized for learning and each week review the teachers' reports. Companies have experimented with profit-sharing plans to make their vision that people and departments should work together visible and concrete and to distribute rewards for joint success.[9]

A shared vision gives much to an organization, but constructing one requires much. A vision breaks out of stereotyped, trade-off thinking and is rational as well emotional, serves the self as well as others, includes the organizational framework as well as the business mission, and is concrete as well as grand. To create such a vision requires a partnership between leaders and employees.

PARTNERS IN VISION MAKING

James C. Penney and other charismatic founders and leaders have been the natural source of visions. From the strength of their personalities, they create an inspiring picture of the future and then use their dynamism to convert employees into believers.

A few leaders take such a commanding role, but more often leaders create a vision through discussion and debate. They exercise leadership by being convinced by employees as well as convincing them.

What is critical is that the vision is shared. It is not enough that the leader is convinced; employees must be convinced for the vision to be alive. An effective vision isn't so much characterized by fancy words and how prominently it is hung on walls but where it fits in the minds and hearts of employees. They must know the vision and believe in its rationale. They can see how by working together they can achieve the vision and believe they can succeed.

The issue is not whether employees should be involved in developing a vision, but how they are. True participation depends on active dialogue and exchange between employees and leaders. Rather than focus on persuading and selling the vision, leaders engage employees in a thoughtful analysis and exploration. The result may be a vision very close to the leader's original position or something quite different.

Employees need to frame the vision of their group out of the company's larger vision. The J.C. Penney's distribution center vision is more specific and focused than the company's. It is different but compatible with the retail division's.

Without such involvement, leaders run the risk that employees "gang up against" official goals and tasks. They see the direction the leader wants as an incursion against them and sabotage it. Highly cohesive groups are particularly able to withstand pressures from managers and work for their objectives, not the organization's.[10]

Visions can divide. A group may be committed to its vision, but not the organization's. Groups in organizations easily adopt a competitive attitude toward each other, and soon see their goals in terms of outdoing and outperforming other departments. They assume outsiders are on the "other" side. Their internal cohesion may be based on distinguishing themselves and seeing the other groups as the "enemy." A vision can also split a company between those who believe and those who do not. A common danger is for top management to be committed, middle management doubtful, and employees unknowing or even suspicious.

The vision is both stable and flexible. The vision must adapt to emerging conditions, but cannot be changed whimsically. The business mission and strategy provide ongoing direction, but must also be updated in light of new opportunities and threats. The organizational framework outlines the basic values and procedures for the company that keep people on the same wavelength. However, the ways the values are expressed and the specific designs and procedures used must respond to the needs of employees and the strategy and objectives of the business.

Success, as well as failure, is threatening. A prosperous company that stagnates encourages rivals to attack and penetrate their markets. Success can lull a company into rigid commitment to its strategy and framework, and leave it unprepared to change when circumstances warrant. Complacency can turn the company's dream into a nightmare.

Employees must adapt the vision to changing circumstances to make it useful and living. The Penney Idea and teamwork integrate the company requirements to serve both customers and employees. The vision though does not straightlace the company into one particular strategy; J.C. Penney recently repositioned itself in the competitive retail marketplace and plans to take advantage of prosperous, underserved international markets.[11] It expects that its values and teamwork will continue to serve the company well into the future.

A vision is much more than lofty sounding ideals ground out by the public relations department. Leaders and employees working together have to forge a vision that fits the company's own particular situation and become committed to it. Both the business strategy and the organization frameworks need to be rational, meaningful, and challenging.

CREATING A VISION

Four key principles guide creating an engaging, uniting common direction.[12] First, leaders and employees set the stage by developing their relationships so that they can begin work on a vision. Second, they challenge the accepted ways of working and proactively seek out the adventure to change rather than wait for a crises that demands action. Third, the processes of developing the vision models the kind of organization framework that the company aspires to: Creating the vision itself furthers the desired teamwork. Fourth, forging a vision is an ongoing process, not a one- or two-step quick fix.

Setting the Stage

What are the conditions that help leaders and employees create an engaging vision? Dissatisfaction and pain have often proposed as needed for an organization to make an effort to evaluate and try to form a more united approach.[13] Yet pain and pessimism can lead to denial that there

---

The Climate Goals Vision at A&W Canada

In the 1970s, McDonalds and other new entries were taking customers away from A&W Canada. Its slide from healthy profitability to huge losses was unnerving and seemingly inevitable. How could its drive-ins compete in a country where the winters drove people inside? Its U.S. counterpart also confronted a shrinking number of restaurants and eventually it abandoned the business. But A&W Canada learned to compete and in the 1990s was taking market share away from McDonald's.

For years the slide paralyzed management. The emotional attachment to the image of the drive-in was strong and the fears of change great. But facing bankruptcy, president Jeff Mooney and other A&W managers recognized that they had to move away from the drive-in formula so successful in the 1960s that was undoing them in the 1970s. They began to experiment with restaurants in malls where people were going to shop and escape the winter.

They also had the key insight that making and implementing this strategy required a deep, practical commitment to people and teamwork. They must move away from the autocratic, top-down management that had kept them stuck for too many years.

In 1977, managers and employees developed a set of climate goals to guide how they were to work together. At the top of the list is Trust and Mutual Respect where "Our actions are open, honest, and caring. We rely on, believe in, and treat each other as partners committed to the

(Continued)

---

is much at stake and change is needed. They also can create a paralyzing sense of powerlessness and withdrawal. Both incentives to change and the confidence that change can be implemented are needed.

A company that has lost money, customers, and support has ample incentives for developing and refocusing the vision. Losing more money than any other company in history in 1981 was clear evidence to Ford management and employees that they should act![14] Involving employees more fully and creating teams throughout the organization in the "Quality Is Job One" program led a resurgence at Ford Motor Company.

Yet even a company that has abundant customers and a healthy bottom line can develop an urgency by ascribing to excellence and taking the long-term view. Boeing in 1989 enjoyed tremendous business in commercial aviation. A few years later it had to downsize in a response

(Continued)

same direction." They also are to "accept responsibility for their own development," "encourage and support people to challenge and question," and have "clear and candid communication of facts, ideas, and feelings between individuals and groups." Ten years later they developed the human resource strategy statement: "To become the Best Place to Work in the fast-food industry where outstanding people at all levels perform to their full potential in a climate of trust."

The climate goals provide a common framework and guidance for everyone in the company. In quarterly climate meetings, groups meet to review their teamwork and brainstorm how they can improve. New recruits are given *The Climate Goals Process* (A&W Food Services of Canada, 1990) which includes examples of behavior consistent and inconsistent with the climate goals. Everyone is to strive to live up to these goals; everyone is responsible for reminding others when they fall short of the climate goals. In this company, all employees have the obligation as well as the right to tell the president when he is not listening.

A&W Canada continues to deepen its eighteen-year commitment to its climate goals. The climate goals are not rhetoric but have clout. The managers reporting to a new senior executive together confronted him for leading in ways that violated the climate goals. The people at A&W are confident that their investment in teamwork has prepared them to compete and provide superior service in the highly competitive fast-food market. They are proud of both their business accomplishments and their open, trusting relationships.

to suddenly harsh market conditions and the credibility of European Airbus products. Might not the Japanese also enter the market? The inevitability of change and the emergence of competitors underlines the need for all organizations to maintain innovativeness and quality.

In addition to the business mission, people must see the need to revitalize how they are organized and managed, and believe they can. Here too, painful conditions can motivate but also debilitate. If people are highly suspicious and hostile, then discussing common goals may well seem at best abstract, and may cause great cynicism as people realize the discrepancy between talk and reality.

A central dilemma is that visions are expected to unite people and groups, but there must be some basic unity in their relationships before work toward a vision will succeed.

Basic steps to set the stage include:

1. *Assess the business mission.* Discussion with customers and industry experts and examination of the competition provide concrete tests of the strengths and weaknesses in the company's business strategy. Listening to American owners praise their Japanese cars helped break down American executives' defensiveness and led them to admit that they had a problem they must confront.[15] Employees must consider the long-term viability and risks of the present course of action.

2. *Reflect on the organization framework.* Employees assess their work relationships, division of labor, and structure and compare their present functioning with ideals. Are they united and empowered behind a common vision? Do people speak out and explore issues in depth? Are they able to function as teams within the organization's hierarchy?

3. *Confront relationship issues.* Managing long-standing conflicts may be necessary before serious work on a vision can begin. Once top management is able to convince employees that grievances and injustices will be considered and dealt with, then employees feel both the need to forge a vision and believe it is possible. Such direct dealing with conflicts also models the team organization leaders want as part of the company vision.

4. *Take first steps.* Incentives to sharpen the vision must be complemented with at least some confidence that the company can succeed. Beginning to improve the quality of the products, strengthening internal communication, dealing with conflicts, and taking other first steps convince people that the company is serious in that it has both the incentive and wherewithal to move forward.

Challenging the Status Quo

Leaders and employees continually search out opportunities to innovate and improve. They understand that, even without any immediate danger, companies must continually revitalize and update. They will be better off if they strive for excellence rather than wait until forced to act. Crises catch people off guard, and while they compel action, that action may not be well-considered.[16] A crisis gives incentives for change and can be a catalyst for learning. However, crises often undercut confidence that meaningful change will happen. One or two crises can unite people as they recognize that they must pull together to survive. However, continual crises lose that motivational value and create a sense of powerlessness and despair.

To challenge the status quo:

1. *Search for opportunities to initiate change, innovate, and grow.* New assignments become challenges to turnaround. People wonder if things could be done differently and better, and, rather than wait for a crisis to hit, find something that is "broken" that they can fix. They break out of the routine and usual, and consider their work an adventure to enjoy.

2. *Use frustrations and conflict.* Employees talk about what their concerns about the business strategy, and what bugs and annoys them about their jobs and work environment. They let one another know what they would like to change.

3. *Take risks and learn from mistakes.* People gather new ideas, try little experiments, model risk-taking, and turn stress into excitement. People recognize that no new effort is risk-free and, while perfection can be striven for, it cannot be assumed or reached.

4. *Present a short-vision statement.* A leader or task force evokes images and metaphors in describing the business mission and organization framework of the company. The leader persuasively and credibly communicates central values and aspirations in a short speech.

A Team Approach

It is a long-standing truism that organizational change does not happen unless the people at the top are committed to change. But it is also true that an inspiring vision is not going to happen unless people at the middle and lower levels of the organization are committed. A vision cannot inspire by itself; managers and workers have to want to be inspired. The vision of the organization needs to be reinforced by a team approach to developing it. Forcing cooperation is a contradiction.

A team approach includes:

1. *Dialogue.* Leaders and employees discuss opposing views to explore the vision and its potential significance for them and the

organization. They are convinced by the reasoning behind it, and appreciate the risks of not changing and the opportunities the vision holds.

2. *Solicit stakeholders.* Customers, suppliers, marketing agents, and investors are asked to state their positions, interests, and suggestions. They indicate the organization's strengths and weaknesses and its opportunities and threats.

3. *Include.* The ideas and suggestions of employees and stakeholders are used to modify the vision to make it as motivating and uniting as possible. The business strategy and organization framework must make sense to employees before they will be committed to them.

Ongoing Strategies

Rapid advances in technology, short life-cycles for products, and the globalization of markets are transforming the business landscape. Strategies must be continually updated to remain current and fresh. Companies realize that to keep on top of changes they need to form strategic alliances and joint ventures to pool resources. New business thrusts require new organizational frameworks. The professional and diverse workforce, employee demands for rights and participation, and changing notions of leadership make authoritarian management styles obsolete.

The organization recognizes that no strategy or design can be assumed to be continually successful. They regularly re-examine their vision in light of new data, environmental changes, and opportunities. In this way, they feel in control of their destiny, not overwhelmed by events.

To keep the vision growing:

1. *Update.* Quarterly, or at least annually, the organization revisits its vision and revises its plans in light of change in and out of the organization.

2. *Confront complacency.* Success is tempered with the recognition that future success is not guaranteed but change is. The organization again hears customers' ideas and complaints, the views of investors, the suggestions of employees, and the predictions of industry experts and reviews the competition.

Set the Stage	Assess the business Reflect on the organization Confront relationship issues
Challenge Status Quo	Find adventures to enjoy Use frustrations Learn from mistakes Describe possibilities
Team Approach	Dialogue Solicit stakeholders Include
Ongoing	Update Celebrate Confront complacency

FIGURE 5.1.   Creating a shared vision.

3. *Appreciate accomplishments.* The organization celebrates its capacity to change and rewards progress toward its vision.

Visions of the highest quality product and working together as a team are not costly, but are not easily established. It may be necessary to deal with an underlying distrust before talk about a vision becomes credible. Their frustrations and inability to manage conflicts must be dealt with before much progress on forming a vision can be made. The vision must be believed, communicated, and lived (see Figure 5.1). People will be tempted to fall back to old ways of thinking and working, and there will be inevitable bumps along the way that must be weathered and overcome. Implementing business missions and developing team organizations are ongoing journeys, not destinations.

VISION TO ENERGIZE AND INTEGRATE FORD

Setting the stage, challenging status quo, dialoguing, and working toward ongoing development are much easier to do with a team of ten than with an organization of hundreds and thousands. But team development focused only on the department can interfere with organizational effectiveness. The team is united, but in a direction that may not complement and could even work against other groups in the organization. The teams feel they are motivated and contributing, and self-righteously denounce other teams for not getting on board. What is needed is for groups within a large organization to be committed to common vision and seeing their roles as complementary.

Gary Jusela and his associates developed an approach at Ford for departments and groups to develop a system vision.[17] In the early 1980s, Tom Page, executive vice president at Ford's Diversified Product Operations (DPO), whose eight divisions made automobile parts for Ford assembly plants, wondered how to get all managers behind the quality and teamwork vision outlined by Ford executives. How can 70,000 employees become committed to moving in one direction? How can middle managers be open to employee input and suggestions?

A team of consultants and managers interviewed potential participants and worked out a design, not to teach participative management, but to build a team around the actual business issues DPO confronted. For each division, they invited the top four levels of managers in each division, which ranged from 80 to 200 people, to attend a five-day seminar, usually broken into a three-day and two-day parts separated by several weeks. Participants worked with those up and down the hierarchy and across departments on the critical business issues of quality, cost containment, and the need to be responsive.

Managers discussed with Tom Page and other executives their hopes and visions. They got feedback from their customers about their products and found out how their errors frustrated assembling quality cars and trucks. They heard testimonies from owners of Japanese cars. They examined the quality of the competition, and could see for themselves their weaknesses. Many groups got fired up about their preferred future state of affairs, and began taking first steps to improve their products for their customers.

The groups also examined how they worked together. They sent "valentines" to reveal their "sads," "glads," and "mads" about each other and publicly declared how they would respond to this feedback. This exchange improved communication and began to deal with long-standing conflicts.

This system approach to envisioning reinforces the message of teamwork. Executives dialogue with managers about their vision, and involve them in shaping and implementing the vision. In this way, executives prepared managers to work as a team with their employees. This system-wide teamwork does not ensure success but it helps Ford compete in the demanding automobile marketplace.

Employees must know and understand the overall mission and organization to work hard to realize it. The vision must be shared. All employees, not just top management, must believe in the vision. They must help the leader formulate the vision and adjust it to fit their particular needs. Employees must be involved enough so that through discussion they come to understand the vision clearly and see how it is rational, promotes their personal aspirations, stretches their abilities, and has value to significant others. They see how the shared vision integrates their own interests with the "bottom line" of their department and organization into a motivating picture of where they are going.

PART THREE

WORKING TOGETHER

> We have grown up in a climate of competition between people, teams, departments, divisions, pupils, schools, universities. We have been taught by economists that competition will solve our problems. Actually, competition, we see now, is destructive. It would be better if everyone would work together as a system, with the aim for everybody to win. What we need is cooperation and transformation to a new style of management.
>
> W. Edward Deming

Leaders can have an enduring impact by strengthening work relationships so that they and employees move toward their shared vision, and serve their customers and themselves. But there is much confusion about the nature of these productive relationships and how can they be created. Chapter 6 uses cooperation theory and research to show that people who believe that they can reach their goals together and are on the same side develop mutual trust and are prepared to help each other be effective and fulfilled. Chapter 7 shows how power can have a constructive, cooperative face where people appreciate and build up each other's abilities.

Employees must build on their cooperative unity and mutual power by actually assisting and coordinating. Chapter 8 identifies barriers to communication and important skills leaders and employees can develop. To have mutual trust and effective cooperative relationships requires that emotions be expressed and managed. Chapter 9 outlines how leaders and employees can share their feelings openly and express feelings to deal with issues that threaten to disrupt work relationships.

6 COOPERATION AND COMPETITION

> Now when I try to explain [NUMMI] to old UAW [United Auto Workers] buddies from other plants . . . they figure going along with the team concept and all the rest was just the price we had to pay to get our jobs back. I explain to them that the plant is cleaner, it's safer, we've got more say on important issues, and we have a real opportunity to build our strength as a union. I explain to them that our members can broaden their understanding of the manufacturing system and build their self-esteem, and that the training we've gotten in manufacturing, problem solving, quality, and so on can help them reach their full potential and get more out of their lives. I explain to them that in a system like this, workers have got a chance to make a real contribution to society—we don't have to let managers do all the thinking. But these guys just don't see it. Maybe it's because they haven't personally experienced the way NUMMI works."
>
> UAW Official, NUMMI

The former General Motors (GM) plant at Fremont, California, once called by a manager, "the worst plant in the world," has become the highly successful New United Motor Manufacturing Inc. (NUMMI), a joint venture of General Motors and Toyota.[1] Under the old system with GM, 20 percent more employees were hired just to make sure there would be enough workers on any given day. The backlog of unresolved grievances often exceeded 5,000. Productivity was among the lowest in all GM plants, quality was awful, and drug use rampant. Finally, in February 1982, GM closed the plant. It did not reopen as NUMMI until 1984.

By the end of 1986, NUMMI productivity was twice as high as its predecessor and the highest of all GM plants. In fact, quality and productivity were nearly as high as Toyota's Takasoka plant. Absenteeism was 3 to 4 percent; drug abuse minimal; participation in the suggestion program reached 92 percent in 1991. Only 700 grievances have been filed over the course of eight years. Recently, 90 percent of employees describe themselves as "very satisfied" or "satisfied."

The system of programs and technology is different, but what has driven the change is a new altitude. An employee described the difference. At GM, "the personnel manager who hired us . . . explained: 'You new employees have been hired the same way we requisition sandpaper. We'll put you back on the street whenever you aren't needed any more.' At NUMMI, the message when we came aboard was 'Welcome to the Family.'"

The old GM system pitted management and industrial engineers against the production workers in a struggle for control of who would tell whom how the job was to be done. Workers would regularly dismiss the directives of supervisors and engineers, doing the jobs as they wanted. They slowed down when being observed by industrial engineers doing time-and-motion studies. A production employee argued, "I don't want the type of union muscle we once had. You could get away with almost anything in the old plant, because the union would get you off the hook. It was really crazy. But it wasn't productive."

In the new system, they are partners in building "the finest vehicles in America." A UAW official put the change this way, "Management is coming to us asking for our input . . . . The old approach was simpler 'You make the damned decision, and I'll grieve it if I want.' . . . . Now we need to understand how the production system works, to take the time to analyze things, to formulate much more detailed proposals. This system really allows us to take as much power as we know what to do with."

NUMMI has invested a great deal in moving from the competitive, win-lose to the cooperative, open style of managing. NUMMI has backed up its attitude of respect and wanting to involve workers. Recognizing that "job security is essential to an employee's well-being," it guarantees "that it will not lay off employees unless compelled to do so by severe economic conditions that threaten the long-term viability of the Company." In 1988, confronted with low demand, workers who were no longer needed on the assembly line were trained and assigned to continuous improvement teams. To support the "we are in this together" attitude, NUMMI has reduced the trade classifications from 18 to two; 80 hourly rates have been collapsed into two.

The common purpose and cooperative relationships in turn have driven continuous improvement and enhancement of standards. Production teams are involved in the ongoing quest to improve quality and reduce costs. In conjunction with industrial engineers, these teams constantly refine their processes. Every job and every machine is examined and modified to maximize efficiency.

The cooperative way of managing NUMMI is both soft and tough. Managers and workers respect each other, but they do not confuse an auto plant with a country club or a beer hall. Nor have they removed all layers of management, left workers to do their own thing, or fostered wild-eyed creativity. Managers are deeply involved in helping employees focus on specifics and build upon and refine procedures and process in the gradual, ongoing pursuit of a high quality, low cost automobile. A team leader said, "Being consistently busy without being hassled and without being overworked takes a lot of the pain out the job. You work harder at NUMMI, but I swear you go home at the end of the day feeling less tired—and feeling a hell of a lot better about yourself!"

Managers in many other organizations have also realized the central value of trust and openness to a successful organization. Tom Peters has concluded, "Relationships really are all there is."

Yet, there is a wide-spread belief that developing these relationships is a very instinctual, haphazard process, not subject to knowable principles that can be persistently applied as the technical aspects of business are. Tom Peters has advised, "Read more novels and fewer business books."[2]

Chapter 4 described effective relationships as productive and oriented to getting common jobs done, where people know each other as individuals, valued their diversity, and respect each other's individuality. But what underlies this kind of relationship? How can they be forged?

For over half a century, psychologists have studied cooperation and we now know a great deal about how to define it, distinguish it from competition and conflict, detail its consequences on how people interact, and specify the effects of these interactions on productivity and relationships. Many studies document that cooperative goals are a foundation for productive, enhancing relationships. Leaders can use this knowledge to create strong cooperative relationships where they and their employees know they are sailing on the same ship to the same port.

CROSS-FUNCTIONAL TEAMWORK

Compelled by market forces and inspired by successful examples, teams of employees are revitalizing organizations by creating a new way of working together. In this spirited teamwork, everyone is important and everyone contributes. Motorola, Texas Instruments, Hewlett-Packard, Merck Pharmaceuticals, Ford, Saturn, and Chrysler have extolled the virtues of their team organizations. These and many other companies have formed cross-functional teams of professionals and specialists from different departments and disciplines to meet pressing business challenges.

Finance and accounting departments are moving away from their roles as controllers and "policemen" to those who help operating specialists to solve problems. At Merck, for example, according to Chief Financial Officer Judy Lewent, finance specialists "work with a very sharp pencil. We are not lax." But they also "attempt to work with the operating units and, in many cases, have been accepted as a partner in the business."[3] Instead of proposing that a new agricultural product was too expensive to meet revenue targets, they worked with those committed to the product to uncover that the packaging was adding too much cost. They fulfilled their mandate of protecting Merck's financial resources but also helped operating specialists make their business viable.

Not surprisingly then, many managers espouse the value of cross-functional, or multidisciplinary, teams as a practical way of integrating professionals with each other and with the organization. The purpose of these teams is not to water down professional identity. Indeed, professionals may be grouped by discipline so that they can update their knowledge. Profitable, high-return pharmaceutical companies encourage their researchers keep active within their disciplines in and out of the company through conferences, joint projects, and publications.[4] But these companies also make sure that these specialists interact with each other and with product and marketing specialists. They discuss each other's projects and debate which ones can be most profitably developed.

Various organizations have put multidisciplinary teams to work. At Motorola's Austin facility, cross-functional teams are improving manufacturing.[5] Once they investigated why there was so much variance in wire bonding using clear role assignments. The upper level manager was responsible to keep meetings focused; the chairperson issued action steps. The team reduced costs and manufacturing time and improved quality.

Dime Savings Bank of New York has used a SWAT team approach to improving information services.[6] These teams have the business consulting, system development, and customer support specialists necessary to evaluate and solve the specific problem and the authority to implement the solution. They have broken down the barriers between information systems professionals and users to improve services in mortgage banking, consumer financial services, and asset recovery while reducing technical support staffing by over 30 percent.

Teams are changing all aspects of manufacturing at Chrysler.[7] Through its cross-functional team organization, its Brandea Assembly Plant in Ontario has, according to Denis Pawley, Executive Vice President of Manufacturing, improved quality, become more productive and flexible, and reduced staff by 18% in just a matter of months. Chrysler is also investing in multi-disciplinary teamwork for product innovation.[8] At the Chrysler Technological Center, specialists in production, design, engineering, manufacturing, and procurement as well as suppliers work together to take advantage of concurrent production and move away from the traditional in-sequence development. Its Educational Center helps these specialists learn to collaborate effectively.

Companies like National Semiconductor, Xerox, Hewlett-Packard, Canon, and Apple Computer are using cross-functional teams to cut product development cycles and reduce time to market.[9] New product teams allow open and early communication among disciplines. They may use concurrent engineering to design the product at the same time as it develops the processes to manufacture and assemble parts and to test and service the product in the field. Following premier Japanese methods of focusing on technology transfer as they begin a research project, these teams are in direct contact with the end user customer as well as with experts outside the company in the disciplines related to the product.[10]

Reengineering has resulted in major productivity advances and profits improvements at such companies as Fannie Mae, Aetna Life & Casualty Co., Franks Nursery & Crafts, Columbia Presbyterian Hospital-New York City, and Levi Strauss & Co.[11] Functional units such as marketing, engineering, and manufacturing are re-formed into cross-functional teams dedicated to delivering valued products to customers. They also use information technology to boost their effectiveness.

IBM developed a selling center to penetrate the factory automation market.[12] Sales people worked with product development personnel to establish demonstration facilities at IBM manufacturing sites. They also involved vendors who provided complimentary products. In this way, they were able to show customers complete solutions to their problems.

Professionals' working together has great potential but getting them to do so can be very difficult. The reality, however, is that professionals and specialists must work together to be effective. Marketing professionals themselves cannot deliver a valued product to customers; informational specialists cannot use their programs to create cost reports; training personnel cannot make managers skilled. Specialists who try to do it all are not specialists. They must apply their specific skills in conjunction with other professionals and employees. They can only be successful together.

COOPERATIVE AND COMPETITIVE GOAL INTERDEPENDENCE

Leaders and employees need a concise, powerful way to understand the nature of productive teamwork. Beginning in the 1940s, Morton Deutsch argued that how people believe their goals are related is a useful way to understand the dynamics and outcomes of collaborative work.[13] He later extended cooperation and competition to analyze the inevitable frustrations, disappointments, and other conflicts of joint work. Hundreds of studies have developed this theory and shown it to be an elegant, powerful way to understand trust and joint effort.[14]

Interaction can take on very different characteristics. People's beliefs about how they depend upon each other drastically affects their expectations, communication, exchange, problem solving, and productivity. Deutsch theorized that whether people believe their goals are predominantly cooperative or competitive affects their expectations and actions, and thereby the consequences and effectiveness of interaction.

The Alternatives

In cooperation, people believe their goals are positively related. As one person moves toward goal attainment, others also move toward reaching their goal. Each individual understands that his or her goal attainment helps others reach their goals; as one succeeds, others succeed. People

FIGURE 6.1.   Cooperation theory.

in cooperation appreciate that they want each other to pursue their goals effectively, for the other's effectiveness helps all of them reach their goals. If one swims, the other swims; if one sinks, the other sinks. They feel like a team and on the same side. They trust that they will use their power for mutual benefit. (See Figure 6.1.)

Their individual achievement depends upon the achievement of others. Cooperation is not based on altruism, but on the recognition that, with positively related goals, self-interests require collaboration. Cooperative new product team members want each other to develop useful ideas and work hard to create a new product that makes everyone feel successful. Cooperative work integrates self-interest to achieve compatible goals.

Alternatively (Figure 6.2), people may believe their goals are competitive in that one's goal attainment precludes or at least makes less

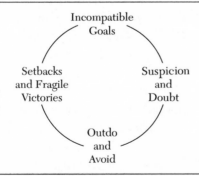

FIGURE 6.2.   Competition theory.

likely the goal attainment of others. If one succeeds, others must fail. If one "wins," others "lose." People in competition conclude that they are better off when others act ineffectively; when others are productive, they are less likely to be successful themselves. Competitive team members want to prove they are the most capable and their ideas superior; they are frustrated when others develop useful ideas and work hard. Competitive work pits self-interest against each other in a struggle to win.

Major Propositions

Whether people conclude their goals are primarily cooperative or competitive, Deutsch theorized, profoundly affects their orientation and intentions toward each other. In cooperation, people want others to act effectively and expect others want them to be effective because it is in each person's self-interest to do so. They trust that their risks and efforts will be welcomed and reciprocated. They believe they can rely on each other and are sensitive and responsive to each other. In short, they trust each other.

This mutual trust leads to discussions to integrate and combine perspectives and interests. Studies document that people in cooperation share information, take each other's perspective, communicate and influence effectively, exchange resources, assist and support each other, discuss opposing ideas openly, and use higher-quality reasoning. These actions in turn help cooperators move forward by completing tasks, agreeing to high quality solutions, reducing stress, fostering attraction, and strengthening work relationships and confidence in future collaboration.

For example, a retail and a computer technologist form a project team to recommend a more responsive system to forecast sales of the company's line of clothing to reduce excess inventory and to avoid lost sales due to inadequate inventory. They conclude that they have cooperative goals because they see each other as fully committed to developing the best possible system. They divide up the work. The retail specialist interviews people knowledgeable about the present system. The computer specialist visits a company with a state of the art system. Expecting that each wants the other to succeed, they freely share their findings. They debate alternative proposals and express their views and ideas with the confidence that the other will use them for mutual advantage. They feel supported, enjoy the camaraderie, and integrate their best information and ideas to make an effective recommendation to their boss.

Conclusions that goals are competitive, on the other hand, lead to the suspicious expectations that people will promote their own interests at the expense of others, and may even actively work to interfere with each other. This mistrust restricts information and resource exchange and distorts communication; people often try to avoid direct discussions and, when compelled to discuss, impose their positions on each other. These ways of interacting frustrate productivity, intensify stress, and lower morale.

However, the retail and computer specialists on the new inventory system project team can conclude that their goals are incompatible and competitive. They believe that their goal is to look more competent and hard-working to their boss than the other. They find it difficult to divide up the work for fear that the other will use his knowledge to make himself look better. In their discussions, they might hold back information that could help the other appear knowledgeable. Alternatively, they try to impose their solution to show the boss that the group's recommendation was really their own individual one. Finding it difficult to integrate, they feel frustrated with each other and are not likely to combine their insights into the most effective system.

The retail and computer specialists have conflict regardless of whether they believe their goals are cooperative or competitive. But believing that their goals are cooperative makes managing the conflict much more constructive.[15]

Conflict is defined as incompatible activities where one person is disagreeing, obstructing, or frustrating another. With cooperative goals, people recognize that it is in everyone's self-interest to promote each other's effectiveness. Feeling trusting, they freely speak their minds, reveal their frustrations, and talk about their anger. People welcome these confrontations and realize it is important to work out settlements so that they can continue to assist each other. They work for mutually beneficial solutions that maintain and strengthen the relationship. They explore each other's perspective, creatively integrate their views, and are confident they will continue to work together for mutual benefit. As a result, they are prepared to discuss future conflicts.

Competitive goals make managing conflict very difficult and can lead to debilitating fights. With competitive goals, people suspect that

The Myth of the Competitive Leader

Robert Helmreich and his associates originally assumed that competitiveness along with other elements of the desire to achieve would characterize successful leaders.[16] They analyzed that the desire to achieve had three parts: Competitiveness as the desire to win in interpersonal situations in which others must lose, mastery as the desire to take on challenging tasks, and work as positive attitudes toward working hard. To their surprise, they found that male scientists who were most successful as measured by citations of their work were high on mastery and work, but low on competitiveness. Competitive scientists apparently get distracted by attempts to outshine others and produce research that is more superficial and less sustained than low competitive ones.

Subsequent studies confirmed the basic findings. Successful (as measured by salaries) businesspeople in large corporations had lower competitiveness and higher mastery and work scores than less successful ones. Similarly, low competitive airline pilots, airline reservation agents, supertanker crews, and students were all more effective than high competitive ones. The researchers were unable to identify any profession in which more competitive persons were more successful. Taking on challenges and hard work are not synonymous with competition. Indeed, it is when competitiveness is low that the desires for challenges and hard work result in success.

self-interests will lead to mutual frustration. They doubt others are interested in their feelings and frustrations, and fear ridicule. Although they often prefer to avoid conflict, especially with their bosses and others with authority and power who can "win" and impose their wishes, the underlying problems continue to frustrate. If they do decide to confront their protagonist, they often do so in a tough, dominating manner that escalates the conflict. Whether they choose to avoid or confront conflict, competitors, although they may believe they have won in the short-term, usually end up feeling that they have lost and only hope that others have lost more.

THE MANY WAYS TO WORK COOPERATIVELY

Cooperation has to do with attitudes and beliefs about how people depend on each other, not a particular style of working and organizing. Many people assume that to be cooperative groups must be structured, leaders must be participatory, and people must be gentle with each other. Cooperation may take these shapes, but not inevitably and not always. We must distinguish between the form and essence of cooperation, between the procedures and core of cooperation.[17]

The essence of cooperation is people supporting each other to pursue their mutual goals, but cooperation takes many forms. Using action teams, sharing resources, and involving people in making decisions are possible ways of working cooperatively. Putting people into teams does not ensure that they feel they are in it together and promoting each other's goals. They may believe that they should use the task force only to defend their department's interests. When leaders ask for input, it does not mean that employees automatically believe that furthering management's interests furthers theirs. They may even think such involvement is a trap to co-opt them and frustrate their aspirations.

Cooperative interaction is much richer and more complex than people being supportive and gentle and holding back their assertiveness and individuality. Open conflict is part of cooperation. People feel more confident speaking their minds and expressing their opinions in cooperation. Teams are effective because they have the potential of combining the perspectives of diverse people, not because people submerge their individuality. As discussed in Chapter 4, people develop their self-confidence and self-esteem through cooperative groups.

Cooperation promotes individual and team accountability and responsibility. Individuals have their own tasks and see how these tasks fit in with others; they are held accountable by their peers as well as their supervisors. Teams are held accountable by other team members and by the executives who advocated them. Effective cooperation requires and fosters individuality, diversity, and conflict management.

Cooperation is both a soft and a tough way of working. People support each other, but they also confront and hold each other accountable. People may be tempted to engage in "social loafing" and "letting George do it."[18] They feel they can get lost in the crowd and their lack of efforts will not be noticed. But there are ways to minimize this possibility.

Killer Bees: A Cooperative Team

Winter in Bridgehampton, New York, is basketball because the Killer Bees have developed a tradition of winning team basketball.[19] Since 1980, the team has 162 wins, 32 losses, qualified for the state championship six times, won twice and finished in the final four two other times. Even more remarkable is that the team has succeeded while the school's population has declined from 67 to 41. The team never has had more than seven players, none of whom has gone on to be a college star.

Team members have a cooperative, meaningful purpose. They are not just winning basketball games, they are uniting an entire community and building its pride. Team members have an incredible work ethic. They teach each other basketball at a young age and prepare themselves to replace those that leave. They get fine coaching, but it is not the coach nor just the players. It is everyone together.

After losing their long-time coach and several key players, the Killer Bees were supposed to be rebuilding. In a critical game, they were losing in the second half to a tough Port Jefferson team. As Rick Murphy reported in the East Hampton *Star,* "And then it happened: the press, full court, in-your-face pressure that has been unnerving opponents for well over a decade was ordered by the [new] coach, Carl Johnson. So effective was the strategy that Bridgehampton had the game in the bag in a matter of minutes. . . . Ken Hunger summed it up best: 'The Bees don't rebuild, they reload.'"

The Killer Bees went on to the state playoff. Murphy wrote, "After all, they are the Killer Bees. They expect to win, and they win. It is a tradition, and the record says it all. No other high school basketball team in the state has been as successful."

Studies document little social loafing when members recognize and notice the contributions of each individual, develop internal commitment to the task, and show real caring for each other. They are convinced that their contributions are unique, needed, and really matter.

Working cooperatively does not mean leaving common sense behind. Some issues are not important, complex, or controversial enough to warrant a group discussion. Five dollar problems do not deserve a thousand dollar process to solve. There are times when time or practical restraints make joint consideration of problems impractical. Crises may demand immediate, unilateral action. Yet even in handling a crisis such as threats to the safety of airplanes, cooperative goals and controversy helped flight crew members return the plane to safe conditions expeditiously.[20]

Example 1: The first officer was apprehensive at the controls as the 737 began its descent. Thunderstorms surrounded the plane; he did not have a clear view of the runway environment from his right side, and he had little experience with the electronic equipment. Fortunately, the other pilot was very supportive and reassured the first officer that the runway was free and the plane on course. Working as a team and trusting each other's abilities, they landed the plane safely.

Example 2: As the 747 descended, the captain was preoccupied with auto land. He should have realized that they were not on the right glide path because air traffic control had not given them clearance to descend. The first officer tried diplomacy by telling the captain their altitude, but the information did not trigger the captain to respond. When they reached 800 feet, the first officer began yelling commands at the captain who luckily followed them. The first officer made all the captain's decisions including talking to the passengers. The first officer realized that his hesitation in dealing with the captain's preoccupation had put the plane in grave danger.

As these examples illustrate, cooperative teamwork and constructive controversy are critical for maintaining the margin of safety in the sky.[21] It has long been recognized that flight crew members must be trained, skilled, and responsible to fulfill their individual roles. But cockpit and cabin crews must effectively communicate information, discuss ideas, and coordinate their efforts to cope with dangers to airplanes.

Confronting Safety Problems Together

We found many examples of flight crew members working together to minimize the threat to the airplane. We coded these examples into categories to identify the major ways that they worked together effectively and ineffectively.

1. Crew members exchanged information to identify and solve a problem. For example, a flight attendant noticed a small engine fire and reported it quickly to the captain. The captain checked his instruments and the second officer inspected the engine. They

soon discovered the cause of the fire and proceeded without further incident.

2. Crew members discussed ideas to create the best solution to the problem. The captain informed the flight attendant that they had a bomb threat. They kept calm and shared their information. Together they discussed how to tell the passengers that they would not be disembarking at the terminal. They decided to tell the passengers that there were technical difficulties at the terminal.

3. Teamwork was also characterized by following procedures and instructions from superiors. After a wing engine failed immediately after takeoff on a Pacific flight, the captain and officers carried out their respective duties. On the captain's command, the second officer proceeded without hesitation to secure the engine and the first officer monitored and advised air traffic control and obtained approach clearance and they landed the plane safely.

4. Crew members gave information and identified a problem so that right person could solve it. After one of the four DC8's engines failed, everyone gave the captain information. He decided that poor weather precluded returning and that it was too soon to dump fuel. Everyone felt free to make suggestions and asked the captain to explain the delay in dumping fuel and agreed that he was making the right decision.

Failed Coordination

The study also identified situations when the failure to communicate and work together left the plane vulnerable.

1. Crew members at times did not follow procedures but this was unintentional. For example, when smoke was detected in the washroom, the first officer took the initiative, but should not have done so without instructions from the captain.

2. People ignored advice and insisted on doing it their own way. The captain was "behind the plane" in not thinking about approach and landing. However, he insisted on proceeding with the second leg of the flight despite poor weather conditions and lightning. The first officer recorded his opposition to the flight on the flight recorder.

3. Flight crew members were unable to discuss their opposing views openly. The captain ordered the first officer to take the plane down a couple of hundred feet, then down another hundred feet, and so on without any apparent reason or explanation. The first officer followed orders without questions. After the flight, the crew wondered what happened and how the first officer kept his cool. The captain apologized for his actions, but did not attempt to explain them.

4. Flight personnel ignored and were indifferent to their responsibilities. The first officer was very nonchalant when confronted by the captain about his failure to check the fuel load and baggage loading.

5. Crew members failed to communicate instructions and identify problems in a timely manner. The captain did not inform the flight attendants who were busy serving a meal that the plane was ahead of schedule. When the attendants realized they were in descent, they did not have time to secure the equipment, make the normal landing checks, or get in their jump seats.

Crew members have important ways they can work together. But they can also interfere and obstruct. What makes the difference? When did flight crew members work together productively and when did they fail to coordinate? Results of the study indicate that when crew members believe they have cooperative, rather than competitive or independent goals, they are much more likely to have coordinated effectively to restore the airplane to safety. Then they are much more prepared to discuss their ideas openly and directly so that they can together manage the crisis.

Most people recognize that organizations and teams must be flexible and appreciate it when their time and the organization's resources are used wisely. In organizations with a cooperative framework, people understand that a decision was made without them because of its costs or inconvenience, not because their ideas and interests were not valued.

More generally, individuals, groups, and organizations must develop their own forms of cooperation that fit their circumstances, goals, values, structure, culture, and personalities. Some teams need to meet five minutes every day; others once a month. Not every group needs to meet weekly to make sure everyone is doing his or her job, but some do. Some sessions require a set agenda; others are more effective free-floating. Procedures to improve team problem solving, such as assigning two subgroups opposing opinions, must be modified to fit the situation.[22]

Cooperation does not prescribe rigid ways of interacting as much as open up possibilities. To make cooperation effective and efficient requires that people have a good understanding of cooperative work. Then they can flexibly apply the idea of cooperation. Employees can work together to create the most fitting cooperative procedures. They use the issue of developing cooperative procedures to strengthen their cooperative relationships. Through cooperative interaction, people best develop forms of cooperation that are appropriate and useful for them.

DEVELOPING A COOPERATIVE CULTURE

At NUMMI, cooperative relationships supported the shared vision of building "the finest vehicles in America" and mutual respect between managers and workers. Slogans and symbols are insufficient. People have to believe the Chinese proverb, "Because we are traveling on the same ship, we will either sail or sink together."

In effective teams and organizations, cooperation is the underlying way that people work. They have a cooperative culture that signals to people that they are in this together and that they help each other accomplish their goals. This cooperative culture can be very productive and useful. As discussed in the previous section, this cooperation takes many forms.

A cooperative culture does not exclude competition and independence for they too play roles. People work independently as part of a cooperative team. Some issues and problems are more efficiently handled by one person working alone. Competition adds variety and spice; two teams compete for the best suggestion to improve safety. Some competition is inevitable; two people compete for the same job. However, they can still remember the cooperative climate in which they compete. They have the cooperative goal to have a "fair, clean" competition in which they present themselves as well as possible. Rather than criticize each other, they help each other retain their reputation and relationship so that they can work effectively after one is promoted. They continue to work on joint projects.

The essence of a cooperative culture is commitment to each other and pursing each other's interests. However, a cooperative culture does not just happen. It requires persistent effort to nurture continually. People in teams and organizations get distracted and default into competition and independence. They may believe that people cannot be trusted to help them, that others do not work in the same superior way they do, or that it is easier for them to focus only on their own goals and tasks. They may get committed to showing that they are more important than others and should be paid more.

People use a wide range of information and experiences to conclude that they have cooperative goals.[23] While we do not have a specific understanding of how people put together these various and sometimes opposing cues, the practical issue is how leaders can develop a strong cooperative culture and framework. Leaders need to work with employees so that they have overlapping reasons to believe that they have very strong cooperative goals in which competition and independence play their complementary roles. Group goals and tasks, shared rewards, connected roles, and complementary resources reinforce expressions of mutual respect and trust.

Group Goals and Tasks

The managers at NUMMI backed up talk about the company as a family with group goals and tasks. Rather than expect individuals to identify and solve production problems by themselves, they were formed into 350 five to seven person production teams. Together they had the challenge, stress, and excitement of learning to do the right things better.

For an effective group goal, people believe they are all committed to it and that success depends upon their all reaching it.[24] They have a common task: the leader asks the team as a whole is to make a set of recommendations, develop and produce a new product, or solve a problem. Team members are to integrate their ideas and develop one solution, and each person signs off on the team's output indicating that he or she has contributed and supports it. Individuals understand how their own job assignments complement each other.

Learning is a particularly valued group goal. Each worker is responsible for keeping his or her own output up and for helping others improve theirs. All group members are expected to improve their skills

---

Gainsharing at Hartzell

In 1990, W. Edwards Deming told Dwain Kasel, president of the die casting and plastic moldings company, Hartzell Manufacturing of St. Paul, Minnesota, that he "will fail. I can't tell you when but you will." Deming had no hope of Hartzell becoming a quality organization because of the factory's individual incentive plans.[25] Employees could also see Deming's logic. Milly Himes, a numerical control operator, described the situation as, "It was everyone for himself." Employees bickered with each other because some machines were easier to get bonuses on than others. Some employees wouldn't learn to operate machines considered less profitable. No worker had a stake in making the whole company better.

Hartzell instituted a factory-wide bonus program. In addition to base pay, employees receive 50 percent of the increases in productivity, which is measured by more parts produced, reduced scrap, less rework, and fewer returned parts. The change has been dramatic. Employees formed teams in which they solved problems together. Dick Bauer, a foreman in the finishing department said, "Ten years ago, I wouldn't have dreamed of grabbing a bunch of bad parts and walking over to someone and saying 'What's going on here?'" The result is that more product gets out faster and fewer parts come back. Employees have a better understanding of how the business operates and, according to Himes, Hartzell is a better place to work.

---

in managing, selling, or operating machinery. Everyone wins when people improve their technical and people skills.

Group Rewards

Leaders use group rewards so that team members understand that their own individual rewards depend upon team progress.[26] If the team is successful, then they will receive tangible and intangible benefits. Either everyone is rewarded or no one is rewarded. The team's accomplishments are recognized in the company newsletter. A party is thrown to honor the team members. Each team member receives a monetary bonus based on the team's success. Each team member receives 5 percent of the first five years' profits for a new product that the team developed and manufactured.

Organizations are adopting the Scanlon Plan and other gain-sharing and profit-sharing compensation programs.[27] Employees meet regularly to analyze their jobs and improve their processes and quality. Together they share monetary bonuses and group recognition for making the plant more effective.

NUMMI had few tangible group rewards, but had reduced unequal rewards blamed for causing rivalry over who should get the most benefits and who was more important than others. However, accepted unequal rewards can still promote unity. Although the task force leader is given 5 percent of the cost savings from the first year's use of a new inventory system, each member accepts 3 percent as reasonable for them because the task force leader was required to do much more work.

Cooperation does not imply that everyone is rewarded and no one is ever punished. Team members hold each other accountable and teams and managers hold teams accountable for meeting their commitments. Although the emphasis is on encouraging people to take initiative, members of a continually unsuccessful team may suffer a consequence. The leader confronts poor quality and takes appropriate action such as noting the group failure in the members performance appraisal reviews. Managers avoid the temptation of blaming a few but hold the group as a whole responsible.

Connected Roles

Although it de-emphasized status differences, NUMMI still had managers, industrial engineers, and team leaders. What managers emphasized was that these roles were complementary. Managers worked to create an atmosphere of mutual respect in which specialists would work with production employees to improve efficiency.

Effective teams have division of labor and specialized roles.[28] Each team member has a role that needs to be performed for the team to function properly. People discuss how their responsibilities supplement each other and how no one can be effective unless others do their jobs. They recognize that they all must fulfill their role obligations to complete the task.

Group process roles can be distributed. In a task force, the leader asks an employee to record ideas, another to encourage full participation, another to be a devil's advocate to challenge common views, and a fourth to observe and provide feedback to help the group reflect on its workings.

Complementary Resources

NUMMI managers repeatedly reminded employees that they had the information, knowledge, and competence to become more productive. Managers did not themselves have the knowledge to identify these

---

Sailing or Sinking Together

Group Goals and Tasks

- Form teams.
- Assign one task.
- Ask for solutions that integrate perspectives.
- Have each person sign off on the project.
- Gain commitment to common goal.
- Encourage group learning.

Group Rewards

- Give bonuses for group success.
- Recognize the team's success.
- Hold an unproductive team accountable.
- Develop a profit sharing plan.
- Encourage employee stock ownership.

Connected Roles

- Show the need for different perspectives.
- Respect each person's contributions.
- Discuss how to coordinate effort.
- Distribute group leadership roles.

Complementary Resources

- Recognize everyone's power.
- Appreciate the limits of one person's power.
- Understand how resources must be combined.

changes nor did managers want to coerce workers into following their ideas.

Leaders remind team members that because each person has only a portion of the information, abilities, and resources necessary to accomplish the task, they must all must contribute. They realize that as individuals they cannot each try to accomplish the task but must pool their resources. Team members identify their own individual abilities and talents so that they appreciate how each one can move the group toward goal attainment.

REALIZING THE POTENTIAL OF A COOPERATIVE CULTURE

Cooperative culture in which people focus on group tasks and share rewards is the foundation for an effective organization, but it is not an easy step. Eaton's Industrial Control Division took eight years to realize such a culture.[29] A gainsharing program was followed by reorganization into 11 large self-managed work teams. With fewer supervisors, it made sense to drop its traditional one-on-one performance appraisals for group ones. The gainsharing and participation were critical to creating, in the words of Steve Sheppard, manager of employee relations for Eaton, a "can-do attitude . . . It is information sharing at its highest level. It gives people the opportunity to actively visit the business plan each month and get some idea of what their contribution was."

Leaders recognize that cooperative cultures fosters the spirited exchange and teamwork necessary for organizations to serve their customers, innovate, and develop the intense internal commitment employees need to be successful. A cooperative culture underlies a productive, fair company that values and listens to all its employees. Leaders put this cooperative culture to work.

The essence of cooperation is not rigid adherence to democratic or other procedures but involves people supporting and cheering each other on as they work to pursue their mutual goals. Together they develop task forces, participative decision-making, work teams and other forums that help them influence each other effectively, value each other's diverse styles and opinions, and combine their energy and insights. To realize these benefits people must actually work together productively. The next chapter describes how power can strengthen the "we are in this together" feeling and joint action.

7 THE FACES OF POWER

If you want one year of prosperity, grow grain.
If you want ten years of prosperity, grow trees.
If you want one hundred years of prosperity, grow people.

Chinese proverb

Richardo Semler[1] is proud of Semco, the Brazilian conglomerate he inherited from his father in 1980. In 13 years, profits soared by 500 percent and sales of $40 million represented a six-fold increase. Most recently, the company has, through deft innovation in products and in management, coped with Brazil's "most lunatic business environment" that is like riding a "Brama bull in an earthquake." But what he is most proud of is that it does not use power to oppress but to liberate people.

When he first took over, Semler himself was intimidated. Though "shocked by the oppression" of workers he found, he took directions from more experienced managers who explained that frequent checks and controls of employees were necessary. He became a "tough guy" who devised a system of docking employees even for a few minutes of tardiness. Unfortunately, employees were not performing and "there was a sense of lifelessness, a lack of enthusiasm, a malaise at Semco." Why, he wondered, did employees have to be treated like children who had to ask foremen to go to the bathroom, bring a doctor's note when they have been ill, and blindly follow instructions? He wanted to practice an "extreme form of common sense" in that it was only reasonable to treat

115

employees as responsible adults, but extreme in that his company would really do it.

He began the revolution by eliminating the most visible signs of oppression. Rather than a demeaning search at the end of the day, a sign, "Please make sure that you are not inadvertently taking anything that does not belong to you," was put up. Small clocks replaced the intimidating big time clock; a reminder not to punch someone else's time sheet replaced the guard. Executive dining rooms, personal assistants, and other perks and privileges were abandoned.

Small changes led to big changes. Groups spontaneously spun off from a factory committee. One team restructured the dishwasher assembly line to a batch process where two or three dishwashers are manufactured by teams whose members have many different tasks, including inventory control. Another group developed a new way to preweld the base of a scale, saving $27 per unit.

"The Kids," mostly young employees, moved the electronics business to a new site. Every morning they met, dressed in all-white uniforms, to find new ways to innovate. They created a board where employees put a green tag for "good mood," an yellow tag for "careful," and a red tag for "not today—please" next to their name. Their just-in-time inventory system and improved processes moved the unit from losing money to Semco's flagship.

Semco has unusual compensation programs. A third of all employees can take a pay cut of 25 percent and then receive a supplement of up to 150 percent of their pay if the company has a good year. Nearly 25 percent of employees set their own salary; however, these numbers are published and a 10 percent pay raise is an exception. Every year or so, professionals are eligible for a sabbatical of weeks or months to learn new skills or get recharged.

It is bosses who are evaluated at Semco. Every six months results are posted. There are no hard and fast rules, but managers who consistently get poor marks tend to leave. In major decisions, such as an acquisition or plant relocation, every employee has one vote. Semler is himself regularly overruled. His office has been moved twice when he was off on his annual two-month leave. A team of diverse people run the company and confidently reject his position 20 to 30 percent of the time. "Nothing is harder work than democracy, I keep telling myself. I don't remember the last time I made a corporate decision alone, nor can I count all the times I've been voted down."

To Semler, it is the "absolute trust in our employees" that lies behind Semco's successful experiment with democracy. As partners, employees share 25 percent of corporate profits and hold an assembly to decide how to distribute it. Ironically, Semco found that by relinquishing direct controls and checks it can influence its employees and involve their hearts and minds in making the company successful.

In 1990, Brazil's minister of finance seized 80 percent of the country's cash to curb inflation, but instead made it impossible for employers to meet payrolls and halted consumer and business spending. It was a severe test for Semco's democracy. With no revenue for months, many divisions within Semco were in deep trouble. The company had to become leaner and more flexible, yet it did not want to renege on its commitment to employees. Semco came to offer employees a chance to form their own satellite organizations to supply Semco. Tax accountants, human resource staffers, and computer programmers first went off on their own followed by many blue collar workers. Soon half the manufacturing was done by these satellite companies. These entrepreneurs took risks and gave up some security but, if they did well, they could prosper. And it was clear to all that the business environment made change necessary. They could still use Semco's plant and machinery and count on at least the business from supplying Semco. Direct employment fell from 500 to 200, with nearly 300 people having a variety of arrangements with Semco.

The system is extremely loose. People come and go as they please; satellites use Semco's machines to make parts for its competitors. The company has little direct control over the people who make most of its components. Semler does feel he has given up governance but not his confidence. He does not envy the iron-fisted executive whose employees leave all the troubles in his lap every night. He has hundreds of leaders all trying to do things better.

INSIGHT INTO THE POSITIVE FACE OF POWER

Semler's insight into the positive face of power created the opportunity for him to lead the way to making Semco a place where all people feel powerful and invigorated to pursue important goals. Management recognizes and enhances the abilities and contributions of employees. Because they feel valued, employees are more open and responsive to the interests of management. The emphasis is on building up the power of employees so that they and management feel motivated, confident, and united. Power is inevitable because managers and employees depend on each other. Organizations must make power a positive force rather than deny or minimize it.

Power is a highly negative force in many companies. Employees feel intimidated because they have little recourse to what they consider their bosses' arbitrary, potentially painful decisions. They believe that power has corrupted their leaders whose goal is merely to maintain their dominance, not to develop a fair, effective team. Their solution is to limit and counter managerial power. Yet in these organizations, managers often feel they lack power and influence. They seek direct ways to control employees to overcome their sense of powerlessness. Employees are better served by powerful leaders who are confident and skilled enough to empower their employees and protect them from unwanted interference.[2]

Whether power takes a constructive or destructive course depends on whether it occurs in a cooperative or competitive situation. When people feel united in a common effort and that they are in this together, they build up each other's power and use it to help them achieve their common goals. When they feel competitive, they try to undermine each other's confidence and power. Unfortunately, it is often assumed that power inevitably involves a win-lose struggle.

Defining Power

Power has traditionally been defined as the capacity to make another do what he would not otherwise do; powerful leaders are able to overcome resistance to get those subject to power to do their bidding.[3] In addition to problems in measuring and observing,[4] this kind of definition assumes that there is an incompatibility between the person with power and the person subject to it; low power persons are "forced" to do what is not in their self-interest. The sociologist Max Weber explicitly argued that power occurs when persons are in competition.

The assumption that power occurs in competitive, win-lose situations very much affects theorizing and conclusions and makes understanding power's positive and negative faces more difficult.[5] It is often hard to distinguish what dynamics result from competition and those from power.

Power is more usefully defined as the capacity to affect outcomes, or equivalently as the control over valued resources.[6] A boss has power over an employee to the extent that the employee sees that her boss has resources that she values. She might value her boss's kindness and compassion, knowledge and suggestions how to get work done, the ability to assign people to projects, and performance ratings and bonuses. Those abilities of the boss that the employee does not see or believe will help or hurt her own success are not sources of power.

Typically, power is two-way, even if unequal. The employee has effort, assistance, ideas, and approval that the boss values to help her develop a successful department. Power is often unequal; for example, an employee feels more dependent on the resources of the manager than the manager on the employee. Power is a measure of the extent of how dependent people are; cooperation and competition measure the kind or direction of their interdependence.

Bases for Power in Organizations

What are the valued resources that give managers and employees power? People in three companies were interviewed on the abilities they needed from each other in specific situations.[7] Although the companies were quite different—one provided computer services for a large retailer, another was a municipal engineering office, and the third provided services for mentally challenged persons—employees valued similar abilities. Knowledge, assistance, and emotional support were mentioned often in all three organizations. Funding, evaluation, and authority were infrequently mentioned.

The people working in these organizations greatly valued information and knowledge; to make decisions, plan how to proceed, and perform many tasks requires the advice and data of others. They also frequently cited willingness to give assistance to complete tasks as important; many tasks cannot be accomplished by a single person working alone. Somewhat surprisingly, emotional support also was seen in nearly half the situations as an important, valued resource, even among such groups as computer specialists, people not typically thought to have strong emotional needs on the job. Even when working with their boss, employees thought that knowledge, effort, and emotional support were more important than official approval. Rewards of bonuses and evaluations, often cited in writings as major sources of power in organizations, were cited infrequently by the interviewees.

Power is central to both the productivity and people sides of organizations. Employees need a rich variety of abilities. They value others' knowledge and effort and often turn to each other for support and encouragement. Power involves the combining of information and assistance needed to complete tasks; it also grows out of the emotional needs people bring to the work place. Power cannot be wished away nor restricted to a few competitive situations. It is very much a part of cooperative work where people assist each other to get things done.

POWER DYNAMICS AT THE TOP

Top management is often portrayed as using power in negative, competitive ways. Executives form coalitions behind the scenes, lobby powerful members, withhold information, and protect turf to try to get their way and promote their special interests. Open, forthright discussions and pursuit of the common goals are mere shells and pretenses. Posturing; fights over budgets and scarce resources; and political infighting, intrigue, and sabotage are the reality.

In their study of politics in top management teams, Kathleen Eisenhardt and Jay Bourgeois[8] interviewed the CEO and his immediate subordinates in eight microcomputer firms in the San Francisco area. Four firms were characterized by competitive power and labeled as politically active; in the four others, consensus and direct controversy were the norm.

The CEOs in the four political firms tried to centralize power in themselves. As one vice-president put it, "When he makes a decision, it's like God." Another said, "Geoff is the decision maker. He runs the show by edit, not by vote." In the management meetings of one firm, it was "as if a gun would go off" as the CEO would "beat up on" people who did not reach their goals.

The executives in these firms lobbied each other before meeting as a group. They used "outlaw" meetings to try to influence decisions before discussions with the president. Rather than form ad hoc coalitions on specific issues, they relied on personal friendships based on office location, previous association, and age to protect themselves and further their interests. Consequently, meetings were more like bargaining and trading sessions than direct exploration of issues. Executives played their cards close to the vest and competed against each other.

Executives in these firms were frustrated; one wished his CEO "would go away for six months." The competitive power dynamics also appear to have greatly impacted the bottom line. One of the firms had declining sales, another was a moderate performer with low growth and modest profits, and the two others later went into bankruptcy.

In contrast, the politically inactive firms decentralized power. They adopted a team-oriented, consensus style of managing targeted for company benefit, not just for one function; super-egos were not tolerated. Executives felt that lobbying before meetings was not a good use of time. Top management meetings focused on important issues, and people changed their minds once confronted with useful ideas and data. Issues were not glossed over: they had many disagreements and some heated conflicts.

These executives were energetic, committed, and successful. One company had sales growing 25 percent to 100 percent per quarter, another tripled its sales in the year of the study, and one had a 50 percent sales growth. The fourth company was still in a start-up mode, but the future looked promising.

Eisenhardt and Bourgeois concluded that centralized power and resulting political activity consume time, distort perceptions, divert attention, result in inferior solutions, and frustrate resource sharing among groups. A cooperative power top management team is empowered and able to explore issues so that it creates and implements a strategy that combines the company's full capabilities.

RESEARCH ON COOPERATIVE POWER

Studies have directly investigated the dynamics and consequences of power in cooperative and competitive situations. Results indicate that the course and effects of power depend not so much on the amount of power but upon whether power occurs in competition or cooperation. Competitive goals lead to undermining each other's abilities, resistance to influence, and using resources to frustrate each other. Cooperative goals foster recognition of employee abilities, mutual influence and profitable exchange, and learning and development.

Recognition and Appreciation

With cooperative goals, people identify and value each other's strengths because they realize that abilities will be used for mutual benefit. It is to one's advantage that others are powerful and resourceful because powerful others help one reach cooperative goals. As having information and ideas is welcomed, cooperators help each other be aware of their ideas, information, skills, and other abilities so that they are in a better position to reach goals and do their jobs.[9]

Mutual Influence and Exchange

Despite having unequal power, people in cooperation have been found to use their abilities to promote each other's success.[10] In cooperation, high and low power people both felt secure in their expectations of each other, exchanged their resources, and strengthened their work relationships. However, with competitive goals, low power persons in particular felt insecure and doubted that they could rely on the high power persons; high and low power persons failed to exchange their abilities and information and weakened their relationships. Powerful people had the capacity to aid the less powerful but only did so when they had cooperative but not competitive or even independent goals. Within cooperation, they encouraged, guided, and gave tangible assistance that aided productivity.

Field studies have found similar power dynamics in various organizations and with peers as well as bosses and within and across departments.[11] In cooperation, managers and employees exchanged their resources and worked effectively to complete their task. With competitive and independent goals, managers and employees withheld resources and made little progress at the task.

Development and Learning

As described in Chapter 2, employees with cooperative goals help each other learn and become more effective to help everyone be successful. They initiate activities and discussion to learn. They coach each other on the job, review information and ideas that aid learning, reflect and learn from their experiences, and provide feedback to learn skills.

Research on cooperative power address David McClelland's[12] call that, while the anti-social, negative face of power has been much emphasized, the positive face of power needs to be documented. Cooperative goals are an important contributor to constructive power in organizations. Within cooperation, peers and superiors are more likely to exchange resources, empower each other, and be productive.

OBSTACLES TO EFFECTIVE LEADER RELATIONSHIPS

Many bosses and their subordinates have developed open, effective work relationships. We have seen how it is the competitive use of power, not power itself, that is obstructive. However, there are important barriers in developing the communication and mutual influence needed for an effective leader-employee relationship. Some of these barriers will be discussed next.

Communication Barriers

Bosses and their employees often have a difficult time expressing their views and feelings openly and directly influencing each other effectively. Because they feel particularly dependent and unable to protect themselves, employees are tempted to restrict themselves to that which supports the boss.[13] They worry that their views might be held against them. They may avoid direct criticism and try to ingratiate the boss to gain favor and avoid punishment.[14] They may not clarify their opinions in order to avoid delaying and upsetting their boss.[15]

Bosses have barriers to direct communication as well. They may feel obligated to protect their superior position and assert that they are more competent than those below them in the hierarchy, especially when they feel unsupported.[16] They do not want to lose social face by revealing their own inadequacies and doubts.

Employees have incentives to understand the perspective of their boss. They want to know the boss's agenda, opinions, and style so that they can adjust accordingly.[17] Although interested, they often do not understand the perspective of their boss because the boss is reluctant to share concerns, fears, and other feelings. Bosses are often distracted and focused on the views of their superiors.

Recognition and Comparisons

With positive power, leaders and employees identify and celebrate each other's abilities and resources to help everyone feel confident and empowered. However, inevitably, some employees will feel that they come up short to those who are more resourceful and knowledgeable. Comparisons are not themselves harmful; people learn about themselves through comparisons. However, invidious ones that create a sense of inferiority and competition should be avoided. Recognition of abilities needs to be well-managed.

1. Skills and achievements are not confused with personal worth. People are intrinsically worthwhile and are not just important because of their knowledge and resources. Having highly valued abilities does not make a person more moral, just as the lack of resources does not make a person unimportant.

2. Recognition is based on facts, not prejudices. Strengths and capabilities are recognized regardless of the sex, race, age, verbal skills, or health status of the employee. Not just attractive people who speak fluently have abilities. Expertise in one area does not automatically confer expertise in another.

3. The emphasis is on joining forces to be successful together. Abilities are recognized to help the team and organization feel more confident and able to achieve, not to see who is a "winner" and who is a "loser."

4. Everyone is valued. Differences in abilities should not obscure the fact that all employees have abilities, are important to the organization, and can contribute to its success. Employees understand that to be successful they must do their jobs well and contribute to the organization.

Identifying abilities and recognizing differences can, if done properly, avoid invidious comparisons and strengthen cooperation. Disclosing and recognizing abilities create a great deal of goodwill. People feel fulfilled and rewarded, and these good feelings lead to a desire to reciprocate, help others, and work together.

Employees easily underestimate the demands on their boss. Bosses are thought to have it easy in that they get other people to do their work. They have their own offices, secretaries, and other amenities. But nearly all bosses have bosses too and often must deal with complex problems in unsupportive environments. With their own frustrations, they may not be very sensitive to employee needs or very open to dealing with employee frustrations.

Influence Barriers

Effective, cooperative relationships demand two-way influence as well as communication. Assuming they are to control their employees, managers can take being open to an employee's influence as a sign of weakness, even if resistance is costly.[18] They must appear strong by resisting being influenced. Managers are tempted to use highly directive, controlling influence attempts that employees resent and resist if they can do so without penalty. Communicating an intention to collaborate rather than control often results in more openness and effective influence than commands.[19]

Bosses get distracted by their power and fail to see that they depend upon employees. They do not feel that they have to consider the employees' perspective. Fixated on their own agenda, they bark out orders, demand compliance, and neglect to listen to employees.

Many bosses assume they need to be highly competent about the full range of issues that confront the group and be able to develop the best answers. Many bosses feel they must demonstrate that they are right, always in charge, and always in control. They come across as egocentric and arrogant and reinforce employee powerlessness. Employees are reluctant to express their opinions and get involved in solving problems for fear of being second guessed and told they are wrong.

Yet some bosses fail to fulfill employees' desire to be led. Feeling uncomfortable about their authority and power, they are afraid of being heavy handed and, in vain attempts to be "participative," they fail to provide needed direction. Not wanting to appear nosy, they do not discuss employee problems. To avoid appearing too harsh and alienating, they delay confronting employees on inferior performance.

Effective work between managers and employees does not just happen. Like other relationships, the leader relationship can be productive or frustrating, formal or informal, personal or impersonal, cooperative or competitive, conflict-positive or conflict-negative. Leaders must work systematically to overcome barriers, develop cooperative leader relationships, and use power effectively.[20]

BUILDING POSITIVE, COOPERATIVE POWER

To make power a highly constructive force, leaders should work with employees to develop highly cooperative goals in which they are committed to each other and to each other's goals. (See Steps to Using Positive Power in a Team.) They recognize each other's abilities, exchange ideas and combine work, celebrate their contributions, and develop each other's strengths and confidence. Competitive goals, on the other hand, make employees and managers reluctant to appreciate each other's abilities, share resources, and build each other up.

Positive power means that employees search out each other's abilities and appreciate their contributions, negotiate and influence each other to exchange resources that will help them both be more productive, and encourage each other to develop and enhance their strengths. This power patterns occurs as employees work on a common tasks with cooperative goals. (See Figure 7.1.)

As they begin, employees can identify previous experiences, achievements, and strengths that are relevant to their task. Shared knowledge about each other's abilities makes it easier to call upon the right team member and to use all the resources available to the group. Throughout their joint assignment, employees continue to identify abilities. Celebrations through praise, giving thanks and compliments convey appreciation as well as recognize abilities. Working together also is critical for developing skills. Coaching, on-the-job training,

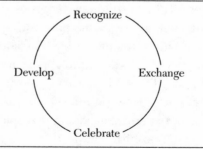

FIGURE 7.1. Positive power.

peer tutoring, and mentoring are important ways for employees to learn and grow on the job.

Leaders can develop company practices that reinforce positive power. To give recognition, newsletters, employee rosters, award ceremonies, and bulletin boards identify the talents, backgrounds, and achievements of employees and celebrate them. To facilitate the exchange of resources, the organization uses project teams, task forces, and other forums in which employees can work together and use their abilities to accomplish common objectives. At the end of meetings, employees reflect on their group processes and plan how they can improve their collaboration. The organization provides workshops, encourages professional activities, establishes networking programs, and subsidizes tuition for courses to develop employee abilities.

INFLUENCING UPWARDS

Leaders have their own leaders. Your success as a leader depends upon your superior as well as your employees. You not only should manage your boss, you have to.[21] By supporting and building their relationship with their boss, without promoting themselves at the expense of others, employees are seen as more valuable and worthy of promotion.[22] To the extent that your boss is confident and informed about you and your group, the more support you will have to be an effective leader. Managing upwards is a critical leadership ability. The foundation of influencing a boss is building an open, cooperative relationship. Without such a relationship, influencing a boss can be most difficult.

Build the Relationship

Yet your boss, like many others, may not understand the value of cooperative power or know how to develop it. Grounded in technical disciplines, many bosses have ill-conceived ideas about the leader's role and are uncertain how they can use their power and authority constructively. They expect that their employees should automatically "cooperate" and fail to realize the difficulties of establishing an effective, cooperative leader relationship.

It is a mistake to assume that a boss should take the responsibility to build leader relationships because she enjoys higher pay and other

Steps to Using Positive Power in a Team

Cooperative Goals

Leaders help each employee understand that her goals are cooperative with her leader and with her co-workers. Employees should know that as others reach their goals, they too are successful. Chapter 6 reviewed basic ways to strengthen cooperative interdependence. Important, cooperative goals lay the foundation for the following activities.

Recognize

Leaders have team members identify the abilities and resources needed for the team to accomplish its tasks and for them to reach the goals. They reveal their own abilities, knowledge, and accomplishments that can help the team work together and accomplish its goals. All team members know and appreciate each other's abilities and accomplishments.

Exchange

Team members indicate how they can use each other's abilities to complete the team's task and meet their aspirations. They agree how they can best coordinate and exchange their abilities in a timely, fair, and efficient manner. Employees let each other know when they need each other's resources. Fairness demands that everyone give as well as receive. Resources are given in ways that the receiver does not feel belittled but helps each person feel that he has important assets and can rely on others for assistance.

Celebrate

The leader helps the team celebrates "small wins" along the way to task accomplishment. The leader and team members continually and explicitly thank each other and show their appreciation. They find appropriate ways to communicate nonverbally their pleasure at being helped and at being able to help others. They create achievement lunches, sport teams, logos, dinner parties, hiking trips, and other ways that they can tangibly celebrate their joint achievements.

Develop

Through success and failure, the emphasis is on developing and refining abilities. Successes are reflected on to build confidence. Mistakes are neither blamed on a scapegoat or ignored and forgotten. Leaders and team members collect data on the effects of their work and assess what could have been more effective. They make realistic plans for improvement. However, they avoid perfectionistic standards; they realize that mistakes are both inevitable and valuable ways to learn.

prerogatives. Developing productive, honest work relationships where people feel on the same side and communicate openly and directly is challenging. Especially because it is so critical and complex, leadership should not be just the boss's responsibility. Employees and managers should do it together. Your boss may well need your assistance to develop a strong, cooperative relationship on which you can influence your boss.

In addition to responding to your boss's overtures, you, recognizing the pressures on your boss, can take the initiative to build the relationship. Make sure you understand your boss's goals and priorities, convey your own aspirations, show how together you and the boss can succeed, indicate how you are promoting your common goals, and discuss what you and the boss can do to help each other in the future. Show your appreciation that your boss has many demands by using her time wisely and making it convenient and rewarding for her to meet with you.

It is very risky to do your own thing, to outdo your boss, or to expose your boss's weaknesses. You have a vested interest in developing strong cooperative links in which you can influence your boss as well as be influenced by her.

Coping with an Intolerable Boss

Sometimes a boss is not just preoccupied and unaware of the need to develop the leader relationships, but is self-centered, nasty, and competitive. Getting a tough, competitive power oriented boss is unfortunate, but it is bad luck shared with many others. Three-fourths of the highly successful executives in three *Fortune* 100 corporations reported that they had a least one intolerable boss during their careers.[23]

How they coped with that boss illustrates that there is no easy solution. Only a few executives openly defied the boss, and fewer successfully mellowed their boss or got the organization to demote him. Believing that reforming him was a long shot, the majority accepted the boss as boss. They reminded themselves that the situation was temporary and tried to do their jobs and protect themselves. Rather than trying to cooperate or compete, they tried to reduce their dependence and minimize the damage.

The executives worked around the boss rather than with him. When they needed to talk with him, they did so when he was in a good mood. They learned his habits; if he did not like disagreement, they downplayed any. Many said that they learned to cope with adversity and be patient with others. They discovered the kind of boss they did not want to be. They appreciated the negative potential of leading and committed themselves to using power constructively.

Cooperative power is at the heart of effective leadership. Leadership is not simply getting other people to do things, but helping them feel they *want* to accomplish what needs to be.[24] Leaders do not take power from employees, but help them feel powerful. Then together they become a vital, united force to get ordinary and extraordinary things done.

8 EFFECTIVE COMMUNICATION

The greatest problem in communication is the illusion that it has been accomplished.

George Bernard Shaw

Knowledge, Peter Drucker has concluded, is the only meaningful resource today; it has replaced hierarchical position as the central basis of power in organizations.[1] Knowledge and power are now much more spread throughout the organization. Front-line employees have insights into customer needs; computer specialists use knowledge to create systems that empower these employees to respond to customer needs. To put their knowledge to work, employees and specialists must communicate and work together. At NUMMI, industrial engineers had to learn to work with production employees to improve quality. Employing technology, developing new products, and reducing costs all require people with diverse skills to communicate and work together.

Communication is vital for the most pressing task of all: preparing organizations to adapt to change and learn more effective ways of working. Levi Strauss CEO Robert D. Haas advised managers to "do as much listening as talking" because "a commitment to two-way communication" is needed to create the "common vision, sense of direction, and understanding of values, ethics, and standards" necessary to empower employees.[2]

The information-based economy has made communication even more important. Telephone and fax lines and computer networks have stimulated the making of a global economy. Walter Wriston, former Chairman of Citicorp, wrote that the "entire globe is now tied together in a single electronic market moving at the speed of light. There is no place to hide."[3]

Recognizing the value of communication does not translate directly to effective communication. Indeed, the explosion of information and communication channels adds to the difficulty of getting a message across. Politicians, business leaders, entertainers, religious leaders, advertisers, and salespeople use television, radio, telephone, fax machines, and the mail to communicate and persuade. With the clutter of so many messages through so many channels, people may end up hearing little.

Even though managers spend most of their day actively communicating in meetings and informal face-to-face encounters, over the telephone and computer lines, and through written correspondence and reports, employees have long complained about the lack of communication. Employees want to feel more included in the work place and be part of the flow of information and communication. How can managers or leaders and employees communicate effectively?

The most serious barriers to communication in the work place are psychological: they reside in fears, misgivings, preoccupations, unrealistic expectations, and mistrustful relationships. Technical skills of word selection and choosing the right channel are also important, but the critical abilities to communicate involve self-knowledge and self-acceptance, and the ability to establish effective, cooperative relationships and put oneself in another's shoes.

GETTING PEOPLE TO TALK TOGETHER: THE DELTA DENTAL PLAN OF MASSACHUSETTS

The Delta Dental Plan of Massachusetts has, since 1987 when it spun off from Blue Cross-Blue Shield as a stand alone company, worked hard to be a total quality company. Thomas Raffio, Senior Vice President of operations, described how it has developed an organization in which people communicate with each other so that they can communicate with customers.[4]

Its vision: "Delta Dental Plan is a customer-oriented organization in which each individual is committed to service excellence through active leadership and teamwork in a supportive, dynamic environment that encourages company pride." Since 1987, the number of subscribers has increased, revenue has increased, more accounts are being retained, overhead costs have decreased, and reserves have grown. Overhead costs as a percent of sales were reduced 18 percent from 1987 to 1991.

In 1990, Delta proudly proclaimed its commitment to "provide the highest level of service to all its customers" and unveiled its "Guarantee of Service Excellence." Delta promised that customers would have 10 percent saving on dentists' usual fees, same or next day resolution of all questions, 85 percent of the group's claims processed within fifteen calendar days, no inappropriate billing, new customers would receive a complete and accurate identification card within fifteen calendar days of enrolling, and companies would receive standard monthly reports within the first ten days of the next month. Each guarantee stipulated the amount Dental would reimburse the customer upon failing to live up to its pledge.

Effective communication and teamwork prepared Dental to live up to these guarantees. The steering committee created the mission statement and oversaw other task forces, which developed new products, new information systems to improve information flow, and the service guarantees. A task force developed a new organization system of cross-functional teams. A few specific examples will illustrate how these cross-functional teams operate.

Operational teams have improved the accuracy and speed of data entry for claims. For instance, after examining the patterns of out-of-state claim processing, the operational analysis team developed a system that reduced the level of suspended claims, eliminated a complete step, and improved claim turn-around time. Now Delta boosts the lowest operating cost per processed claim of all Delta Plans that have more than $15 million in revenues.

The design committee benchmarked its processes to install new customers against Mutual of Omaha, Xerox, IBM, Paul Revere Insurance Co., and ODS Health Plan. It put Delta standards for critical processes equal to or better than the benchmarked companies. It has improved its best practices rate by at least 10 percent.

After benchmarking for telephone customer service, the design committee, based on the customer service team concepts of Federal Express and L.L. Bean, formed teams each with a resource team leader, a telephone service associate, and a research associate. The office was redesigned to facilitate communication within and between these teams.

These teams can call upon "reserve teams" at peak call periods. The result has been that percentage of calls answered by customer service associates within ten seconds has improved by 100 percent without adding staff or increasing turnover. Its rate of 85 percent is much better than the 42 percent considered the best standard for the insurance industry.

The marketing committee includes operations people; a team determines payout for service failures; teams deliver quality at Delta. And effective communication and teamwork keep pushing the quality program forward. Teams have analyzed the causes behind reimbursements for service failures and implemented steps to reduce the payout. Groups identified and described every activity—how they answered phones, processed claims, and handled relationships. Then cross-departmental teams analyzed the data and presented their findings on the strengths and weaknesses to the company. Action groups were then formed to address training, benchmarking, continuous improvement, and key indicators to make Delta a stronger company that takes care of its customers and its employees.

COMMUNICATION TAKES TWO

Delta has realized that effective communication involves mutual, ongoing give-and-take. It has structured teams to facilitate the flow of information among employees and between employees and management. Leaders at Delta know that if they want employees to listen to them, then they should listen to employees.

Leaders cannot communicate by themselves. No matter how elegant the speech or persuasively framed the message, leaders cannot communicate unless someone is willing to listen. Although talking can be one-way, communication has to be two-ways.

Communication means sending a message from one person to another. One person tries to let another know what he is thinking, feeling, or believing. Accurate communication occurs when there is a good fit between the message the sender wanted to send and the message the listener actually received. Effective communication, though defined simply, is difficult to accomplish.

Communication is an integral part of people and their relationships. When we listen to a boss, we are not just listening to anyone. The boss has power over us and may give us directions. But our boss is not just like any boss. He has his own reputation and style that we consider. And we have had our own experience working with him that may have solidified his reputation or challenge us to reassess him. We bring our own concerns and misgivings: How might he react to the decision we made after he went home last night? Such attitudes as believing that we must keep this job or that we will move to another also impact our communication.

Unfortunately, many leaders ignore the reality that it takes two to communicate. They talk and when they discover the employee has not understood, they blame the employee. They complain that everyone wants to be kept informed, but no one bothers to listen. But like most difficulties in organizations, it is not simply that people are not trying. The problems of miscommunication go far beyond the lack of motivation. Ineffective communication is a signal or a sign; underlying causes of miscommunication are many.

A shared direction and cooperative goals set the stage for effective communication. To the extent that leaders and employees know each other, show interest and respect for each other as individuals and convey they want to help each other pursue their interests and goals, then communication is more likely to be open and effective. People are more prepared to make the effort to understand each other and allow fewer fears and misgivings to distract them.

Developing a strongly cooperative relationship is absolutely critical for effective communication.[5] People in cooperation compared to competition express their views openly, listen to the views of others open-mindedly, and focus on the problem; they are empathetic, spontaneous, and descriptive. In competitive relationships, people suspect each other's motives, want to prove they are right, attempt to claim superiority, try to control and force their views, and evaluate and judge each other. Not only do they mislead and misunderstand each other, but they become more mistrustful, making future communication even more difficult.

Some leaders dismiss the idea that people need strong, cooperative relationships to communicate and coordinate. They aim to rule out concerns about relationships. People are expected to be rational and businesslike. They should be mature enough to communicate so that they complete their responsibilities, regardless of their relationships. But demands to be impersonal do not change people's character; they only drive relationship concerns underground where they cannot be discussed.[6] Although people feel misled and mistrustful, they have no direct way of getting relationship issues addressed so that they can improve communication. The "hard-headed" attitude to be impersonal and not let personality and relationships interfere with communication turns out to be an impractical, unrealistic ideal.

COMPLEXITIES AND BARRIERS

In addition to developing a cooperative, mutually respectful relationship, communication also requires sensitive skills and determined effort. Sending a message from one person to another, even if they are both open-minded and cooperative, is a complex undertaking.

Communicating seems like one act, but actually has several parts. To communicate her doubts about the proposed revision to the performance appraisal system, a task force member must first try to put her hunches, thoughts, and information into words, symbols, gestures, and expressions that she believes will accurately communicate them. Then she must speak up and act consistently with these intentions. Her fellow task force members in turn use these verbal and nonverbal signals to decode the message to understand her objections.

What does it take to communicate? A sender encodes an internal message, selects a medium or channel to send the message, and uses the channel. The receiver must receive and interpret the message as intended and react to it.[7]

It is no easy matter to encode, send, and decode. For example, the task force member may have misinterpreted her unease; she was really worried that managers and employees would not be able to discuss their performance conflicts effectively but she encoded her misgivings into objections that the rating format was not objective. Task force members then began to argue the virtues of different rating systems.

Noise and barriers also occur in the channel. She may have talked too softly for the hearing impaired manager or so loudly that the people near him concentrated on adapting to the volume. Whispering by another task force member or outside noises may also distract.

Decoding can also lead to miscommunication. Task force members may have different meanings for the words used. When one member said the ratings weren't objective, they thought that he meant that there was no research behind the proposed format. They interpreted his smile as indicating that he was not serious about his message; he was using the smile to appear open-minded and reasonable.

Nonverbal communication—hand gestures, facial expressions, posture, and tone of voice—are particularly vulnerable to miscoding and misinterpretation. Yet we rely on these nonverbal signals very heavily and tend to accept them as the true message when they are in contradiction to the verbal messages. Despite her intent that her misgivings be considered thoroughly, the task force member's smile communicates that they can be dismissed. She leaves the meeting believing that despite being warm and gracious when she makes a serious point, others do not care about her or her possible contributions.

No wonder so many people complain about the lack of communication and they talk at great length about how important and critical it is. Even with strong, cooperative relationships—highly underdeveloped in many organizations—communication can be inaccurate and alienating.

TRAPS FOR LEADERS AND EMPLOYEES

Leaders have special pitfalls in communicating effectively, for example, the belief that because they are the leader, people will listen and understand them. Leaders are in a position to demand the attention of employees who risk reprimand and punishment if they fail to listen and understand. Anyone can neglect that communication takes two, but leaders are particularly susceptible. But employees are often allies in disrupting communication.

Leader Arrogance

Studies have repeatedly documented that leaders talk the most frequently in meetings and other settings.[8] They feel free to jump into conversations, even interrupt others, speak when others are reflective, and in other ways dominate conversations. Though this dominance means they are engaged in the discussion, it can easily convey a disinterest in listening to others. How can they listen when they are talking all the time?

More generally, leaders are tempted to be uninterested in understanding the perspective of employees.[9] They focus on their own opinions and feelings, assuming those of employees are less critical for the issue at hand. Employees, on the other hand, are keen observers of their bosses because they know they must adapt and respond to the views and plans of these leaders.

Yet all the talking by leaders and the interest of employees do not mean that effective communication is taking place.[10] Leaders often restrict their messages so that they do not convey weaknesses and fears. Leaders feel an obligation to demonstrate their competence and hesitate to convey their doubts and questions. They may also be reluctant to make their relationships too close and personal for fear that employees may not respect them and they will be unable to exert discipline on friends.

Leaders often believe they must show they are in charge and in control. But coercive, controlling influence creates resentment and a struggle over who is to be in charge.[11] Feeling competitive, employees resist the leader's ideas.

Leader-employee communication is highly evaluative. Leaders are continually looking for problems to be solved and mistakes to be corrected. Many employees assume that they should only bother their leader when there is a problem to report. Leaders have been repeatedly advised that they should be more willing to reward and praise employee successes. However, this tendency to evaluate and judge interferes with communication. Employees try to put the best possible light on their actions and defend themselves from criticism. Leaders quickly point out errors and find someone to blame, rather than explain their perspective fully and begin to develop ways to prevent future errors.

Employee Avoidance

Employees help leaders miscommunicate. They are reluctant to bring up "hot" issues out of fear that an irritated boss will blame the messenger. Taking the short-term view, employees hope that somehow problems will work out; in the meantime, they will keep their heads down, collect their paychecks, and, if things get bad enough, look for another job.

Despite incentives to figure out their boss, employees often under appreciate the pressures on her. The life of a boss may well seem much rosier and richer than their own, but in many organizations bosses must be on guard against rivals and mischief-makers, form alliances for self-protection, and cope with their own difficult boss. Many bosses feel besieged by problems and negative issues. Because of their years invested in the company, any misstep may seem very costly. And many leaders feel pressured to keep their frustrations bottled-up for fear of worrying employees.

Employees unrealistically assume that the boss is in the position to know their ideas, feelings, and frustrations. They tell each other, "If the boss wanted to do something about my plight, then she would do something." Yet the manager may not even know that an employee is angry, let alone the reasons behind the anger. The boss may well assume that the employee would take the initiative if there was a problem. When confronted with a problem, leaders often feel they must have a quick answer least they appear incompetent, even though the problem deserves thorough consideration by several people.

Leaders and employees help each other avoid open communication and stay out of touch. However, frustrations do not disappear. They fester, distort, and pollute their work relationships and cast doubt that they can trust each other and are on the same side.

LEADING BY EXAMPLE

Presented with the urgent need to communicate and the difficulties of doing so, many leaders jump to the conclusion that it is a problem that they should identify and fix. They will remind people that communication is important, ask them to improve their communication, and offer training in communication skills. But the most powerful action leaders can take is to change their own behavior by demonstrating the interest and the ability to communicate, in particular, to show that they are listening to employees.

An executive found a way to signal that he wanted two-way communication. "I was a marketing guy sent to start up the first computerization project our company had every attempted. . . . I faced this group of computer fanatics ready to revolutionize our operations. Maybe my ignorance saved me because how could I posture when I knew nothing? Anyway, this is what I said, 'Let me tell you guys three things. One, you've got a leader who knows nothing about computers and a lot about marketing, so we've both got a lot to learn from each other. Two, I'm not afraid to say I don't know and ask stupid questions, and don't you be either. Third, let's not worry about our differences too much. Let's see what we can do to set up this system and while we're at it let's move the art of marketing twenty years into the future.'"[12]

Rather than demand that everyone else take communication training, leaders model the way and change their behavior. They take formal training in communication skills and demonstrate that they are practicing these skills on the job. They use effective communication skills even in difficult, trying circumstances when crises have to be managed and conflicts faced.

The leader listening to employees makes it easier for employees to listen and understand her. It is ironic that often the best way for a leader to get a point across is to for her to understand the employee's point. Just repeating a message gets in the way of communication. Listening reduces employee misgivings that the leader is too arrogant and pretends to know too much. When leaders show concern and listen, employees focus on the leader's message.

PUT YOURSELF IN THE OTHER'S SHOES

Communicating effectively is a complex art built on many skills. Becoming a skilled communicator is a life-long effort. Effective communicators know themselves, accept their feelings, and have developed the skills to express themselves directly and unambiguously. They are forthright and credible as their nonverbal communication reinforces their verbal.

Perhaps the most vital of all communication abilities is a receiving one, not a sending one. Learning to take the perspective of another is absolutely critical to communicating. Putting yourself in the position of others helps you listen to understand their message as well as encode and express yours.

Research has demonstrated the power of perspective taking.[13] Demonstrating an understanding of messages of others by rephrasing their views contributes to communication effectiveness, relationship development, decision-making capacity, and conflict management. Taking the perspective of people helps them feel more understood and accepted and helps the perspective-taker become more open-minded and aware. Perspective taking stimulates intellectual development and moral reasoning, awareness of the goals and aspirations of others, and sensitivity to a range of feelings.

Taking the perspective of others helps send accurate messages. Leaders who can anticipate how people will react to their verbal and

---

Keys to Communicate

Sending	Relationship	Receiving
Self-knowledge	Cooperative	Attend to other
Self-acceptance	Mutually accepting	Stop talking
Consistent nonverbal	Respectful	Understand, not judge
Ask to take perspective	Common language	Perspective take
Confront	Openness	Interview
"I," "my" statements	"You are important"	"What I understand you to mean is"

---

nonverbal messages are more able to communicate effectively. They phrase their message so that listeners can decode it consistent with their intentions.

Strategies

Rephrasing another's verbal and nonverbal messages demonstrates active listening. It reminds the sender that the listener is engaged and working to understand him. The listener begins with "What I understand you mean . . ." or a similar phrase. By accurately reflecting back the message, the listener conveys an interest in the other person as well as knowledge of his views.

There are more common, abbreviated ways to show an attempt to perspective take, such as simply nodding one's head or saying, "I understand, I see your point." However, these methods are easily overused and lose their impact. The sender may conclude that rather than an invitation to be more forthcoming, head nodding is an attempt to appease and brush off his concerns.

Taking perspective is a complex, challenging task. A person must put away her own concerns and issues to focus on the employee's. Then she must attend closely to the verbal and nonverbal messages and decide how the sender encoded the message. She must conclude both how the sender intends to use the words and nonverbal signals and what the sender might be trying to convey implicitly. Then she must encode her own understanding and communicate that to the listener. No wonder people rely on head nodding and agreement to convey perspective taking!

Cross-cultural communication highlights the difficulties of perspective taking.[14] If the sender is from another country and culture, then it is especially challenging to decide what the verbal and nonverbal signals are meant to communicate. Does head-nodding and a quiet "yes" mean agreement? A willingness to consider the idea? A desire to be a friend who does not disagree openly? Learning to work with people of different backgrounds requires a great deal of perspective-taking effort to know how they send messages.

Individuals within one culture are more likely to estimate accurately how people are using words and gestures. Yet this relative ease of communication can lead to an illusion of understanding. People within one culture also have different ways of signaling a message, but because they assume they have similar ways, they never check out their understandings and are left feeling misunderstood.

Rephrasing another's message can be poorly done. It can be used when inappropriate, such as when the message is very straightforward without many feelings. "What I understand you mean is that you just got yourself a glass of water," for example, is seldom effective. A larger danger is that reflection becomes a formula. The listener begins with "what I hear you saying is . . ." and then simply repeats the words of the sender.

Showing that you, the leader, have taken an employee's perspective may seem too time consuming and complex for already pressured leaders. But perspective taking mirrors the challenges of communication. It is not a new demand, but an integral part of being a leader who communicates. What appears to be time consuming may be time saving in terms of the final outcome.

Interview to Perspective Take

Interviewing is a powerful way to understand another's perspective. Most interviews in the work place are informal: the supervisor asks an employee to explain what happened on the night shift. Formal interviews are often used in hiring and handling grievances.

Much more interviewing should be done between leaders and employees. Informal interviews where the leader listens and tries to put himself in the employee's shoes can be very useful to help an employee express her excitement, fears, and troubles. Leaders may also want to make a formal interview of each employee a regular part of the work place.

Interviews help leaders demonstrate that they care about employees. Interviews break down stereotypes and misunderstandings so that people understand each other's needs and perspectives. Interviews can help make motivation knowledge concrete and useful. Employees talk about their achievement, affiliation, and power needs and how they are trying to meet them. What do they find valuable in their jobs and how can these rewards be reinforced?

As with "managing by walking around," the emphasis in interviewing is on understanding and positive feedback. Interviews also uncover problems and difficulties. Employees identify what are the obstacles and distractions that get in their way of working productively. The leader and employee brainstorm on how to overcome these roadblocks.

Employees should also interview. Many leaders have used informal brown bag lunches and question-and-answer sessions to communicate their perspective and priorities. Employees' taking turns interviewing each other can develop trust as well as help discover effective ways to work together.

Guides for Interviewing

Successful interviewing requires that people feel able to recall information accurately and disclose it willingly. There is no magic formula or set phrase for success. Interviewing involves complex skills learned through experience. Remember the central ability is to put yourself in the other's shoes and to demonstrate this to the interviewee. You are listening to understand, not trying to judge and evaluate.

In the first part, the interviewer should work to establish a climate of respect, openness, and confidentiality. She indicates the purpose of the interview and the ground rules for how the information will be used and in what ways it will be confidential. She shows warmth and interest in the other person and invites him to express any concerns about the interview.

The second part begins the probing and listening. Typically, the interviewee will want to ask open-ended questions focused on the issue of the interview. The interview is not a time for the interviewer to talk and tell her views, but to listen carefully to those of the interviewee. General opinions and evaluations are important, but they should be followed up with the background experiences and logic that resulted in these conclusions. The interviewer asks for specific examples and situations that give a picture of what led to the interviewee's feelings and opinions. Throughout, the interviewer demonstrates listening and responds to the interviewee's feelings.

In closing, the interviewer expresses her thanks for the interviewee's openness and summarizes what she has learned. She reaffirms the purpose of the interview and restates how the information will be used and in what ways it will be held confidential.

EARNING CREDIBILITY

Leaders seek to be credible, but they can not demand it. They communicate their values and let employees know who they are as persons. They follow up their ideals. They do more than "talk the talk"; they "walk the talk." They take opportunities to describe their vision and inspire people to work together. Forthright, consistent communication builds credibility.

Leaders should also remember that by listening closely and putting themselves in the shoes of employees they also build credibility. Employees reciprocate their leader's respect and caring. They are prepared to solve problems and create an organization that deserves their loyalty.

How practical is it for leaders to take perspective and model good communication, given the pressures to get things done and the need to evaluate performance? Leaders must deal with low performing employees, reject employee recommendations, and give performance appraisal ratings. Leaders must at times judge, but it is not necessary that people generally feel they must be on guard because their leader is evaluating and critiquing them. Leaders create a climate in which people feel accepted and able to express their ideas, hunches, and feelings. The next chapters explore how leaders and employees can express irritation and other feelings and how they can manage conflicts constructively.

9 FEELINGS AND THEIR EXPRESSION

Anyone who keeps the ability to see beauty never grows old.
                                                    Franz Kafka

Jack Welch, CEO of General Electric, has discovered the value of open communication throughout an organization. Key to GE's future is "an open, trusting, sharing of ideas. A willingness to listen, debate, and then take the best ideas and get on with it."[1] GE's "enormous advantage . . . [is to be] as a laboratory for ideas. We've found mechanisms to share best practices in a way that's trusting and open."

His commitment to open communication is based on business logic, not on sentiment. He got the nefarious reputation as Neutron Jack because he was reputed to have restructured and downsized GE by eliminating people but leaving the buildings standing. His credo is leaders must face reality and their only choice is to control their destiny or someone else will.[2] The "way to control your destiny in a global environment of change and uncertainty is simple: Be the highest value supplier in your marketplace."

Welch defends using toughness and power. Indeed, employees "don't like weak managers, because they know that the weak managers of the 1970s and 1980s cost millions of people their jobs." His biggest mistake "by far was not moving faster. Pulling off a Band-Aid one hair at a time hurts a lot more than a sudden yank. Of course, you want to avoid breaking things or stretching the organization too far—but generally human nature holds you back. You want to be liked, to be thought of

145

as reasonable. So you don't move as fast as you should. Besides hurting more, it costs you competitiveness."

He advised leaders that they have "got to be hard to be soft. You have to demonstrate the ability to make the hard, tough decisions—closing plants, divesting, delayering—if you want to have any credibility when you try to promote soft values. We reduced employment and cut the bureaucracy and picked up some unpleasant nicknames, but when we spoke of soft values—things like candor, fairness, facing reality—people listened. . . . Before you can get into [teamwork throughout the organization], you've first got to do the hard structural work. Take out the layers. Pull up the weeds. Scrape off the rust."

Now that GE has scraped away the rust, Welch is building GE's future on mutual trust and respect.[3] "The autocrat, the big shot, the tyrant" who forces rather than inspires performance must change or leave because "trust and respect take years to build and no time at all to destroy. . . . More and more we're cutting back on useless titles and we're rewarding people based on what they contribute—the quality of their ideas and their ability to implement them, rather than on what they control."

Welch understands that "trust is enormously powerful in a corporation. People won't do their best unless they believe they'll be treated fairly—that there's no cronyism and everybody has a real shot. The only way I know to create that kind of trust is by laying out your values and then walking the talk. You've got to do what you say you'll do, consistently, over time."[4]

But Welch does not consider trust a wishy-washy sentiment. "I have a great relationship with Bill Bywater, president of the International Union of Electronic Workers. I would trust him with my wallet, but he knows I'll fight him to the death in certain areas, and vice versa. He wants to recruit more members for the union. I'll say, 'No way! We can give people everything you can and more.' He knows where I stand. I know where he stands. We don't always agree—but we trust each other."

Welch has found no inconsistency between being tough and being responsive to people. To create "an environment where we must have every good idea from every man and woman in the organization, we cannot afford management styles that suppress and intimidate." Strong relationships where ideas, feelings, and values are communicated are necessary. "If you're not thinking all the time about making every person more valuable, you don't have a chance. What's the alternative?

Wasted minds? Uninvolved people? A labor force that's angry or bored? That doesn't make sense!"

"Any company that's trying to play in the 1990s has got to find a way to engage every single employee. Whether we make our way successfully down this road is something only time will tell—but I'm sure as I've ever been about anything that this is the right road."

VALUES AND FEELINGS IN THE LEAN ORGANIZATION

Organizations must be disciplined and management tough to be successful in the competitive marketplace. Welch and other leaders have learned that, although at first this emphasis suggests promoting productivity over people, it actually requires developing a trusting environment where people express themselves fully and develop open relationships.

Welch argued that "every organization needs values, but a lean organization needs them even more. When you strip away the support systems of staffs and layers, people need to change their habits and expectations or else the stress will just overwhelm them. We're all working harder and faster. But unless we're also having more fun, the transformation doesn't work. Values are what enable people to guide themselves through that kind of change."

The lean organization must break away from the traditional stereotype that being rational, mature, and businesslike means suppressing feelings. Traditionally, feelings have been considered counterproductive; showing feelings should be left to after-work socializing, retirement parties, and retreats on the company's vision and teamwork.

But feelings do not get in the way of effective action. It is the suppression and other harmful approaches to feelings that disrupt people and their work. Employees angry about being terminated with no appropriate way of expressing their feelings have turned to violence, even shooting, to vent and retaliate.[5]

Cooperative, mutual power relationships and effective communication skills help manage feelings successfully. This chapter explores the pervasiveness of emotions in organizations and how to resolve the values of openness and inhibition of feelings. Feelings do not just happen, but develop from how people think about and interpret their experiences. Feelings do not force behavior, but people have choices in how to feel and express feelings. Expressing emotions well buttresses rational thinking, productivity, and innovation.

REALITY OF EMOTIONS

Leaders and employees have strong feelings whether they are supposed to or not. The emphasis on rationality only drives feelings underground, making it more difficult for people to manage them constructively.[6] It is irrational to expect people to be only rational without emotion on the job.

Leaders and employees feel supported, committed, invigorated, but also anxious, lonely, and angry in organizations. Some people embrace the excitement of change; others deplore their losses. Feelings are internal reactions to experiences.[7] Experiencing rejection makes the heart beat faster, increases energy and thoughts of crying, running away, or fighting. Experiencing acceptance can slow the heart beat, create a warm glow of feeling okay, and build energy and commitment to help others. Feelings are inside but they seek outward expression.

Futurists had predicted that employees would have to cope with a great deal of boredom and monotony in their work. Workers would be pressing buttons to operate technology and machines, waiting until the end of their shift. Their challenge would be to use their considerable leisure time. It has not worked out that way. Few people complain that their work life is too slow-paced or that they have too much time to relax and unwind.

Rapid, continuous change provokes strong emotions. People worry that their company is losing market share and they might lose their jobs. Others are thrilled by the prospects of increased sales. Some workers doubt that they can master the new technology whereas others are energized to use it. Employees in some organizations feel empowered and united to confront the challenge to be more productive; employees in other organizations are frustrated and demoralized because they are so divided and unfocused. Some managers are angry because top management plans to restructure; others are relieved that top management is finally committed to change. Indeed, one person can feel both excited and worried, optimistic and pessimistic in the face of change.

Much emotion in organizations is hidden. The feelings are there but appear not to be. An employee hides her anger from her boss for fear of derailing her career. An employee does not want to bother his coworker by talking about his frustration. Pretending to be working happily along, they feel unappreciated and devalued inside. People smile on the outside, but rage on the inside. The result is people are unsure where they stand with each other.

Behavior that communicates a lack of involvement and feeling may be generated from strong feelings. Much is discussed about how people want to take it easy and "free ride" without contributing.[8] They do as little as possible and just do not care. However, often intense feelings have paralyzed them. Believing they are unable to contribute, they use their energy in self-doubt and fear the risks of revealing their insecurity. Or believing their colleagues have belittled them and pushed aside their ideas, they seethe with anger and withdraw from work as a way to take silent revenge.

Feelings are important in organizations because organizations are important to us. Working in organizations is not a vanilla-flavored, take-it-or-leave-it experience. Violence, crises, and strikes provoke strong feelings, but so too do everyday events. Achievement, affiliation, and power needs, our development as secure and self-confident people, our self-image as contributors to society and to our families all depend on our work. We identify with our profession and organizations and they become part of our self-identity. We must deal with the rich complexities of relationships with peers, employees, and bosses. Indeed, as our communities become more fragmented and our families more dispersed, we expect more from our jobs and work relationships. With more invested, we have stronger feelings that are alternatively energizing and enervating.

Despite persistent efforts, feelings cannot be denied and pushed aside.[9] However, our stereotypes and demands to hide feelings have meant that people are unskilled about how to manage on-the-job feelings. So much energy has been devoted to pretenses and defenses and so little to the constructive expression of feelings. The most accomplished managers and professionals often feel at a loss even to identify their feelings, much less to express them. They turn away from feelings and issues of people and relationships to focus on what they believe they can do, namely, get specific jobs done. But such narrowly focused leaders, Welch has reminded us, are not up to the challenge of mobilizing everyone in the organization.

Organizational leaders have begun to appreciate the reality and power of emotions. They see that contemporary demands require people to commit their hearts as well as their heads. To get extraordinary things done, they must encourage their employees to think long-term, take risks, and persist to overcome obstacles. A paycheck and a pin every five years is simply not enough. People need public recognition, genuine praise, and warm support if they are going to continue to give so much of themselves to their work.

Welch argued that leaders should set "the bar higher than people think they can go. The standard of performance we use is: Be as good as the best in the world. Invariably people find the way to get there, or most of the way. They dream and reach and search. The trick is not to punish those who fall short. If they improve, you reward them—even if they haven't reached the goal. But unless you set the bar high enough, you'll never find out what people can do."[10] Going through the motions does not result in superior customer service, new products, and reduced costs necessary to stay competitive; spirited, driven, emotional teamwork is necessary for organizations to survive and prosper.

OPENNESS AND INHIBITION

The advice of Welch and other leaders for more open communication in business organization is an extension of the social movement toward openness and genuineness. Psychotherapists and family psychologists have advised people to express their feelings more openly as key to well-being. The capacity to feel is as important to being a human being as the capacity to think and act. Expressing affections, even irritation and anger, can be enhancing experiences. Stuffing feelings inside harms people and their relationships.

Today's leaders want people to feel good about their company and care about its products and customers and each other.[11] Teams have gone on wilderness trips to strip away artificial barriers. Through the struggles of climbing mountains and forging rivers, team members are able to reveal themselves as they really are. Celebrations and hoopla are becoming more accepted in many businesses.

Expressing feelings is valuable and important in itself.[12] People feel better after telling others about their disappointments. Talking does not change that the salesperson lost the sale the company was counting on, but it helps him keep perspective on it. He also has much more fun celebrating a sale with his colleagues than alone.

Talking about feelings builds a sense of trust and mutual sympathy that underlies productive work relationships. People get to know each other as individuals and understand their agendas and thinking. Expressing feelings helps identify issues and focus on resolution. People stay in touch and become aware of the difficulties that potentially disrupt their relationships.

Leaders are relying on feelings and intuition in making decisions, not just the techniques of analysis. After or even despite the rational analysis of the problem, they must feel right about the decision. A university president argued that he felt he had to go along with his team when everyone but himself agreed. However, upon reflection, the decision invariably proved ineffective when he did not go with his gut feeling.

Feelings are windows to people's inner lives. By sharing feelings, people know each other's experiences and thinking. They see how they are interpretating and reacting to events. People who know each other become effective at predicting how they will react to situations.[13] Even a short expression of feeling can reveal a great deal about a person.[14]

Yet the value of open feelings is not easily extended to the world of organization. Many managers shudder when they envisage people openly expressing their feelings. Such openness, they believe, would only increase the already too much chaos and disruption in the work place. They sense that they and employees have too little knowledge and practice to express their feelings directly and constructively.

The choice is not between being open or inhibited with feelings nor between being rational or emotional. Leaders and employees must be able to be both open with their feelings and able to inhibit them. Leaders and employees must manage their feelings in rational, effective ways. They must know their choices about how to express and deal with their emotions and the purposes for which various options are useful. A first step is a good understanding of how people develop feelings.

THINKING AND FEELING

A most common and most misleading belief is that feelings and thinking are separate and distinct from each other. People think with their brains and feel with their hearts and guts. Since Freud, psychologists have argued that people often rationalize their feelings: they project that their ideals and thinking guide their behavior, but their feelings and desires actually do.

Thinking and feeling are not separate and divorced. How people interpret and understand an event very much affects how they react and feel about it.[15] If they believe a colleague is talking with others about their illness because he is worried about their health, they react one way. If they believe he is gossiping to make them look weak, they react quite differently. Other people and events do not directly cause our feelings; how we think about people and interpret their actions do.[16] Because we can change our thinking, we can change our feelings.[17]

Often feelings, especially those of others, just seem to appear and can be easily dismissed as irrational experiences that with luck will soon pass. "My employee must have gotten up on the wrong side of the bed this morning and next week he won't be so upset." But feelings develop from how people think about their experiences. Once the reasoning behind them is understood, feelings seldom seem irrational and crazy.

Anger does not just come over a person, but develops from thinking (Figure 9.1). How people interpret an event very much affects their feelings about it. The boss asking an employee to work late and miss a son's piano concert can cause anger if the worker believes the boss could have easily foreseen the added work and made other plans. However, it may be only annoying if the added work was thought to be necessary and unpredictable. Indeed, the employee might also feel grateful that she has an opportunity to reciprocate for the time off the boss had given her when her son was sick.

Recently, we began a team-building session by asking the three women in the group to discuss the feelings they had now and what lay behind them. Sarah talked about her frustrations that she was not going forward in her career. Her life outside of work was finally in good shape but she worried about her future. How could she translate this job into a long-term career? Georgia revealed that she was preoccupied with an upcoming performance appraisal session. She had many issues and conflicts with her boss. With so many high hopes and fears about the performance review, she felt on hold, waiting for the big day. Marlene, the newcomer, said she was frustrated because she and the group were not

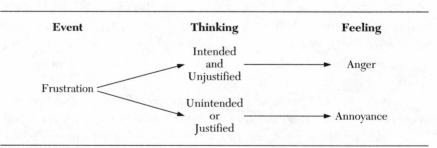

FIGURE 9.1.   Feeling angry.

making progress on their special projects. She hated trying to keep herself busy doing small tasks and not taking the initiative to do the long-term projects that would make a difference to the organization. She was tired of putting out fires. Was this a job that would allow her to have an impact on the whole organization?

Although the three women were friendly with each other, worked side-by-side, and had labeled themselves a team, they had not shared their feelings. Sarah and Georgia did not want to demoralize the others with "down" talk. Marlene felt awkward as a newcomer to bring up her concerns; she did not want to intrude.

After they discussed their feelings and what lay behind them, they quickly saw how their failure to communicate feelings had frustrated them and their work. They brainstormed ways that they could help each other deal with their issues. They doubted that Georgia was realistic in expecting to handle so many conflicts in one performance session and identified other forums to discuss issues with her boss. They also renewed their joint effort to manage conflicts with their boss more openly and effectively. They encouraged Marlene to step up and take more leadership for they too wanted to have an impact on the whole organization. Sharing feelings led to productive joint action.

GENERATING FEELINGS

Feelings arise from our experiences and how we think about them. Although it typically seems like only one step, developing a feeling is more complicated and can be described as a five-step process.[18]

1. People gather information about what is going on through their senses. They see, hear, touch, taste, and smell to determine what is happening outside them. This information describes what appears to be taking place, but it does not give a meaning to it. They see their boss's withdrawn eyes but they can give that many interpretations.

2. People interpret the information to decide what it means. This interpretation goes on inside; the events and people outside them do not determine how they interpret them. They believe that the withdrawn eyes means that their boss feels sad and lonely, or that she feels angry and upset. It is up to them to decide, based on the

information and their own ideas and assumptions, the meaning the event has.

3. People have an internal reaction based on this interpretation. When they see their boss walking around the office not smiling, they may interpret that to mean that she is lost in thought about how the department can best respond to the budget reductions just announced by the CEO. Or they may conclude that she just does not think her employees are important and valuable enough for her to pay attention to or that she is upset with their handling of the broken pump problem. Their interpretation of the boss's behavior affects their internal reactions; they may be grateful she is willing to confront the budget problem, demoralized that she is uncaring, or angry that she will not discuss the pump and see their side of the situation.

4. They decide how to express this feeling externally. Feelings generate energy and a push for an outlet. They suggest plans for action and immediate goals that will give expression to the feelings. Gratitude to the boss makes people think they want to smile and encourage her; feeling unvalued leads to thoughts of complaining to their peers about their arrogant boss, and anger suggests that they should take a drink or a long run and try to forget about work and the boss.

5. People express their feelings. They smile and laugh, frown and grimace, gossip and complain. They seek out their boss for a talk, or they work hard to avoid her. They feel energized to get the assignment done or defend themselves. They mope and look at the employee opportunities section of the want ads.

Marlene saw her colleagues withdraw from eye contact and conversation and heard them grumble. Based on this information, she concluded that they were upset and did not want to work on their special projects or discuss their feelings. She felt frustrated and hampered. She decided to express her feelings by not bothering her colleagues. She busied herself trying to find little things that needed to get done. Seeing her busy, Sarah and Georgia concluded that she was doing okay and that they should not engage her in their feelings of frustrations and interfere with her by talking about their feelings. The result was more misunderstood feelings and ineffective work.

EXPRESSING FEELINGS

Feelings press for expression. Trying to hide them and keep them inside so that no one knows is hard work and very difficult to do completely.[19] Suppression leads to conclusions that one is dependent, unable to influence one's destiny and undermines physical health.[20] Feelings are powerfully communicated by tone of voice, facial expressions, and body movements. Avoiding someone often communicates a great deal. Trying to conceal feelings typically provokes speculation. Sarah and Georgia did not want to express their frustrations, but Marlene drew her own conclusions about their feelings and what lay behind them. The issue is not so much whether to express emotions but how to express them.

People have choices in how they express feelings. Relationships very much affect the communication of feelings.[21] Indeed, people find it easier to control what they do than control how they think about emotional situations. In a study of anger, people were found to verbally lash out and punish, but they also talked to the person without hostility, talked to others to get their perspective, ventilated, gossiped to get back, and took their anger out on others.[22] People are by no means programmed to deal with anger and other feelings in one way; they have options.

How can people express feelings directly and openly? How can they show their feelings in ways that help others reveal theirs?

Creating cooperative relationships where people value each other's abilities is the foundation for the constructive expression of feelings. When people feel they are on the same side and valued, they trust that they can share their reservations and doubts as well as joys. Communication skills of showing empathy and concern for each other's perspective also lay the groundwork for the skillful expression of feelings.

Communication Skills

A fundamental, but often forgotten, skill is to identify the feeling as your own. Use a personal statement with "I," "me," or "my" to indicate that you own and take responsibility for the feeling. You communicate that it is you that feels exhilarated, angry, or lonely. Personal statements recognize that you have made interpretations of behaviors that have resulted in your feelings. Identifying your feelings this way communicates clearly and avoids blaming others for your feelings.

Feelings need to be identified, often simply by labeling it. "I feel humiliated." "I feel proud of our accomplishments." "I feel confused." People have many colorful, vivid ways of identifying feelings through figures of speech. "I feel as happy as a bear in a salmon spring." "I feel like a cloudy day."

People use descriptions. "I feel like I just got a shot of adrenalin." "I feel like I've just been kicked in the stomach." People also identify what the feeling makes them want to do. "I am so upset I could scream." "I feel like giving you the biggest hug." Recognizing, labeling, and describing feelings are fundamental expressing skills.

Nonverbal Communication

Posture, body language, facial expression, tension, eye contact, hand and body movement and gestures, tone of voice, rate and pauses in speech, spatial distance, and touch all communicate.[23] Ralph Waldo Emerson wrote, "When the eyes say one thing and the tongue another, a practical man relies on the language of the first." The boss's ignoring a proposal makes those who prepared it angry. An employee's absence from the company party perplexes his colleagues. But nonverbal communications are subject to widely discrepant interpretations.

"Actions speak louder than words" is often said and often believed. Estimates are that more than 65 percent of the social meaning of a message is communicated through nonverbal cues and less than 35 percent by words.[24] A grimace overshadows a verbal apology. Smiling at the same time as identifying anger confuses and downplays the feeling. Nonverbal communication is key to expressing feelings fully and accurately.

Nonverbal cues are powerful but blunt and ambiguous. Smiling typically communicates acceptance, interest, and liking for another, but it also can seem like a smirk that communicates disdain and disrespect. Direct eye contract is usually thought to mean an interest and commitment to the person, but it can be construed as an attempt to embarrass and overpower.

Individuals, social groups, and cultures have different rules about how to use nonverbal communication.[25] Social distance in some cultures is a mark of respect; in another it communicates aggressiveness or fear or aloofness. Touching in some groups is a sign of warmth, but in others it is a powerplay. Downcast eyes may communicate deference but to others disinterest.

There are many ways that the same feeling can be communicated nonverbally. Happiness can be communicated by shouting, jumping up and down, crying, and glowing. Anger can be communicated by shouting, jumping up and down, crying, silence, demanding, and glowering.

The power of nonverbal messages needs to be channeled to support the direct verbal expression of feelings. The major principle is to make nonverbal messages consistent with verbal ones. Words are used to clarify and specify the feelings. A leader smiles when he tells an employees he likes her work. An employee shows a serious face and erect posture when she describes her anger at being insulted.

Ventilate

The direct, open expression of anger to an intolerable boss, affection to a new customer, concern for a preoccupied colleague, or frustration with a stressed employee may not be wise or practical. Even when direct expression is possible, it is often useful to express feelings, especially anger, indirectly first so that they do not overpower.

Techniques for releasing feelings include:

- *Exercise.* Vigorous and active activities such as running, swimming, racket sports, and fast walking are useful.[26] Shouting, screaming, crying, throwing things, and punching pillows release energy.

- *Talking to others.* People spend a great deal of time confiding, complaining, and gossiping. When others listen, such talk helps reduce the power of feelings.

- *Resolve the situation in your mind.* After deciding that you do not want to feel so intensely, find ways to view the frustration as something you can live with. Give up telling yourself that the other should act more fairly and justly. Focus on relaxation rather than revenge.

Sometimes leaders and employees have to keep their frustration and anger to themselves. They may conclude that expressing feelings directly is unwise and may not have an appropriate way to realize them indirectly. Generally, though, they ventilate to reduce the pressure of a negative feeling rather than hold on to it and bear a grudge.

CHANGING FEELINGS

Feelings can be changed. Change the interpretation of an event and the feeling is changed. Feelings are real and vital and people have reasons for their feelings. However, their reasoning may be faulty because of inadequate information or biased consideration. Leaders and employees must at times confront their interpretation of an incident and change their feelings about it.

Checking Interpretations

Incomplete, misleading information leads to faulty interpretations and confusing, destructive action. Employees did not see that their boss was just told that her daughter must undergo serious surgery. With this information, they would analyze, react emotionally, and behave much differently to her downcast eyes and avoidance. Information is seldom complete. Employees cannot see inside their leader and know all the information and ways she is interpreting and deciding how to communicate her feelings.

Interpretations can be faulty because of competitive relationships. People conclude that a competitor's smile is insecure and his offer to assist is a trick. Indirect ways of expressing feelings also lead to misleading interpretations. As we have seen, nonverbal communication is powerful but easily misinterpreted. Despite these problems, often people quickly and confidently become convinced that their interpretations are right and their feelings justified.

Realizing the dangers of reaching conclusions based on limited data, leaders and employees should search for information to make a more realistic assessment of events. They ask their colleague if he realized that he interrupted them three times at the meeting with their boss? Did he mean to imply that his views were more important than theirs? Does he understand that his actions conveyed that message? With answers to these questions, they are in a much better position to decide whether they are insulted, how frustrated and angry they are, and how they should respond.

Checking the intentions and feelings of another helps people examine their own thinking and reasoning. Why did they conclude that their colleague was trying to make them look bad in front of their boss by interrupting them? It may be that the colleague was actually very uptight because he felt the boss was blaming him for the miscue.

Beliefs about a person very much influence reasoning and feelings. If employees have concluded that their boss is arrogant, her walking by their office without speaking quickly reinforces their views. If they assume that the new CEO is trying to make a mark by making big changes, they might conclude that the boss is trying to decide the best way for the department to adapt and are grateful she has that job. Checking interpretations can help people see the need to change their assumptions.

Challenging Unrealistic Assumptions

In addition to beliefs about specific people, general assumptions about ourselves and other people also impact interpretations and feelings.[27] Sometimes these assumptions are unrealistic and result in continual depression or anger. But these assumptions can also be changed.

Feeling frustrated, low, and angry are natural and inevitable, but some people find themselves feeling depressed or frequently angry. Depression and anger would seem like opposite conditions. But there is a strong link between the two. The major difference is that depressed people tend to blame themselves for their situation whereas highly aggressive people blame other people.

Depressed people are not just feeling blue for a few days, but feel low for weeks and months. They feel lethargic, as if they cannot move. Angry people may be abusive, alienate friends, as well as continually upset their own mood.

Unrealistic assumptions underlie the feelings of deep depression. They lead to interpreting events as losses and undermining the ability to cope with them.[28] Common assumptions include:

- I am a good person; everyone should like and respect me. If they do not, then I must be a bad person.
- I should be able to do everything perfectly. If I do not, I am a worthless person.[29]
- Because I am frustrated now, I will always be frustrated and never feel fulfilled.

Angry people also use assumptions to interpret events as losses and that people are committed to their intentional, unjust frustration that precludes their fulfillment. Common assumptions are:

- Every person who gets angry at me has acted unjustly and unfairly.

- Every criticism is designed to make me look foolish and weak; my self and social respect demand that I counterattack.[30]

- I have the right to an uninterrupted lunch hour (or chair, traffic lane, or whatever), and anyone who infringes on this right is wrong and no longer a worthy person.

Employees should know their own assumptions, realize how they affect their interpretations of situations, identify assumptions that lead to depression or overly angry feelings, dispose of these assumptions, and replace them with more reasonable ones. As people realize they have made faulty interpretations, they become aware of unrealistic assumptions. Then they can develop more useful assumptions, and argue with themselves until they adopt them. People have learned misleading assumptions; they can replace them by learning more useful ones.

Constructive assumptions include:

- Although I am a good person, I will do things that will upset and frustrate others.

- People who get angry with me often value me and our relationship and want to deal with problems and make our relationship stronger.

- Criticism and negative feedback can help me become more self-aware and stimulate the motivation to improve my competence and upgrade my skills.

- It would be nice if I was left in peace for my lunch hour (no one used my chair, no one cut me off in traffic), but interruptions are nuisances that I can easily live with.

Remember, self-examination and appraisal of your personal assumptions and the development of more constructive ones requires deep honesty and ongoing effort.

FEELINGS IN HIGH-PERFORMING ORGANIZATIONS

Jack Welch and other leaders appreciate that the open, trusting climates are necessary to help people find direction and cope with the intense stresses and demands of today's organization. People can find great value in sharing their frustrations, exchanging their hunches, and celebrating their triumphs together. Mutual trust and respect are not simply nice; they are essential if organizations are to mobilize every man and woman to give high value to customers.

Unfortunately, people have had much more practice in trying to suppress than express feelings. Their relationships are too closed, impersonal, and competitive to be as enhancing and productive as they could be. They express their feelings in indirect ways that confuse and alienate. People are unsure whether their colleague is angry or demoralized. They feel insulted that their boss was so punitive in his anger.

But the skillful expressing of frustration, anger, and other feelings can begin to identify and solve problems. Leaders and employees believe that together they can confront and deal with their conflicts. Part Four describes the benefits and procedures of using different points of views to solve problems and manage conflict constructively.

PART FOUR

MAKING USE
OF PROBLEMS
AND BARRIERS

The intellectual equipment needed for the job of the future is an ability to define problems, quickly assimilate relevant data, conceptualize and reorganize the information, make deductive and inductive leaps with it, ask hard questions about it, discuss findings with colleagues, work collaboratively to find solutions, and then convince others.

Robert B. Reich

Organizations and teams, even those who have laid the foundation of cooperative goals and mutual power and have developed procedures and skills to communicate and express feelings, inevitably hit barriers. Opposing positions and viewpoints prevent reaching decisions; frustrations and irritations threaten to divide people. These difficulties are not inevitable roadblocks but can be opportunities. Chapter 10 shows how the constructive discussion of opposing views very much contributes to digging into issues and creating viable solutions to problems. Chapter 11 describes how the open discussions of conflicts focused on cooperative, mutually beneficial solutions help make conflict a highly positive force by improving procedures and strengthening work relationships.

A formidable challenge in many organizations is to develop self-directing teams. Controversy and conflict abilities, as well as cooperative goals, communication, and managing feeling, help teams manage themselves. Chapter 12 shows how leaders and employees can negotiate responsibility and hold each other accountable to realize the potential of self-managing.

10 MAKING DECISIONS

Loyalty to a petrified opinion never yet broke a chain or
freed a human soul.

Mark Twain

Peter Johnson learned through the crucible of ongoing crises that organizations can no longer rely solely on their technical expertise and authority to make decisions and expect them to be accepted.[1] Organizations
must involve those who have a stake in the decision in open dialogue and
use the clash of opposing views to forge effective, accepted decisions.

Johnson was Administrator, Bonneville Power Administration
(BPA), which had built and operated a 15,000-mile electric transmission
grid between Canada, the four states in the Northwest, and California.
BPA had a proud tradition of contributing to the economic and social development of the region. One employee recalled, "It was really an honor
to be a Bonneville employee, because we did so many good things."

By the early 1980s, BPA's world had changed but Johnson and the
agency had not. Johnson "viewed conflict with people outside the company as an annoyance I'd do almost anything to avoid. I had enough on
my plate without environmentalists, politicians, special interests, or the
general public second-guessing my decisions and interfering with my
operations." But people affected by BPA's decisions were demanding "in
any way they could—lobbying to curtail BDP's authority, taking BPA to
court, or aiming rifles at BPA surveyors—the father-knows-best approach to decision making was completely unacceptable."

165

It turned out that involving adversaries in full, honest ways helped BPA make better decisions. "By listening to people's concerns and soliciting their advice on how to reconcile vast differences of opinion and conflicting needs, our operations did not come to a screeching halt. On the contrary, by involving the public in the decision-making process itself, we gained authority and legitimacy, avoided costly lawsuits and political challenges, and arrived at creative solutions to seemingly intractable problems."

But the movement to this more open, productive decision making was trying and difficult. Johnson and others at BPA had to "let go of outmoded attitudes, face up to underlying fears, and hope that 'outsiders' would do the same." The realization that they needed to change came through crises that threatened to undercut BPA's presence and role in the Northwest.

When BPA announced plans to build a transmission line linking power-generating plants in Montana with the Pacific Northwest, people in Montana were outraged. They disrupted every meeting, denouncing the plan. BPA employees did not dare identify themselves in public and needed unmarked cars to travel. One ranger got the attention of project surveyors by aiming a rifle at them. "Bolt weevils" unbolted transmission lines to collapse them.

There was controversy inside BPA about how to respond to this new reality. Lawyers argued that public involvement would force premature release of important documents, jeopardize the attorney-client relationship, forfeit flexibility, give outsiders unreasonable influence, and leave the agency vulnerable to lawsuits. Johnson's assistant for external affairs, Jack Robertson, advised him that the outcry to make BPA more accountable was not going away and that political pressure could paralyze the agency.

Johnson decided that the agency had to find a way to manage the risks of public involvement. But the controversy within BPA did not end with Johnson's decision. While Johnson described the agency as open to real public involvement, some parts resisted and reminded people that BPA would make final decisions. Johnson was confronted by an outsider, "Which way are you heading? We don't see you walking the talk."

Johnson had to manage the controversy inside BPA before public involvement would be seen as genuine and organization-wide. He initiated a policy review where for two years the whole organization debated and considered the need for public involvement. Awards were handed out for involving the public; BPA people were trained in speaking and writing.

To respond to the crisis in Montana, BPA began a program where it listened to everyone with an opinion and responded openly. The result was that BPA relocated transmission lines off scenic agricultural lowlands and behind forested ridges, used special treatment to reduce the visibility of the lines, and compensated local communities for road maintenance.

One crisis had passed but BPA was just at the beginning of change. BPA began to restore its reputation—the media even held it up as a model for self-improvement—after releasing a report on its public involvement process. The report concluded that the agency was "arrogant, insensitive, and uncaring." BPA accompanied the report with a letter recognizing its shortcomings and detailing how it would address them. The public did not expect perfection, but it detested arrogance and complacency.

Johnson and others at BPA were breaking out of the habit of the hard sell. It was "no longer appropriate to put the best spin on everything BPA did. The job was now to be open and honest so that people were well-informed." The agency issued backgrounders and issue alerts, not just impenetrable technical reports.

But the hardened adversaries—rate payer advocates, environmentalists (sometimes referred to as the "crazies")—were unconvinced. They wanted to meet with top management and set the agenda. Johnson agreed, and "that's when things got really interesting."

There was tension in the air at the first meetings. Johnson was worried that the meetings might blow up; the adversaries were leery and suspicious. Johnson worked hard not to react too harshly, even when facts were misinterpreted, and he tried to show he could be forthright. Once agency officials and their adversaries realized they could have a frank discussion on any issue, the tension dissipated. Soon they relaxed and were enjoying their debates. They spotted concerns before they became major issues and had fewer conflicts based on misperception and misinformation. "Most important, we began to trust and respect each other."

Learning how to involve people and use controversy to make decisions paid off handsomely in developing a rate that kept the Northwest aluminum plants operating and using BPA's power. Because of the nuclear power debacle at Washington Public Power Supply System that left BPA paying for three plants that could not produce electricity, its industrial users had confronted a 304 percent rate increase between 1980–84. None was hit harder than the aluminum industry. In five years, rates were eight times higher. Aluminum plants had moved to the Northwest to take advantage of cheap electrical power from federal dams. They took the surplus power generated at the spring run-off and were willing to be shut off at peak times to get reduced rates.

Not only had costs skyrocketed, but the world price of aluminum fell dramatically. The industry which used 30 percent of BPA's production and provided $640 million in annual revenues and employed 9,000 workers in the area was threatened. BPAs other hard-pressed customers would challenge any break in the rate to the industry in the courts. Johnson felt helpless, especially when people pleaded, "There must be something you can do" and hundreds of students wrote begging him not to take away their parents' jobs.

Initial discussions with communities and unions brought only minor gains. Casting the net wider, an advisory group of 75 people from utilities, local governments, state agencies, public interest groups, labor unions, aluminum companies, and private citizens was formed. Brochures about the industry's problem were distributed to 15,000 people. Then suddenly the situation did not seem hopeless. After a symposium in April 1985, where all kinds of experts and community members had spoken, there was an "Unspoken assumption that helping the aluminum industry would help everyone in the room. We had finally moved beyond arguing; we had agreed that there was a problem, and we were ready to talk solutions." They believed they could find a win-win solution.

BPA staff drafted a number of options, and held 13 public meetings which 4,600 people attended. The most supported option was a variable rate that tied the price of power to the price of aluminum, an idea that in a litigious, adversarial climate would have been a nonstarter. But now people who disagreed had enough respect for the process that they did not object at rate hearings. The result of the variable rate was that the smelters remained open and BPA had $200 million in revenues it would not otherwise have. "From that point on, we knew it was possible to make decisions that would count."

Johnson's major lesson: "With external stakeholders now exerting substantial influence on organizations in every sector, conflict is inevitable. The only choice is whether to dodge the controversy or learn to harness it.

"Those who harness it by including third parties rather than trying to vanquish them will have the opportunity to consider new possibilities and to test out new ideas in the heat of dialogue. While others are mired in disputes and litigation, astute practitioners of public involvement will have hammered out an agreement and gotten on with the project. In short, they will have made better decisions and found a new source of competitive advantage."

UNDER THE FIRE OF CHANGE

Johnson's BPA had to create effective decisions to deal with emerging changes and opportunities. Indeed, it had to create a new way of making decisions that would increase its legitimacy and authority and pave the way for acceptance of its decisions. Johnson and other leaders are discovering that open dialogue and controversy within the company as well as with those outside is key to solving problems. Natural resource and power companies are asking environmentalists for assistance. Consumer companies are including customers with marketing, engineering, and production specialists to design and develop new products. BPA used controversy inside the organization to develop its public involvement programs so it could use controversy with its stakeholders to make quality, accepted decisions.

Today's tough, complex issues need the combined consideration of people with diverse perspectives and outlooks. New products must make sense to production as well as to marketing. Reducing costs while maintaining quality cannot be mandated, but must be worked out by people up and down the hierarchy. Improving customer service is more than front-line employees smiling more but requires the integrated work of executives, trainers, computer technologists, supervisors, and employees to deliver more value to customers.

Effective decision making, always important, is now absolutely essential for organizations to prosper in the turbulent, fast-paced marketplace. Without the ability to solve problems, new conditions will control and overrun an organization. Being profitable and celebrated now does not exempt the company from the need to make hard decisions to prepare for the future. Some organizations have become "fat" and undisciplined as they dominated a marketplace and charged high margins. When the market changed—as inevitably it must—they were unprepared to confront their sloppy habits and adapt.

Sensing and identifying the problem, creating and evaluating alternatives, and selecting and implementing the decisions are major problem-solving steps. Groups and organizations can falter in any of them. Problems are not anticipated early enough for a considered response; the problem is misdiagnosed leading to implementing a nonsolution; the first plausible solution, usually based on tradition, is accepted without brainstorming new possibilities; risks are dismissed because everyone apparently agrees; people charged to implement the solution are uncommitted to it.[2] However, biased decision making is not inevitable.[3]

BPA's investing in forming cooperative relationships with its stakeholders, recognizing their abilities and value, and developing the skills to communicate and manage feelings paid off when they confronted the likely decline of the aluminum industry. In cooperative, open relationships, people keep each other informed and act as early warning devices. They feel free to create new solutions and break away from old habits. They assess risks directly, avoiding macho or timid decision making. To realize the potential of these relationships, leaders must encourage and structure constructive discussion of opposing views.[4]

Controversy is critical for organizations and groups to explore issues and make decisions. When organizations discourage the open discussion of opposing views and ideas, individuals feel intimidated and the organization suffers. When controversy brings out ideas and information, the organization identifies and grapples with problems fully and integrates views to create new, valuable solutions. People are more able to incorporate various ideas and perspectives and think more flexibly and complexly about problems.[5] Though the pull to avoid controversy can be strong, constructive controversy has proved to be the key to unlocking the power of organizational decision making.[6]

LEADERS' CHOICES

Managers have been repeatedly advised that they should be more participative and democratic and less autocratic and unilateral. Involve employees so that they feel ownership of decisions. This has become a credo for the modern manager. Leaders want to capture the full range of employee perspectives to identify problems and create solutions. Yet the focus on the choice of how participative to be has obscured the critical issue of how to involve employees so that together with leaders they make successful decisions.[7]

Employees participate with leaders regardless of whether leaders want them to or how they structure their participation. Even in the most autocratic companies, the top person making the important decisions gets information from others and needs their compliance to carry out decisions. Leaders can decide but, if others do not comply, not much will happen.

In the most democratic and participative systems, leaders are still very central in decision making. Leaders must understand and be committed to important decisions as are those who will implement them. Leaders cannot tell the CEO, customers, and the public that they do not support a significant decision because "my team made it." Even if it is not their choice, leaders must be convinced that the decision is viable and be able to defend it.

Making decisions on important issues is something that leaders and employees do best together.[8] There are choices regarding who should be listened to and who should be at the meetings. However, how they interact as they discuss issues, identify problems, create options, and select and implement a solution often has a greater impact. Without such effective exchange, the most elaborate scheme of involvement may result in poor solutions and frustrated employees and leaders.[9]

THE POTENTIAL OF TEAM DECISION MAKING

Corporate management committees, departmental meetings, and other sessions are used to advise executives and managers. Informally, managers often discuss issues with others and get feedback before they act. Most important issues are discussed over time, with people expressing their opinions, giving information, and making suggestions in different ways.

But is this reliance on team decision making useful? Having several persons discuss issues may just water down the decision to make it more palatable but less effective. Do people reinforce each other's biases or overcome them? A great number of studies indicate that team discussion and responsibility have considerable potential for solving problems.[10]

Team meetings provide opportunities for an enriching analysis and creative solution making. People can challenge and correct each other's errors and biases in reasoning, present a variety of information that no one person has or can adequately remember, and combine ideas and perspectives into new solutions not previously considered.[11]

In addition to quality solutions, teams can generate the commitment to follow through.[12] People who explicitly committed themselves to implement a decision resist attempts to persuade them to lower their efforts and comply with requests for assistance. As they encourage and persuade others of the value of their decision, they strengthen their own internal commitment.

Managers are not simple-minded information processors. They can step out of their framework, use varied criteria, and seek out additional and conflicting information. Well-managed teams have created new products, strategies, and service delivery systems. Teams are practical ways for organizations to respond to rapid changes.

However, there are pitfalls that prevent groups from realizing their potential and make them frustrating and ineffective.[13] Individuals may inhibit communication of information and generation of ideas, reinforce each other's biases, and undercut energy and commitment. Calling people together as a group does not necessarily result in effective decisions. For teams to explore issues thoroughly and create solutions, they must master the skills and procedures of constructive controversy.

THE VALUE OF CONTROVERSY

Controversy avoidance has resulted in major fiascoes. President John F. Kennedy and his advisors pressed foreign policy experts to suppress their reservations about the invasion of Cuba.[14] The Bay of Pigs invasion remains a blot on American foreign policy. Learning from this experience, Kennedy insisted on controversy in the Cuban missile crisis, and his actions still earn him high marks.

Suppressed controversy contributed to the Challenger disaster early in 1986. Engineers and managers apparently did not discuss their opposing views on the safety of flying the shuttle in cold weather.[15] The explosion seconds after take-off cost lives and crippled the American space effort.

Failure to discuss opposing views is also a major contributor to commercial airplane crashes. Flight crew members often have the information that could avert crashes, but hesitate to challenge the pilot in command.[16]

Investors and corporate raiders have argued that boards of directors do not have the independence, courage, and information to challenge management, and, as a consequence, do not defend the rights of shareholders properly. Harold S. Geneen, former CEO of ITT, argued that too often in the past boards failed to protect stockholders and seldom acted until the company was near ruin. Boards are becoming more assertive.

The costs of ineffective controversy are not limited to disasters or the boardroom. Employees often avoid discussing their strongly held views and frustrations directly with their bosses, and continue to work in unproductive ways. Managers find it prudent to pretend to agree, withhold information, and fail to challenge inadequate decisions. Alternatively, they badger, fight, and build coalitions to get their position accepted to make themselves look good. The more powerful, cunning, and persistent win, but their decisions may be wrong.[17]

Diversity of people, perspectives, and ideas is an important advantage for an organization. However, it is not simply open controversy that is so useful for making decisions. *Constructive controversy* and its dynamics and steps have been identified. It is this constructive controversy that gives organizations an advantage. (See Figure 10.1.)

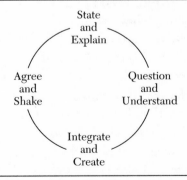

FIGURE 10.1.   Cooperative controversy dynamics.

CONSTRUCTIVE CONTROVERSY DYNAMICS

Developing cooperative relationships sets the stage for a constructive discussion of opposing views. But leaders and employees must have the skills to use their perspectives to dig into issues and create effective solutions. In cooperative, constructive controversy, people argue their position, question and seek to know opposing views, combine contrasting ideas, and reach an agreement worthy of mutual commitment.[18]

State and Explain Your Position

As they begin to disagree over a problem, decision makers state and explain their own position and ideas. They identify their positions and use facts, information, and theories that validate their theses and provide a logical structure that links the facts to the conclusion. They share new information, present ideas and their rationales. As they elaborate, they can understand their own position more fully. Often people appreciate their own positions, assume that their positions are superior, and want to prove their ideas are "right" and that their position should be accepted.

As the controversy is engaged, other people press and explain their views. Proponents may feel frustrated and argue their positions and develop their arguments more completely and forcefully. They repeat old and add new information, present more ideas, and elaborate on their positions.

Question and Understand Opposing Views

In the clash of opposing ideas and positions, people search and refute each other's arguments. They critique and point out weaknesses and possible strengths in the arguments. They rebut counterarguments and elaborate, but they also come to doubt the wisdom and correctness of their own position. The ideas and logic of others creates internal, cognitive conflict questioning whether their original position is as useful and sensible as they had assumed. They avoid feeling that because it is a crisis they must demand conformity.[19]

People become uncertain about the validity of their original thesis.[20] With this conceptual conflict, they actively search for new information. They read more relevant material, gather new information, and ask others for information. They question their protagonists to clarify their positions and rephrase their arguments so that they can understand the opposing position more thoroughly.

Because of their curiosity, they consider and evaluate the arguments, reasoning, and facts that support alternative positions. They can take the perspective of their opponents, anticipate how they might think about future issues, and identify the kind of reasoning they like to employ.

Integrate and Create Options

The elaboration and search leaves people open-minded and knowledgeable about the issue. They have approached the issue from several perspectives and are not rigidly fixed to their own. In making decisions, people generally use inductive reasoning in which they use available information to "jump" to a conclusion. This conclusion must be held tentatively because there will be new information and ideas that can be used to revise and improve conclusions.

With constructive controversy, decision makers synthesize and bring together different ideas and facts into new positions.[21] They sense new patterns and new ways to integrate ideas. They incorporate others' information and reasoning into their own and form new attitudes and judgments. They develop positions responsive to several points of view and use more mature ways of thinking.

Agree and Shake

These dynamics have been shown to result in high-quality, innovative solutions and agreements.[22] The mix and clash of the discussion creates new positions not previously considered. These positions combine the arguments and perspectives of several people in elegant ways.

Controversy encourages people to adopt more adequate ways of reasoning and gain a deeper understanding of the problem. The increase in the number and quality of ideas and higher levels of stimulation facilitates creativity.

Controversy is critical for successful participation in which people "own" and feel committed to decisions. People are satisfied and feel they have benefited from the discussion. They enjoy the excitement, feel aroused by the challenges of the conflict, and develop positive attitudes toward the experience. They are committed to the new agreements and positions because they understand how they are related to their own interests and positions, and why the adopted position is superior to their original one.

Cooperative controversy also fosters a camaraderie that reinforces commitment to the group's position. People have fully voiced their opinions, listened to each other, and enjoyed the excitement of disagreeing together. They feel better about themselves and about their team members.

The rewards of cooperative conflict in problem solving are rich indeed. They are much more than proving that one is right or that one's position should dominate. Constructive controversy stimulates intellectually and results in effective solutions and strengthened work relationships.

USING ADVOCACY TEAMS

Often managers try to encourage controversy by asking all to speak their minds freely. Structuring advocacy teams and assigning them different positions is a defined, thorough way to develop cooperative, constructive controversy to analyze a problem and create and evaluate alternatives.

Major steps as illustrated in Figure 10.2 are:

* *Phase 1:* A problem important enough to warrant the time and resources needed to explore it comprehensively is identified. Organizations have used advocacy teams to decide whether to acquire another company and whether to build a new plant or modify the existing one. Simple, unimportant problems do not deserve

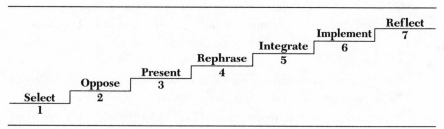

FIGURE 10.2.   Advocacy teams.

extensive exploration and take time and attention away from significant issues. Focusing on unimportant issues can demoralize and frustrate. Short advocacy teams procedures are used to begin to explore major issues or to resolve less significant ones.

- *Phase 2:* Advocacy teams are formed and each one assigned a major alternative. The teams are given the time and resources to find the supporting facts, information, evidence and reasons for their alternative. They plan how they can present their arguments so that everyone is well aware of the strengths of their position. Their goal is not to win the debate by getting their position accepted, but they still want to present their arguments forcefully and thoroughly so that their position is seriously considered.

- *Phase 3:* Teams present their arguments and position fully and persuasively. In this free discussion, they develop their own arguments, advocate their positions, defend it against refutation and counter opposing arguments. They take notes and challenge inadequate facts and reasoning.

- *Phase 4:* The teams open-mindedly listen and present each other's position. They rephrase each other's position and arguments to demonstrate that they have paid attention and understand. Throughout the discussion, they remember their purpose is for the whole group to develop as strong a position as possible.

- *Phase 5:* Teams together strive to create an integrated decision. The subgroups drop their assigned position, and using all the facts and arguments identified, reach a general agreement on the best course of action. They change their minds because of the logic and evidence, not because others are more powerful or argue more loudly. The decision reflects their best joint reflected judgment.

- *Phase 6:* The group as a whole approaches management and others to make and implement their decision. Making a decision in an organization is more than getting the right answer. Decisions are not puzzles to be solved; they are part of the stream of working and managing. The solution must be accepted and implemented, its impact assessed, and new problems identified.

- *Phase 7:* The group reflects on their use of conflict to make decisions. Though advocacy teams can be exciting, involving and worthwhile, they are not easy. It can be tempting to fall back into the typical mode of trying to dominate and "win" by getting one's position accepted. Team members can easily get caught up in believing they are in a debate to prove they are right and the other wrong. They have to remind themselves that what counts is not who was right at first but that the team is right at the end.

The advocacy teams procedure should be used flexibly and efficiently to fit the issue and circumstances. The decision to invest in developing a new product line may deserve extensive research and repeated discussions over weeks before people feel informed and confident about a decision. But advocacy teams can be used for twenty minutes at a meeting to get people thinking about an important issue or to solve a relatively minor one. For example, rather than just ask people at the regular management meeting whether the company should follow a price reduction by a competitor, advocacy teams can be used to generate discussion and ideas and move the group to a resolution.

PROCEDURES FOR CONSTRUCTIVE CONTROVERSY

It is critical for managers and employees to aim for open discussions of opposing ideas within cooperation. In addition to advocacy teams, they can turn to other ways to develop these productive controversies.

Emphasize Cooperative Context

- *Commit to a common task.* Decision makers want one effective decision that will promote their shared vision for the group and company. Controversy can help them create the solution that will best promote their common interests.

- *Share rewards.* Decision makers realize that they will be rewarded to the extent that the group is successful. Financial rewards, evaluations, and prestige are given for the group's success, not for independent work, appearing better than others, or proving that one is right. Rewards are shared for success; shared responsibility for failure is accepted.

- *Convey cooperative expectations.* Decision makers communicate that they are committed to working for a solution that benefits all. Efforts to pursue individual objectives at others' expense are discouraged.

- *Show personal regard.* Decision makers believe they are accepted and valued as persons even though others criticize their ideas. They listen to everyone's ideas respectfully, and criticize these ideas rather than attack an individual's motivation and personality. Insults or implications that challenge another's integrity, intelligence, and motives are avoided. Communication of interest and acceptance is accompanied by disagreement with another's current position.

State and Explain Your Position

- *Develop openness norms.* Everyone should be encouraged to express his or her opinions, doubts, uncertainties, and hunches. Ideas should not be dismissed because they first appear too unusual, impractical, or undeveloped. Affirmation of the right to dissent and free speech reduce fears of retribution for speaking out.

- *Structure opposing views.* In addition to advocacy teams, one person can be assigned to be a devil's advocate who takes a critical evaluation role by attacking what appears to be the group's solution. Managers can actively seek to encourage various viewpoints and assure others that they are not rigidly fixed to their present position. Requiring consensus decision making encourages full participation and people with doubts to speak out. Majority vote can degenerate into attempts to get a majority and force that decision on others.

- *Include heterogeneous members.* People who differ in background, expertise, opinions, outlook, and organization position are likely to disagree. Independent thinkers and people outside the department and organization make controversy more likely. For example, Pacific Gas & Electric decided that not only did environmentalists block some of their projects in the 1970s but they had learned from them. Now it seeks dialogue with them inside and outside the company.

Question and Understand Opposing View

- *Ask questions.* In cooperative conflict, people want to hear each other's arguments and reasoning directly. They explore opposing positions and try to understand the logic and facts that support it. They avoid the illusion of understanding.

- *Conduct research.* Decision makers read articles and materials that the opposing side is using to defend their positions. They visit sites and interview people who believe in and are using opposing ideas.

- *Influence and be open to influence.* Decision makers try to influence each other, but avoid dominating. Controversy requires people to persuade, inform, and convince to make the discussion stimulating and involving. People have the conviction and willingness to argue their positions forcefully and to persuade, but they avoid dominating and coercion. They say, "I want you to consider this seriously" and "You will probably find this convincing," not "You must accept this point" and "You have no choice but to agree." There is give-and-take, not dominance or passivity.

- *Demonstrate understanding.* Decision makers continually put themselves in each other's shoes to understand the opposing arguments. They show their understanding by accurately paraphrasing opposing ideas and thereby convey acceptance and interest in another as a person while disagreeing.

Integrate and Create Options

- *Strive for "win-win," cooperative solutions.* Decision makers say, "We are all in this together" and "Let's see a solution that is good for everyone," not "I am right, and you are wrong." Decision makers avoid looking for winners and losers but focus on a productive solution to the common problem.

- *Combine ideas.* Rather than assume that there are only two solutions and that these are mutually incompatible, people in cooperative conflict try to integrate parts of the positions, ideas, and facts of all sides to invent an array of possible decisions.

- *Use rational argumentation.* People reason logically, listen open-mindedly and change their positions when others are persuasive. They move away from simplistic, "right or wrong" thinking to recognize that they must continually integrate new evidence and ideas as they develop richer understandings and more reasonable conclusions.

Agree and Shake

- *Select a high-quality solution.* The decision should best promote the shared vision and the common interests of the group and organization. It is not selected just because the most powerful favor it.

- *Implement the solution.* The most elegant solution will not be much good unless people are prepared and able to implement it.

Reflect and Learn

- *Assess implementation and effects of solution.* Successful solutions are implemented as intended and the consequences are in line with expectations.

- *Be prepared to recycle through more controversy.* A solution that appears satisfactory one week proves ineffectual the next; a solution thought to be easy to implement turns out not to be. A new round of cooperative conflict can incorporate new information and perspectives.

- *Discuss the process.* Decision makers give each other feedback and identify the strengths and areas that need improvement to solve future problems more effectively and efficiently.

- *Joint celebrations.* Using conflict to make decisions is challenging, but the rewards are considerable. People recognize their abilities and efforts, the quality of the solution, and confidence in their relationships. They jointly celebrate their success.

Traditional notions that the leader stands above the fray and makes the tough decisions are increasingly misleading. Leaders are not aloof, but take part in the give-and-take of team decision making. Rather than pontificate, they structure participation so that people inside and outside the organization express their views open-mindedly and together dig into issues and forge solutions responsive to many different viewpoints. Leaders do not seek to show that they are right, but provide the climate and exchange needed so that the organization and team strive for the best solution possible.

To be effective problem solvers under the pressure for change, BPA's Johnson and other leaders and employees must let go of outworn notions that conflicting opinions should be smoothed over. They must be convinced that they can use their diverse perspectives to advantage. Chapter 11 shows that conflict more generally can be a highly positive force in organizations but, to be so, leaders must help to manage conflict.

11 MANAGING CONFLICT

> The fear factor was our biggest problem when we first got started in the quality movement. . . . I don't think that there's a company in the United States that doesn't have this problem . . . Unless a company is involved in the quality movement, I would expect that their fear factor is extremely high. That is the way we have all been brought up to run a company. The prevalent attitude is "Either you are going to do it my way or else."
>
> John Wallace, CEO, Wallace Company,
> Malcolm Baldridge National Quality Award, 1990

The emphasis of previous chapters on the value of mutual respect and power, cooperative relationships, openness, and ability to discuss opposing views constructively may seem desirable, but too far removed from the reality of many work places. How can people engage in constructive controversy in organizations where people are hostile and unforgiving? The production team believes the computer team is arrogant and closed-minded; the information systems group thinks the production group is competitive and aggressive. Employees find the boss too coy; the boss finds the employees too passive.

These prejudices have grown out of ineffective conflict management.[1] The production people have concluded that the information system group is arrogant because it brushes aside their issues and tries to impose its computer solutions on them. The information systems people believe production employees are mean because they bark out their demands and make other employees look foolish. Employees consider their boss coy because he does not give straight answers to their concerns. The boss considers employees passive because, while they do not complain, they do not embrace his direction.

The path to reduce these negative attitudes and hostility is for people to manage their conflicts openly and strive for integrated solutions that help them all be more effective. Information systems people who listen and incorporate the production department's views into the design of the computer systems won't be seen as arrogant. Production people who voice their frustrations directly without blaming won't be seen as aggressive. Employees and bosses who discuss their conflicts directly and constructively will begin to see each other as open-minded and capable. Through managing conflict, people can develop and maintain cooperative relationships where they combine their different perspectives to solve problems.

THE NEED TO MANAGE CONFLICT

Leaders and employees have a choice: either manage conflict or have conflict manage them. Either they are in charge of conflict or conflict will be in charge of them. Too many organizations and teams are so preoccupied with avoiding conflict that they remain frustrated and stymied, getting up just enough energy and courage to deal with conflicts that interfere with immediate tasks. Not only do their frustrations remain, they are pessimistic that they will find a reasonable way to deal with their grievances. They must work to hide their feelings and conclude that their team members are too closed-minded or too uncaring to discuss the issues that divide them.

Leaders are told that they must confront reality to succeed. They cannot afford to pretend that a shrinking market, dissatisfied customers, and disgruntled work force will disappear. Conflicts are the means for confronting reality. Through conflict, organizations stay in touch with their customers and leaders with their employees. Conflict identifies issues, creates incentives to explore them, and provides a medium to move toward resolution. It is through conflict that agreement, unity, and justice can be reached. Conflict is not part of the problem; conflict is part of the solution.

Yet avoiding conflict has great appeal. Might not the conflict dissolve itself? Why take the risks of appearing to be a complainer and overly emotional? Words that cannot be taken back may do irreparable damage to an already frail relationship. Might not our conflict partners wilt under the pressure? Perhaps they will counterattack.

However, trying to avoid conflict often leads to escalating, debilitating conflict.[2] After frustration and pressure have built, angry words are exchanged and a "I'm right, you're wrong" fight is engaged. After this win-lose approach to their conflict deepens their burdens and suspicions, they again return to avoiding. Avoiding and escalating are not so much opposing approaches to conflict as alternating, complementary ways of handling conflict.

It is not just when people believe each other to be arrogant, aggressive, coy, and passive that they must manage conflict. Relationships are not static, but are either becoming more or less united, more or less trusting. Kurt Lewin analyzed the current state of a relationship as the balance of forces pushing in opposite directions. Sharing the success of a completed task, spending an evening together, and using opposing views to solve a problem creates more unity. However, there are always forces to undermine relationships. Doubts that the other person really cares, questions why the person has not called recently, an unintended slight, a failure to complete a project push people apart. Managing conflict helps people deal with destructive forces and build upon constructive forces.

The assumptions that harmony can prevail and that conflicts can be avoided are unrealistic and impractical.[3] Managing conflict is built on the reality that frustrations and debates are inevitable and pervasive. It recognizes that there will be misunderstandings, mistrust, disrespect, even arrogance. But managing conflict is idealistic in that it offers the hope of using difficulties to change and improve so that we feel unleashed and confident that together we can deal with future dilemmas.[4]

BECOMING CONFLICT POSITIVE

Conflict management puts in bold relief how contemporary leadership has moved beyond traditional expectations for leaders. Leaders were thought to exert their decisive role by minimizing conflict and eliminating it quickly. Their charge was to develop a harmonious, efficient department; they were to step into any conflict and find a quick solution that restored the department to efficiency. Now leaders are to empower employees to become a synergistic team and encourage opposing views to make decisions. They are to use frustrations, grievances, and other conflicts to solve problems and innovate. Managing conflict is a hard-headed as well as soft-hearted approach to leading.

Moving to this more open, positive approach to conflict requires challenging many traditional assumptions and developing new values, practices, and skills.[5] Rather than be a judge and arbitrator, a leader is a mediator who assists employees to discuss issues and frustrations openly and together work out solutions. Rather than avoid and gossip about their protagonists and try to get their leader on their side, employees must confront each other honestly, openmindedly consider each other's feelings and positions, and consider how they should change.

Although becoming a more conflict-positive organization is difficult, a return to the command-and-control system is probably impossible. Telling and selling do not result in the inner conviction and drive needed to meet contemporary challenges. Employees are less willing to accept autocratic resolutions of conflicts as legitimate. They want to be involved and to have their voices and feelings listened to and respected. They want to feel cared for before they will care for the company. Conflict is intensifying as specialists are asked to work together on task forces and new product teams and as the workforce becomes increasingly diverse. There is no realistic alternative to learning to manage our conflicts more effectively.

Developing cooperative relationships, communicating fully, managing feelings, and dealing with opposing views to create solutions all contribute to constructive conflict management. Managing a conflict is a test and, if handled well, it strengthens relationships and reaffirms abilities. But managing conflict can be a beginning. A poorly managed conflict exposes mistrust and communication failures; it underlines the need for strong, cooperative work relationships; it creates incentives for change; and it can be the first step on a journey to build conflict management abilities.

COOPERATIVE CONFLICT THEORY

A useful, valid conflict theory is critical to diagnosing present attitudes and approaches and understanding how to improve conflict

Cooperative Conflict's Benefits

- *Identifies problems.* Discussing frustrations identifies competitive relationships, poor quality, excessive costs, injustices, and other barriers to effectiveness.

- *Improves solutions.* Debating opposing views digs into issues, searches for information and insight, and integrates ideas to create solutions responsive to several perspectives that people are committed to.

- *Drives productivity.* Managed conflict reduces the time wasted by brooding and redoing tasks and results in more efficient use of resources.

- *Stimulates creativity.* People retain ideas and understand their implications through elaboration and listening. They become more creative as they explore alternatives and integrate different points of view.

- *Manages change and innovation.* Conflict creates incentives to challenge and change outmoded procedures, assignments, and structures.

- *Reduces day-to-day frustrations.* Employees release their tensions and stress through discussion and problem solving. They feel confident that they have faced difficulties together and their relationships are strong and open.

- *Increases awareness.* People learn what makes themselves and others irritated and angry and what is important to them. Knowing what people are willing to fight about keeps them in touch.

- *Facilitates personal development.* Managers and employees learn how their style affects others and the competencies they need to develop.

- *Strengthens self-acceptance.* Expressing frustrations and important feelings helps people accept and value themselves. Others' listening and responding to feelings builds self-esteem.

- *Prompts psychological maturation.* People take the perspectives of others and become less egocentric. They feel confident and powerful they can cope with difficulties by dealing directly with them.

- *Makes interacting fun and exciting.* Employees enjoy the stimulation, arousal, and involvement of conflict, and it can be a welcome break from an easy-going pace. It invites people to examine and appreciate the intricacies of their relationships.

management. Unfortunately, people have various, often misleading, theories about conflict.

Defining Conflict

Perhaps the idea that most obstructs understanding is that conflict occurs because people have opposing interests. Conflict inevitably means that people are working against each other; what one wants is incompatible with what another wants; their goals are competitive; what one gets comes at the expense of others. The best that can be accomplished is a compromise where each gives up something in order to receive something.

A much more useful definition is that conflict involves incompatible behaviors; one person is interfering, disrupting, or in some other way making another's actions less effective.[6] Controversy is a particular kind of conflict where proposing different alternatives interferes with reaching a decision. Defining conflict in terms of incompatible

---

Need to Manage Conflict for Total Quality

"If the management team desires to help us out of this quagmire, listen to us, develop a definite plan of action, resolve problems, get things done, obtain the supplies we need to do our jobs, then our efforts will be justified. If, on the other hand, we sense the runaround, the putoff, the condescending attitude that has prevailed all too often in the past, we will be worse off than we are now. Management will retain the reputation of not to be trusted, morale will surely plummet, and some of us will certainly feel foolish.

"We expect—no, we demand honesty on management's part with no b.s. Management must listen to the things we have to say, regardless of how mundane or ludicrous that they may seem at the time. After all, they're important enough for us to mention them in the first place, and management should put forth a sincere effort to help us resolve the problems and conflicts that are sure to arise."

Joe Campau, machinist,
on his company's push for
total quality management.[7]

activities rather than goals may seem minor and academic, but it has vast practical implications.

People with compatible, cooperative interests can be in conflict as they argue about the best means to accomplish their common tasks, distribute the benefits and burdens of their cooperative effort, and determine how they are to treat each other. Task force members all want to improve company profitability, but some want to market the product now and others to redevelop it. They may be irritated that others are not listening to their views carefully enough. Within organizations, the majority of conflicts occur when people have cooperative interests. People can reach their goals when others also reach theirs; they must be successful together.

The assumption that conflict is based on opposing interests leads to viewing conflict as a struggle to see whose will and interests will dominate and whose interests will be subordinated. We must fight to win, or at least not lose. The assumption of largely cooperative goals leads to viewing the conflict as a common problem to be solved for mutual benefit, which in turn makes it more likely that the conflict will be constructive and that people will improve their conflict-handling abilities.

Cooperative and Competitive Approaches

Cooperative conflict theory is elegant and powerful. It suggests the kind of relationship that conflict partners want to establish as well as the actions that complement these relationships. When people believe their goals are cooperative ("We are in this together." "We swim or sink together."), they are committed to promote each other and help each other be effective. ("We trust and rely upon each other.") Then they are prepared to consider each other's ideas to try to combine them into a mutually beneficial solution. They use the conflict to get the job done and strengthen their relationship.

Studies show that cooperative conflict builds people up, strengthens their relationship, reaches agreement, and gets things done.[8] Cooperative conflict is a practical way to integrate the needs of people and the requirements of work. (See Figure 11.1.)

Competitive goals, on the other hand, create the suspicion that people will promote their own interests at others' expense and interfere with each other. Their mistrust restricts the exchange of information and resources and distorts communication; people often try to

FIGURE 11.1. Cooperative conflict theory.

avoid direct discussions and, when compelled to discuss, try to win and impose their positions and to avoid losing. This avoidance alternating with escalating conflict frustrates productivity, intensifies stress, and lowers morale.[9] (See Figure 11.2.)

Competitive goals make managing conflict very difficult and can lead to debilitating fights. With competitive goals, people suspect that self-interest will lead to mutual frustration. They doubt others are interested in their feelings and frustrations; they fear being ridiculed. Although they often prefer to avoid conflict, especially with their bosses and others with authority and power who can "win" and impose their wishes, the underlying problems continue to frustrate. If they do decide to confront their protagonist, they often do so in a tough, dominating manner that escalates the conflict. Whether they choose to avoid or confront conflict, competitors, although they may believe they have won

FIGURE 11.2. Competitive conflict theory.

in the short-term, usually end up feeling that they have lost and only hope that others have lost more.

MAKING CHOICES

Success in managing conflict requires making wise choices. Some minor conflicts should be ignored. Giving in and accommodating on issues unimportant to oneself but important to the others can be very sensible. Other conflicts need to be avoided because people do not have the time, skills, or relationships to make direct negotiations productive.

Understanding cooperative conflict helps make wise choices. There is a viable approach to important conflicts that can improve productivity and relationships. Knowledge of cooperative conflict makes the alternative of win-lose, competitive negotiations clearer. Not all conflict negotiations are similar; win-lose negotiations have different dynamics and consequences than cooperative ones. Studies confirm, what most mature managers know, that the cooperative approach is much more useful because in an organization and in the world of business "what goes around, comes around."

Resolving a conflict by creating a loser means that not only might you have an enemy, but the agreement does too because the loser may be getting prepared to undo your victory and the agreement. Jean Sartre wrote, "Once you hear the details of victory, it is hard to distinguish it from defeat." Research has not been able to document many organizational situations in which competition is effective.[10] Success in negotiations to resolve conflict comes from knowing what the other wants, knowing what you want, and showing the other how to get what the other really wants while you get what you want.

PHASES OF COOPERATIVE CONFLICT MANAGEMENT

Negotiating conflicts productively requires persistence, skill, and ingenuity as well as knowledge of cooperative conflict. The phases are similar to those of constructive controversy.

State and Explain Your Position

Negotiation begins when at least one person directly communicates that there is a conflict that he wants to discuss and resolve for mutual benefit.

The conflict partners sit down to identify and define the conflict. Each side describes the other's actions and why they have concluded that the other's behavior is interfering or frustrating them. Rather than blame and evaluate, they share their perceptions and feelings. They recognize that they are not mind readers, but need direct information about each other's feelings and beliefs. Rather than seeing the conflict as a win-lose struggle, they define it as a mutual problem to be solved. No one loses when you solve a mutual problem.

It is critical to focus on needs, feelings, and goals, not just describe one's positions.[11] Cooperative negotiators state why they are proposing their resolution and how it will help them accomplish their needs and strengthen their relationships. They do not assume that because positions and proposals are incompatible that basic goals and interests are. They seek solutions that further the needs of both persons so that both are committed to resolving the conflict. They see that they have more to gain by a negotiated settlement than by continuing the conflict.

Question and Understand Opposing View

As the protagonists elaborate on their positions, they listen to learn more about each other's needs, interests, and feelings. They argue to show how their proposals can meet the needs of both persons. They critique opposing solutions and point out their inadequacies. They ask "why?" and "why not?" to look behind positions and proposals. They realize that an advantage of conflict is to confront their colleagues' and friends' personal, unique perspectives and to identify both the differences and the similarities involved. To create a mutually beneficial agreement, negotiators have to maintain an accurate assessment of their own and the other's perspectives.

There are important obstacles to this understanding. We can misjudge the other's motivation and the emotional intensity he brings to the conflict. We can exaggerate our differences and discount our similarities. Moreover, people in conflict often feel they are not understood and must repeat their arguments in stronger and louder terms. They become intransigent or give up because the other is not listening to them or respecting them and therefore no agreement suitable to them can be arranged.

The communication skill of putting yourself in the other's shoes by presenting the other's position and reasoning contributes significantly to cooperative conflict management.[12] The other recognizes that you are trying to understand him and gives you feedback and additional information to improve your perspective taking. The other is also more prepared to stop repeating arguments and listen and consider your views. Then both negotiators are in a better position to develop effective resolutions.

Integrate and Create Options—There Is No "Fixed Pie"

Through open discussion, negotiators move toward a shared understanding of the conflict which helps them create options that promote mutual goals. But the obstacles to creating solutions are formidable.[13]

Perhaps the most common one is fixation on your original proposal as if that were the only one that could satisfy your requirements. As both people or teams are rigidly committed to their own position and either/or thinking, the issue is often defined in terms of "my way or his way."

Similarly, there is a tendency to assume a fixed pie in which the more one gets, the less the other gets, often accompanied by a short-term perspective. However, a truly fixed pie rarely occurs especially in the long-term. Management and labor have competitive interests in regards to wage settlements, but both will benefit from a stronger relationship in which they join forces to reduce costs, improve quality, resolve grievances, and strengthen the firm's security. Both management and labor want fair wages that increase people's commitment to the organization. Generally, the more one gets, the more the other gets.

Premature evaluation also frustrates creating alternatives. Some people are so prepared to pounce on the drawbacks of any new idea that others are reluctant to brainstorm and propose ideas for fear of being shot down.

To create alternatives and overcome these obstacles, negotiators brainstorm and invent as many options as they can. The more ideas, the more likely a good one can be selected. Later they evaluate ideas to the extent they promote mutual benefit.

Negotiators can bundle ideas together and propose package deals. They reach agreement on several issues simultaneously so that all persons can see that at least on some issues their interests have been protected and promoted. Similarly, negotiators can reach agreement on different issues in which a settlement to one issue is linked to a settlement on another.

Guide to Managing Conflict

Foster Cooperative Context

- Develop realistic attitudes that working together cooperatively requires conflict management.
- Focus on working together to deal with the conflict.
- Work for win-win solutions.
- Calculate the losses of continuing the conflict and the gains of resolving it.

State and Explain Your Position

- Arrange a time and place to discuss the conflict.
- Identify ideas and feelings behind positions.
- Be hard on the problem, soft on the person.

Question and Understand Opposing View

- Probe and ask questions.
- Put yourself in the other's shoes.
- Show respect and acceptance as you disagree with the opposing position.
- Follow the golden rule of conflict of using the approach you want others to use.

Integrate and Create Options

- Define the problem together.
- Be firm in furthering mutual needs, but flexible in how to do that.
- Brainstorm options.

(Continued)

Agree and Shake

Effective agreements meet the important, legitimate interests of both sides. To the extent possible, the agreement satisfies their mutual needs and reconciles their opposing interests. The negotiators must be able and committed to implementing the settlement. No matter how elegant the solution, it is not going to solve the conflict unless it is abided by. The agreement should be durable and help the negotiators put the conflict behind, get the job done, and prepare them for future collaboration.

(Continued)

Agree and Shake

- Agree to an option.
- Reaffirm the agreement.

Reflect and Learn

- Give each other feedback and support.
- Celebrate.

Pitfalls to Avoid

- Seeing conflict as a problem that must be blamed on someone.
- Assuming every conflict is a fight to win.
- Focusing only on what you want.
- Conveying it is "us versus them."
- Assuming sole responsibility to resolve the conflict.
- Assuming it is sole responsibility of the other to resolve the conflict.
- Repeating arguments in a louder voice.
- Surprising and overwhelming.
- Hitting your protagonist hard to overcome, then running to avoid getting hit back.
- Returning every slight with rebuke.
- Pretending to listen.
- Using the other's arguments only to strengthen your position.
- Assuming it is "his way or my way."
- Using "either/or," fixed pie thinking.
- Equating success with getting your way.
- Gloating over your victory.

Proceeding successfully through the prior steps is critical for arriving at these agreements.

Ideally, the conflict should be resolved on the basis of an objective criteria. The proposals are evaluated according to standards of fairness, efficiency, community values, and scientific merit. They may decide to use the standard of equity in which rewards are distributed according to how much effort each person had made. Then they evaluate options and make a decision based on the principle of equity. When no agreement on principle is possible, people can agree to other methods such as taking turns, drawing lots, or letting someone else decide.

The agreement should indicate that the conflict will end, describe how people are to behave differently in the future, stipulate what should happen if people fail to live up to the agreement, and identify times to discuss the resolution to see if further steps can be taken to improve the relationship. They are prepared to open up negotiations if the present solution proves ineffective. They remember that success in negotiations comes when, to the fullest extent possible, both sides get what they really want.

Reflect and Learn

The protagonists reflect back on their negotiations to learn more about how they approached the conflict and their relationship.[14] By discarding the dysfunctional idea that somehow they should be able to manage their conflict perfectly, they seek to deepen their sensitivities and improve their abilities. They ask for and give each other feedback and the support needed to consider and use the feedback. They celebrate their successes and plan how to change shortcomings. They see how learning to manage conflict binds them cooperatively together.

MEDIATING CONFLICT

Managers are thrust into the roles of mediators of their employees' conflicts. A recent survey by Accountemps, a division of Robert Half International, Inc., found that vice presidents and personnel directors of 100 of the America's largest 1,000 corporations exert much effort and time in handling problems with conflicting employees. Executives indicated that they spent 9.2 percent of their time attempting to deal with employee conflicts and the difficulties they cause. They may spend even more time trying to smooth over conflicts.

Mediators have many specific strategies.[15] Cooperative conflict suggests two powerful, integrated ways that managers and others can help people discuss and manage their differences. The first is to help the conflict partners develop a cooperative context in which they understand that they have important, positively related goals. The second method involves helping them learn cooperative negotiation strategies.

Recognizing Cooperative Goals

In an ongoing, difficult-to-resolve conflict, people usually have emphasized their competitive interests at the expense of their cooperative ones. They fight over who would win the fight and who should be seen as more important and valued. Yet in the world of work, they typically need each other's effective work to get their own jobs done well; they need each other's respect to feel competent and successful at work. Even their inability to manage the conflict effectively without their leader underlines their cooperative goals. Each needs the other to learn how to manage conflict. Each has much to gain when they both learn to deal with the present and other conflicts. Their common needs to manage conflict binds them cooperatively together.

In addition to reminding the conflict partners of their cooperative goals, mediators can strengthen the cooperative context by having them assess their goals and how they depend on each other. The conflict partners break away from discussing the conflict at hand and examine their relationship. The steps in this interdependence assessment are:

1. The protagonists list their major objectives and aspirations independently. These can be global, "to feel respected," or specific, "make more commissions." Learning to manage conflict should be included for both persons.

2. They brainstorm how they can help each other reach their goals and how they can get in each other's ways. They are to assess their potentials rather than measure their actual behavior. Avoid having them blame each other for failing to help each other reach goals. List these "failures" as possible ways that they can get in each other's ways.

3. They negotiate and reach agreements about how they can help each other reach their goals. These agreements should be specific and doable; they should be fair and mutually agreed upon. Successful follow-up should be recognized and rewarded and violations dealt with.

    The mediator can guide the protagonists to understand that, though they have incompatible activities, they still have many cooperative goals. They may also see that they put different values on goals and can "logroll" so that each person gets what she considers her most important goals. They may formulate superordinate goals which require both of them to work together to achieve.

4. The participants reflect upon these activities and discuss what they have learned. They should be able to see concretely how they will both be further ahead helping each other rather than working against each other. They can also discuss the extent that they negotiated their agreements for mutual benefit. They have begun to put into practice their agreed upon procedures and ways to manage their differences. They are jointly reaching agreement about fair and effective ways for them to work through conflict. They have concrete evidence of the value and their ability to learn to manage their differences cooperatively and productively.

The mediator has asked the conflict partners to put aside discussion of the conflict at hand to focus on their more cooperative interdependence. However, the exercise is not a way to avoid discussing the conflict issues, but to prepare them for it. They are asked to discuss how they can use the present conflict to strengthen their cooperative goals and relationship.

Teaching Cooperative Negotiation Strategies

A strong cooperative context facilitates but does not ensure productive conflict. The protagonists must still hammer out resolutions. Encouraging and teaching cooperative negotiation strategies can help the protagonists deal with the specific issues at hand and reduce competitive feelings.

The previous section described the major cooperative skills of elaborate position, search and demonstrate understanding of the other's views, create options, and decide on a settlement. Mediators model these strategies and urge protagonists to adopt them. The protagonists also study and discuss conflict strategies together.

1. The conflict partners read a paragraph describing each cooperative conflict strategy and discuss the strategies with each other.
2. They identify what the behavior "looks like" and what it "sounds like" to make their understanding more concrete and specific.

3. They identify related behaviors that they believe will be useful for them.

4. They discuss to reach a consensus that they should use these strategies as they deal with the conflict at hand.

5. They reflect at the end of each session to identify the extent they have and have not used these cooperative conflict strategies. The mediator helps them focus on helping each other learn to use these strategies more appropriately and frequently.

If appropriate and time and resources are available, the mediator can provide a training program for the protagonists. For example, they could develop a clear understanding of the need to develop cooperative conflict skills and their nature, observe a behavioral model of cooperative conflict, discuss the effectiveness and uses of this approach, practice role playing cooperative negotiations, and receive feedback and support to continue to learn.

Reflect and Learn

Leaders want to empower employees by having them develop the skills to deal with future conflicts. The lack of a shared framework, as well as the pressure to reach an agreement to the immediate issue, frustrates this learning. The theory of cooperative conflict gives mediators and conflict partners a common understanding. Then they have a shared ideal for how they are trying to discuss their differences and can give each other feedback and support to improve how they deal with present and future conflicts.

ARBITRATION

Arbitration is a viable alternative to negotiations. Most leaders rely on informal arbitration as their method of choice in dealing with employee conflicts. Arbitration seems more efficient than mediation and fits leaders' view of their role as those who solve problems and make decisions. However, this informal arbitration is usually carried out in abbreviated, ineffective ways.

An arbitrator is to take an unbiased role to become familiar with the problem and opposing positions and to examine all the evidence. Then the arbitrator renders a judgment about how the conflict should be resolved. The process includes:

1. The conflict partners both agree that they will abide by the arbitrator's decision after they have had a chance to present their side of the conflict.

2. Both sides submit their positions and how they want the conflict to be resolved to focus the discussion and decision.

3. Both present their positions and supporting evidence without interruption. Each side has an equal opportunity to present its case.

4. They refute and provide counter evidence to the other side's arguments and evidence. They try to persuade the arbitrator through facts and logic.

5. Both sides make a closing statement.

6. The arbitrator announces the decision and its rationale.

Ideally, arbitration is voluntary. Two companies agree to ask an arbitrator to decide a breach of contract and abide by the decision. Two countries agree to let the World Court resolve a territorial dispute. But within organizations, employees typically assume that they must submit to informal arbitration by their boss. The traditional hierarchy gives managers the authority and responsibility to settle disputes and ensure smooth coordination. Indeed, passing a conflict up the hierarchy is, after avoiding, perhaps the most popular way to deal with conflict in organizations.

But managers are seldom prepared to arbitrate effectively. They are not without prejudice, but bring strong attitudes and biases toward the conflict partners and their conflict. Feeling they do not have the time to proceed through the steps of arbitration thoroughly, managers often short-circuit the process by making a decision after listening to one side. They dismiss preparing positions as time-wasting, and refuting each other's arguments as squabbling.

Employees are also often unprepared. They are angry but are unsure why and what the resolution should be. Even when they know, they might be embarrassed to write out their position and discuss it with the manager. They remain fixated on their position, and when that is not completely accepted, feel they have lost, blame the manager as unfair, and withdraw from work.

Arbitration is overused and mediation is underused in organizations. Although both can result in poor solutions and weakened relationships, cooperative negotiation provides more face-to-face opportunities to present and understand each other's point of view, to create new alternatives, and to reach an agreement that people believe is fair and effective. Negotiations and mediation also provide more opportunities to practice and learn the complex skills of conflict management.

Becoming Conflict-Positive

Becoming conflict-positive requires breaking away from the old assumption that conflict is inevitably competitive. People see "strong" members as aggressive, stubborn, arrogant, closed-minded, and determined to win. They see "weak" members as too passive, coy, and fragile to be open and face losing a conflict. Although they are willing to deal directly and helpfully with problems and differences, they assume others are committed to winning or to avoiding. These attitudes and assumptions make productive conflict very difficult and improbable. While learning to manage conflict is useful even when a conflict partner is unwilling to change, the most powerful impact occurs when people learn to manage conflict together.[16]

Conflict partners can work together to move away from competitive conflict ideas and habits to create a cooperative conflict team and organization. Discussing the benefits of cooperative conflict and the price each side is paying for the destructive conflict can convince them that they should invest in improving their conflict abilities. Then they can study cooperative conflict to understand how it is an alternative to viewing conflict as a competitive fight over opposing interests.

People can commit themselves publicly to managing their conflicts openly and cooperatively. They realize that they cannot transform their ways of working overnight, but credibly convey that they are motivated to learn cooperative ways of managing conflict. In this way, team members move away from seeing each other as arrogant or passive to believing that they are direct, open-minded, and responsive people who want to manage their differences.

They need to follow up this commitment with action to put cooperative values, procedures, and skills in place. The team identifies the rules for discussing conflicts and problems, allocates bonuses and other rewards, and undertakes the training that will support their handling conflicts cooperatively. They agree they have a right to speak their minds and to disagree with each other.

Leaders and employees together learning to deal with their conflicts is a wise, practical investment. Such learning is, as we will see in the next chapter, critical for empowerment and self-management.

12 MOVING TO SELF-DIRECTING TEAMS

> A tyrant refuses to work for a common cause, and is patho-
> logically afraid of rivals. He suppresses every superiority,
> does away with good men, forbids education and light, con-
> trols the movement of the citizens, keeps them in perpetual
> servitude, wants them to grow accustomed to baseness and
> cowardice.
>
> Aristotle

Our family business has moved from a complex hierarchical structure toward a self-directing team organization. Like many other companies, we
realize that we must create new ways of working to survive and flourish
in a turbulent, demanding environment. Rather than just working
harder, we must find ways of working smarter so that we continuously
improve the quality service we deliver to our elderly and developmentally disabled clients as well as reduce costs.

From the beginning, our organization has emphasized cooperative
teamwork and managing conflict. Employees have come to expect to be
asked to solve problems in task forces and identify issues and work toward resolution in advisory groups. The clients they serve have councils
to manage their homes and groups to promote learning. Employees have
access to grievance procedures, open door policies, and training to
manage conflict. Nevertheless, our experience has been, like that of
many other companies, that the road to self-managing teams is difficult
and conflict-filled as well as exhilarating and liberating.

Changing an organization adds burdens. People must still do
their tasks and manage the inevitable crises, but now they have to

203

learn to operate in a new mode. There will be miscues and misdirection in the movement to the new way of working; these must be identified and corrected.

Self-managing is particularly challenging because people not only must accept more responsibility but also be willing to be held accountable for setbacks and to take the lead to fix them. They must not just get along with their peers but develop ongoing, open, conflict-positive relationships. It can seem easier to let others do their own thing rather than confront a team member with one's doubts that his decision is only a stop gap solution. Groups often find it easier to blame problems on other groups, rather than to deal with their own internal tensions and conflicts.

People have quit our company because they did not see how self-managing could pay off for them. Despite assurances of job security and no decrease of pay, they felt unable to accept what they saw as lost power and status. Some employees long for the "good old days" when they had to worry just about their own jobs and could fall back on the safety net of their boss.

Leaders also had to be prepared to change. They developed coaching and facilitating teamwork skills. They had to learn to encourage initiative, support people even when mistakes are made, and hold them accountable. More work was needed to clarify and communicate the vision and mission of our organization. Groups had to rethink their direction—where they were going and develop the confidence and resources to get there.

Performance appraisal, selection, and compensation systems are being modified to foster cooperative self-directing teams. Conflicts continue over who is to make decisions. What issues should a team decide itself and what issues must be discussed with other teams and leaders?

No simple plan to "let go" or neat blueprint exists to become self-directing. Moving to self-management exposes the critical need for leaders and employees to have considerable psychological knowledge, sensitivity, and skills to work together productively.

THE POTENTIAL OF SELF-DIRECTING TEAMS

Companies in a number of countries are using self-managing teams.[1] In 1990, nearly half of Fortune 1000 companies reported that they were using self-directing teams and even more indicated that they planned to increase their use.[2] Usually carried out on the shop floor, these groups give workers considerable authority to determine their day-to-day work. They can decide the pace of work, division of labor, breaks, recruitment, and training of new members.[3] Typically, the work team members have related subtasks that require coordination, diverse skills needed to complete the task, and feedback and evaluation on the performance of the entire group.

Minimal critical specification is an underlying principle of self-managing work teams. Employees are expected to work more effectively without external supervision and are in charge of their own internal matters. The self-determination of working without supervision is intrinsically motivated and satisfying, which results in more ownership and pride in one's work. The outcomes are expected to be improved group productivity, strengthened mental health, and reduced turnover.

Self-Directing Versus Traditional Work

Texas Instruments, Xerox, and many other successful organizations believe their considerable investment self-managing teams have paid off. Teams with the responsibility to determine their own priorities, divide up their work, and develop their abilities have been found to be able to deal with organizational tasks and problems and involve employees and gain their commitment.

Wall, Kemp, Jackson, and Clegg found that autonomous work groups at a new plant in a British confectionery company had a long lasting impact on employee intrinsic job satisfaction.[4] A new plant was designed to allow from 8 to 12 people to work in groups, all of whom were expected to carry out all the jobs necessary to produce candy. They collectively allocated jobs, reached production targets, and met quality and health standards, solved local problems, and recorded production data for the company information system, organized breaks, ordered and collected raw material, delivered finished goods to the warehouse, called for engineering support, trained new recruits, and participated in their selection. Each production group was responsible for its own product line. In addition to informal discussions, they met formally once a week. No supervisors were hired because the work teams carried out all supervision functions.

Results indicate that the self-managing teams, compared to control groups at established sites within the same company, had specific rather than general impact on attitudes and outcomes for the company.[5]

Workers clearly appreciated these groups and indicated a high degree of involvement and intrinsic job satisfaction. The company also benefited because supervisors did not have to be hired. However, self-directing groups were not found to improve employee job motivation, commitment to the organization, work performance, or turnover. In fact, there was higher turnover in the self-managing groups. Managers also experienced more stress in overseeing these groups.

Other studies indicate that self-directing teams can have a positive impact on attitudes and behavior.[6] Cohen and Ledford conducted a careful comparison of 50 self-managing and 50 matched traditionally managed teams in a telecommunication company.[7] The self-managing teams indicated higher levels of job, social, group, and growth satisfaction than did traditionally managed groups. Self-directing teams were rated more effective than traditional ones by managers.

Self-managing groups have been found to improve productivity, commitment, worker attitudes, and safety, but these groups increase stress for managers.[8] Meta-analysis of research indicates that self-managing teams and similar interventions can improve productivity and attitudes but usually these impacts are modest and mixed.[9] Self-directing teams have potential but are not panaceas or inevitable fixes; they must be used appropriately and managed effectively to pay off for the organization and employees.

Capacity to Self-Manage

Giving employees the leeway to direct their own groups does not assure that they can effectively do so. Workers, like managers, need encouragement, guidance, feedback, and other support to manage themselves and work effectively as a team.[10] Poorly run self-managing groups can be oppressive, undermine individual initiative and self-autonomy.[11] Employees must develop the skills to lead themselves.

Self-directing teams need cooperative goals and constructive controversy to be effective. A Midwestern manufacturing plant had implemented a self-managing team structure for five years and was interested in using cooperation theory to analyze their teams.[12] The 540 employees involved in the 65 teams who participated in the study performed painting, assembly, and wiring functions. Teams were responsible for scheduling, housekeeping, safety, expense purchases, accident investigation, and quality, and all teams had weekly meetings facilitated by a team leader.

Teams characterized by highly cooperative goals were found to discuss their opposing views openly and skillfully. The teams with cooperative goals and constructive controversy were rated by themselves, their team leaders, and supervisors as more careful, productive, and innovative than were teams with more competitive and independent goals and less open discussion of conflicting positions.

Self-managing team members must be leaders and need the ideas and skills discussed in previous chapters. They must strive to see how they are cooperatively interdependent and swim or sink together. Two-way communication skills and managing intense feelings contribute to the capacity to self-manage. Team members need to discuss their opposing views openly and skillfully manage their conflicts. The next sections discuss how self-directing teams might meet the challenges of working with other groups, negotiating appropriate responsibility, and holding themselves and be held accountable.

SELF-DIRECTING IN AN INTERDEPENDENT WORLD

A major dilemma in making self-managing teams effective is that although they have autonomy—and sometimes even are called autonomous groups—self-directing groups are highly dependent upon the organization. Indeed, studies have documented that they challenge and frustrate management. To make self-managing teams effective, organizations must change their values, managerial skills, and compensation systems.[13]

Self-direction implies that teams provide their own directions and work with a great deal of autonomy. They feel in charge of their own destiny, make their own decisions, reap the rewards of success, and feel accountable for failure. People believe they can make a difference. Yet self-managing teams cannot just do their "own thing." Organizations are too interdependent for that. Self-direction requires mutually supportive relationships, not strict independence and autonomy.

Self-managing proponents argue that the freedom to be self-determining is highly motivating. Employees want to move away from the boredom of repetitive jobs and the constraints of being told what to do. They find value in making decisions about their own jobs and how they work and welcome the opportunities to build up their feelings of self-efficacy.

However, the autonomy to make decisions and manage oneself does not itself make people believe their own work will lead directly to success. Few individuals in an organization have the illusion that they can make a substantial impact by themselves. If they believe others do not have or are unwilling to share necessary information, they do not feel energized and empowered. If they believe others are shirking their responsibilities and engaging in social loafing, they are apt to conclude that their hard work will be wasted.[14]

Before people in organizations persist and work hard, they want assurance that their goals are valuable and important and that they have the capabilities to accomplish them. They want to know that their work is important for customers and colleagues and that they will be given the necessary resources to get the job done.

Recognition of the interdependence in organization has lead to the emphasis on developing self-managing teams. The team will believe that it can accomplish its goals by combining the knowledge and energy of individuals into coordinated, effective work. But giving teams more autonomy does not lead directly to their feeling that they "can do it." Other individuals and teams affect whether teams believe their goals are valuable and whether they have the means to be successful.

Self-managing requires the combined efforts of leaders and employees. Leaders help employees appreciate that their efforts will be valued and reciprocated and that they have the abilities and resources to be successful. The stereotype is that managers give up their authority and get out of the way. But the reality is that leaders must work continually with individuals and teams to become self-managing.

Credible top management support is needed to move to self-management.[15] Leaders and employees both must be confident and committed to making self-direction work. Top management support helps teams believe that their efforts will be recognized and appreciated and they will be able to get the resources to complete their tasks and the acceptance needed to implement their recommendations.

Individuals must feel empowered and able to manage themselves within their teams; teams must manage themselves within the context of other groups and the organization as a whole. Self-managing does not mean autonomy from others but requires developing cooperative, empowering relationships throughout the organization. Then people feel directed and resourceful so that they can be successful and have an impact.

THE GIVE-AND-TAKE OF RESPONSIBILITY

Self-direction holds that teams should be responsible for their own success. Leaders cannot just bestow self-management on employees; nor can employees just accept it. They have to be engaged in ongoing negotiations and dialogue.

Traditionally, managers assumed that employees were extensions of themselves. They would decide what needed to be done and how it would be done; then they would direct and cajole employees to implement these decisions. They relied on telling employees what to do and employees expected to be told. By observing employees, they could see whether they needed more complete instructions. Managers frequently checked their work and advised employees how they should adjust to unforeseen circumstances. They had many opportunities to "micro-manage."

In self-management, leaders must be prepared to help employees understand the whole task and how it fits into what the organization is trying to do. Leaders must be explicit about the desired end state of the project and in the specific ways that it complements the work of other individuals and groups. Employees cannot adjust to circumstances and use their own creativity effectively without a clear understanding of the ultimate purpose of their work.

Leaders must also help employees become internally committed to their tasks and see the value to the organization and to themselves of doing those tasks successfully. They will no longer be able to reassure themselves with frequent checks that the needed work is being done. Leaders must trust that employees can become internally committed and then work with them so that they are.

Employees must also develop skills to accept responsibility and reassure their managers that they can be trusted. Traditionally, employees focus on their own particular assignments and get frequent feedback from their boss on their progress. They could be reassured that their boss would step in and instruct them if their jobs were not done properly. With self-management, employees must take the long-term view. They must work to make sure that they understand their assignments and how they are intended to support the work of others and the vision of the company, believe they can complete them, and tolerate the lack of immediate feedback from their boss on their progress.

Actions that leaders and employees can take to promote effective responsibility include:

1. Leaders and employees discuss how their team's tasks complement and further the business strategy of the organization. Employees know that top management wants them to succeed. They feel in step with the rest of the organization and believe their success will have a critical impact.

2. Leaders back up the talk about the importance of the self-directing team with assignment of people and budget. Team members believe that they have among them the personal abilities, finances, information, and knowledge to be successful. They have both the technical and the interpersonal abilities to coordinate and work together. They are confident that they can negotiate to get resources they really need.

3. Team members discuss their previous accomplishments, experiences, and credentials, and in other ways realistically disclose their personal strengths. They point out and recognize how individuals have used their abilities in the service of the team. Using preliminary estimates of what the task requires, the team identifies how it can apply its technical skills, money, and other resources.

4. Team members take courses, read books and journals, and discuss ideas to keep current in their specialities. Readings, workshops, and reflection on experiences develop skills in dealing with conflicts and other group issues.

5. Regular meetings, proximity of offices, electronic mail, and computer systems help team members exchange information and keep each other posted.

HOLDING ACCOUNTABLE

Self-directing is more than having responsibility and accepting the praise for success. People must hold themselves and be held accountable for shortcomings and failures; they need to take the leadership to solve their problems. Although leaders avoid micro-managing, they expect people to produce and confront unacceptable performance. It is also vital that team members confront each other when expectations are not reached.

Contrary to the popular notions associating cooperation with harmony and "live and let live," working cooperatively requires confrontation. In cooperation, team members want each other to perform effectively, for that helps everyone accomplish the team's cooperative goals. The better one does her job, the better off others will be. Team members support each other efforts and praise them for success. However, when one does not perform effectively, team members are frustrated and seek to change the inadequate performance.

Such confrontation promotes the cooperative good. In effective confrontation, leaders and team members are legitimately holding people accountable to do their assigned, fair share of work. They are not imposing their will and being tyrants. They seek to promote the interests of the confronted employee, too. They want him to succeed and are working with him so that he can succeed. To keep an employee on the job though he is performing inadequately might undermine self-confidence and well-being. The employee feels frustrated because he failed to meet his needs to achieve and succeed; he may feel isolated and unappreciated because people did not value his contributions.

Cooperative work makes confrontation more likely. People in competition are actually "better off" and more likely to "win" when their competitors are performing inadequately. In cooperation, people have a vested interest in helping, cajoling, and demanding effective performance from each other. People in cooperation are much more likely to discuss their frustrations with each other than those in competition. True partners and supportive bosses are those who tell us when we are being ineffective and work with us to improve.

Confronting Individuals and Teams

Although blaming is avoided, the team holds individual members accountable. In the division of labor and assignment of roles, they have been assigned particular responsibilities. Those who have not fulfilled them are confronted and the reasons for their inadequate performance explored. The team has a shared responsibility to work with the individual, help remove obstacles, and provide the resources for individual and group success. Often individuals have not performed because they have not felt supported or adequately informed. Individuals who continue to refuse to do their jobs risk punishment and expulsion.

Each team member reports on her activities to the group and shows her personal responsibility. Individual performance is compared to role expectations and assignments, and contributions to the team monitored. Individuals who complete their assignments are recognized. The team confronts individuals who fail to fulfill their obligations, and may decide to encourage and give assistance, or warn, or reprimand and punish the individual. In difficult cases, the team involves their manager in mediating a resolution.

Cooperative teamwork does not imply that everyone is rewarded and no one is ever punished. Although the emphasis is on encouraging initiative and learning from mistakes, managers need to confront unproductive teams, not cover up by rewarding them. If a group continues to be unproductive, then having it suffer some consequence can be useful. Managers avoid the temptation of blaming a few, but hold the group as a whole responsible.

Effective Confrontation

Effective confrontation requires making the situation "win-win." Those confronting need to stay focused on the cooperative goals even though the confronted person does not. They show the patience and discipline of supportive confrontation and managing conflict constructively.

They remind the individual why his task is important and how other team members rely and count on his work if the team is to succeed. They work with him to identify roadblocks and facilitate getting his job completed on time. They demonstrate a desire to have the person succeed and provide technical and other support that are needed to succeed.

Disciplined, they do not allow themselves to get sidetracked and obscure their cooperative intentions. They do not criticize the employee as a person nor call into question his intentions. They recognize his other contributions and reassure him that he is respected and valued as a person.

CREATING THE "CAN DO" ORGANIZATIONAL CULTURE

Throughout many organizations, people are increasingly expected to work without much direct supervision. They are to use advanced technology and computers to stay informed and complete important tasks by themselves. Middle managers, now considered less needed, have been

Becoming Self-Directed

Lay the Foundation

- Build cooperative goals.
- Foster two-way communication.
- Express and manage feelings.
- Discuss opposing views constructively.
- Manage conflicts productively.
- Develop cooperative, productive relationships with other teams.
- Show credible top management support.

Develop Responsibility

- Leaders and employees discuss how their team's tasks complement and further the business strategy of the organization.
- Employees understand the goals and purposes of their tasks and become committed to them.
- Leaders back up the talk with assignment of people and budget to the team.
- Team members identify their accomplishments, experiences, and personal strengths.
- They use formal and informal learning methods to build their abilities.
- Employees feel empowered that they have the authority and resources to be successful.
- The team plans how to apply its skills and resources to achieve its goals.
- Regular meetings, proximity of offices, electronic mail, and computer systems help team members exchange information and keep each other posted.

Hold Accountable

- Each person describes his contributions to the team.
- The team celebrates individual contributions and team successes.
- Leaders and employees confront unacceptable performance.
- They help the confronted person remove obstacles and provide resources.
- The emphasis is on "win-win."
- They reaffirm their acceptance of the confronted as a person.
- They use the confrontation to be a stronger cooperative team.

terminated in great numbers as organizations downsize and reduce costs. The challenge is to create the "can do" organizational culture where employees manage themselves.

The opportunity to self-direct can be highly motivating for employees. It unleashes them from the constraints of traditional bureaucracy and hierarchy. Employees resent micro-managing and resist being pawns. They want challenges and autonomy to develop their abilities and prove their worth. Self-managing builds up the internal commitment lean organizations need to meet today's challenges.

Yet, critiquing hierarchy and painting a bold picture of the self-directing future have proved easier than realizing it. Managers are often blamed for resisting change; they are too committed to control to let go. They easily talk the language of self-management but withhold information and interfere to reassert their authority. Leaders complain that employees want responsibility but not accountability when quality tasks and service are not delivered. Employees talk of job challenges but cannot take the heat of possible failure.

Effective self-managing requires much more than the willingness of managers to let go and employees to accept responsibility. Managers do not simply give up authority but have to exercise a new kind of leadership. Giving employees the autonomy to make decisions does not give them the ability to manage themselves. Trained and oriented in hierarchy, executives and employees alike are often unprepared for the rigors of self-directing.

The "can do" organization is action-oriented; action is needed to create it. Less recognized is that knowledge is also critical to expose myths that frustrate progress. Self-direction is more than the absence of direct supervisors or allowing people to exercise self-control, because employees must manage themselves with other individuals and teams in the organization. Leaders do not just let go, but need to work with individuals and groups so that they accept responsibility. Leaders and employees need to confront and hold each other accountable as well as celebrate their common successes. Employees need more than autonomy to be self-managing. They and their leaders must be psychologically skillful and adept.

PART FIVE

BECOMING LEADERS

Whilst he sits on the cushion of advantage, he goes to sleep.
Ralph Waldo Emerson

Leaders and employees must learn if their organizations are to adapt successfully to rapid changes in technology and the marketplace. Learning psychology is most fundamental because it helps people develop powerful, cooperative, conflict-positive ways to work together so that they adopt new methods, implement new technologies, and develop new products and services. Chapter 13 describes how employees can learn and apply psychology to strengthen their cooperative relationships. They invest in their future productivity by creating a learning organization. Chapter 14 shows how learning leadership and teamwork prepare organizations for the uncertainties of the future.

13 BECOMING A LEARNING ORGANIZATION

> The person who grabs the cat by the tail learns about 44 percent faster than the one just watching.
>
> Mark Twain

Managers like Ralph Strayer of Johnsonville Foods (Chapter 2) found that they needed to teach to become leaders. Teachers have also become corporate leaders. Rosemarie B. Greco knew without a doubt from sixth grade on that she would be a teacher.[1] But when she took a job as a secretary at Fidelity Bank in Philadelphia to help her family and pay college tuition, she had no idea that her teaching would be in a bank. In the late 1960s when she began, and now as CEO of a $5.7 billion bank, her teaching skills of setting standards, communicating values, and imparting knowledge have proved valuable for forging a common culture and helping people have the confidence and skills to cope with a changing marketplace.

In her first three months as a secretary, she learned all she could about bank operations, filling a three-ring binder with notes. Because there was no formal training program, she volunteered to train new managerial hires using her book. She was teaching and getting paid for it; she did not mind that she was training men who would make twice as much as she would. When a teaching job came up, she tried to quit. A vice president insisted that she stay to train people in his area and raised her salary. She could also get tuition reimbursed for working toward her degree in education.

217

Two years later, she sent her boss a memo outlining training programs that the bank needed. Hearing nothing directly, she was surprised when the bank introduced some of her ideas at the very top of the organization. When confronted, her boss admitted that he had used correction fluid to replace her name with his on the proposal because, he argued, it would not be implemented coming from so far down the ladder and surely she wanted her ideas used. Greco was confused, shocked, and angry.

After graduating magna cum laude in education, she took on the job of training operations people. To get prepared to write instruction booklets, she first taught day and night shifts to learn the critical jobs of bookkeeper, proof-machine operator, and stop-payment clerk. Discovering that operations people did not understand the importance of their work, she produced a video that showed how interdependent and important each job and area were. The video and booklets helped reduce turnover from unbearable to manageable levels. Her boss simply said, "You were right," and gave her the $10,000 salary she had earlier requested.

In the early 1970s, the bank was hit with a sex discrimination, class action suit. Through several turns of events, she became head of human resources. She moved quickly to change the corporate culture. Her most popular move was to fire the manager who had whited out her name on her training proposal. He had not changed his ways; his staff was as demoralized and fearful as when he was her boss. Her motive though was not vengeance, but as always "to do what was right for the bank."

When the bank had to downsize, she insisted that women not suffer an unfair share of the terminations, despite the protestations of line managers that she was interfering. A master teacher had once told her, "They don't have to like what you say, they only have to learn from what you do." In teaching values, a teacher and a leader must have an "unwavering commitment to doing the right thing—and the ability to grow a second layer of tough skin." A decade later, the bank was honored as one of the 50 best organizations for working women.

In 1978, a new CEO named Greco head of branch banking. When reminded that she had never made a loan, he told her that she could learn the business, but she needed to "teach people how to change." A survey revealed that the business owners ranked the bank as inferior to its competitors. She and a small group defined goals and performance standards and an incentive program to reach them. She needed commitment. Those who would not accept the new scheme left with a severance package. Three years later, the survey revealed the bank had become a customer favorite.

In December 1988, the bank faced a crisis for which Greco had to call upon all her experience and learning. As she went up on a makeshift stage, she had devastating news. Real-estate loan problems and a power struggle at the parent corporation had resulted in the firing of the admired CEO and vice chairman and the acquisition of the bank. "I saw that these officers needed to be comforted, encouraged, and most of all, led. I promised them we would get through these difficult times together. I assured them that our bank was safe and sound and gave them a critical assignment—to convince our customers that they had made the right choice in banking with us." For months, she met with people from early morning until late at night, emphasizing service to the customer and respect for each other.

The bank employees came through and she was promoted to CEO of the new bank. In September 1990, she again went to the same makeshift stage to the playing of "Hail to the Chief" with balloons and hundreds of smiling faces. She had known many of them for half her life and 22 years at Fidelity. She told them that they had earned her new title. She also saw that she had taught all the lessons that she could teach them. Six months later, she left to become president and CEO of a bank across town. "The first thing I did was buy a notebook. And I began again."

MOVING TO A LEARNING ORGANIZATION

Learning to lead is an ongoing pursuit, not the mastery of a few techniques or being born with the right genes. Greco and other leaders must also teach. To be credible, they lead by example to develop people and the business. They ask, support, and cajole employees to improve as they too take risks and learn.

The link between learning and organizational performance is becoming clear. Traditionally, the world of action and knowledge have stood in opposition. Professional education and training are carried out in classrooms and workshops removed from the action of the boardroom and shop floor. Now the demands to respond to changes in technology and the marketplace and to improve continuously are so high and visible that many leaders and employees want to become learning organizations.

More than just knowing ideas, "learning organizations" put ideas to work to improve their performance.[2] They dig into issues and collect valid data, generate solutions, implement a high-quality solution, gather data on its effects, revise, and re-implement. They reach out beyond their boundaries to benchmark how successful organizations accomplish objectives and identify how they can develop even more effective procedures and processes.[3]

Learning organizations take advantage of their mistakes. Boeing appointed a high-level employee group, called Project Homework, to compare the development of two troubled airplanes, the 737 and 747, with the more successful 707 and 727.[4] These lessons informed the development of the 757 and 767, the most successful, error-free launches in Boeing history.

LEARNING IN THE LEAN ENTERPRISE

To be competitive today, the enterprise as a whole, not just one company or the manufacturing department, has to be lean and effective. The key to improving customer value while reducing costs is teamwork, not just on the shop floor but between manufacturing, suppliers, and marketing distributors. The key to this effective partnership in turn is learning together.

In the lean enterprise, groups, functions, and legally separate but operationally interdependent companies collectively analyze a value stream and work together to ensure maximum value to the customer.[5] But too many managers are so focused on their own areas that they fail to see the value stream and the need to work together with other functions. Compared to one hour at Toyota, Mercedes-Benz requires three hours to engineer and manufacture a comparable luxury car, largely because engineering functions won't talk to each other. The result is many labor-intensive loops in development and little attention to manufacturability in the design and development process.

Lean enterprise is also stymied because many companies react to market downturns by protecting themselves rather than developing the total enterprise. Nissan in Great Britain had a great deal of trouble with the launch of its Primera because key suppliers did not deliver. Rather than punish the suppliers, Nissan lent some of its best engineers to improve their processes. Two years later, these suppliers were its best, most effective partners in the launching of Micra.

Britain's Unipart Group, a 1987 spin-off from Rover, has established Unipart University so that its divisions and functions teach each other best practices. The auto parts manufacturing taught important lean principles to other areas. The Information Technology Faculty, part of the information systems company, upgrades IT skills through Unipart. The Deans of the Faculties are heads of the business. John Neil, CEO, argued, "Our vision is to build the world's best lean enterprise. That means continuously integrating . . . learning, into the decision-making systems of the company."

Teamwork Is the Basis

Learning the psychological abilities and sensitivities to work as a team is the basis of becoming a learning organization. Teams help to reflect on mistakes and learn from experience. Team members help each other feel confident that they can deal with their conflicts.[6] Members of Boeing's Project Homework had to collect and analyze complex information and debate and integrate views to hammer out their recommendations. Then they had to inform and persuade engineers to implement their recommendations.

Delta Dental Plan (Chapter 8) and many other organizations are benchmarking to learn from companies using the best practices. They identify companies that have developed successful processes even though they may be in different industries, and interview and observe them at work. But benchmarking requires teamwork. Several people are needed to identify successful companies, understand their processes, and adapt them to their own situations. Then departments and groups must be receptive and implement the new processes.

Marketing people learn production and production specialists learn marketing through discussing issues and solving problems together. Young managers must be willing to listen and observe if they are to benefit from the expertise of more experienced ones. Cooperative goals, mutual power, two-way communication, managing feelings and conflicts, and using controversy constructively are needed to empower people to work together to help their organization adapt and learn.

By helping people learn to work together, leaders have a powerful, enduring impact. With strong team relationships, employees are better able to borrow and learn ideas, implement new programs, and learn each other's expertise. They get in the mode of learning and continuous improvement.

Learning to Be an Executive

There is much to know to become an effective leader. In studies involving six major corporations, 191 successful executives were interviewed on key events in their career that made a difference in the way they manage. They gave a total of 616 events and 1,547 lessons.[7] Psychological abilities of self-confidence and working with people were critical to their development; they learned these abilities through rich, demanding experiences and years of reflection.

In their journey to becoming successful executives, the interviewees indicated that they had learned the valuable lesson that they could not manage everything by themselves. They had given up the notion that they could master all areas and be expert doers and realized that they could have a larger impact by helping others get things done.

Because they had learned that they did not have the expertise, and often not the authority, to tell people what to do, they had become adept at understanding the perspectives of others, an ability that allowed them to motivate and direct employees. They had learned to negotiate conflict and confront employees. Because of pressing demands, they realized that they needed to empower and develop employees if the challenges were to be met.

They had learned to take the perspective of an executive who knows the business and thinks strategically. They broadened their understanding that an organization must respond to customers, competitors, government regulations, and stockholders to be a successful business. Experiences helped them solidify their professional skills, build and use structure and control systems, and find innovative ways to solve problems. They had to cope with the ambiguity of managing, especially in a corporate head office job without a specific bottom line.

Self-knowledge and confidence were highly valued lessons. The firing line had made these executives aware why they were excited about their work. They were not just doing a job, but believed in what they were doing. Making it through adverse situations convinced them that they could survive and be strong and tough when necessary. They could cope with ambiguous situations, quickly get up to speed on emerging issues in new assignments, and deal with situations that were beyond their control. They persevered through adversity and took charge of their own careers.

Yet their self-confidence was not allowed to become arrogance; they had already learned that they must remember their limits and blind spots. Though tough, they also had to learn to be sensitive people who avoid using other people as instruments for their own will.

Learning on the Job

Demanding job challenges drove the interviewees to draw upon their inner resources, gain insight, and experiment with new ways of leading. Being thrust into heading a visible task force with a restricted budget and time table was valuable in getting the executives to think like leaders who form and galvanize a team to get something extraordinary done. Moving from line to staff also helped move them away from being technical doers who get tangible things done by themselves.

Starting an operation from scratch required them to build something from nothing. Executives had to learn about organizations by creating their own, including selecting and training their own staff. Fixing a business in trouble was an important developmental experience. The managers had to be tough and disciplined to attack the problems that were bleeding the organization to death. Then they had to rebuild it.

They learned working with bosses and others. There is much to be learned from observing up close a leader who is proficient at developing a team that gets things done. But coping with a difficult, intolerable boss made these executives more compassionate and respectful when dealing with their own subordinates. Even losing out in political warfare helped some executives recognize their own personal limitations and scale back unrealistic career and promotion expectations.

Reflecting on mistakes and disasters could be very useful, especially when they could understand the underlying reasons. For example, they came to appreciate the destructiveness of mistreating people because they would then withhold information and let them fail. They realized their own limitations and because of the need to rely on others they must develop mutually respectful relationships.

Barriers to Learning

Despite the emphasis on the learning organization, many managers and employees remain highly focused on getting the task done without a firm recognition of the need to build and maintain the relationships needed for continuous improvement. They see sharing technical information and solving task problems as highly legitimate and useful; their education and experience have built their task abilities and confidence. However, they consider sharing feelings about how people are working together difficult and obstructive.

The crushing emphasis on the short-run and crisis management reinforces the neglect of relationships. Managers and employees often feel under the gun to get a letter out by 5 o'clock, the project done by Friday, and the profits in by the end of the quarter. Competitive pressures in the marketplace and investor pressure on stocks can make this short-term orientation seem even more important today. From this perspective, spending time having people talk about their feelings toward each other and complaining about their conflicts may seem superfluous, perhaps a bit crazy. From a long-term view, however, discussing how people can strengthen their communication and teamwork to be increasingly effective is a wise investment.

Chris Argyris argued that professional education reinforces values and beliefs that result in defining interpersonal issues as "undiscussable."[8] Though managers espouse openness and cooperation, they act to exert unilateral control, to win, and to hide feelings. The discrepancy between action and ideals is a double-bind message that immobilizes managers and employees. Employees conspire to let managers maintain the illusion of participation and collaboration. To reflect openly and talk about feelings would reveal the manager's competitiveness and control-orientation, expose employees' duplicity, and embarrass everyone. Managers and employees experience a deep sense of hypocrisy between the ideal and the reality, but the very discrepancy prevents them from discussions that would reduce it.

The short-term, get-things-done orientation coupled with fears of offending people and being offended result in a "if it ain't broke, don't fix it" approach to interpersonal issues: Let's hope that people will work together and that any problems will naturally sort themselves out. If relationships explode and it becomes obvious that the job is not getting done, we'll try to pick up the pieces, hire a consultant, and have a weekend for team-building. But by then suspicions and anger can be so intense that finding and dealing with underlying issues is very emotionally trying and time-consuming. The team may be stalled in a quagmire with no practical means to extradite itself.

Employees at times develop highly cooperative, learning relationships without much help from leaders. The demands of an immediate, clearly valuable task, and the chemistry between people can be enough. However, in our fragmented, suspicious world, leaders are increasingly needed to help people learn to work together synergistically.

Psychological Ineffectiveness and Executive Derailment

Job challenges and reflecting can help managers become leaders. The failure to use experience to develop skills in working with peers, superiors, and subordinates can be disastrous. Major reasons why executives derailed and failed to fulfill their potential include:[9]

1. Insensitivity to others.
2. Coldness, aloofness, and arrogance.
3. Untrustworthiness.
4. Playing politics and pushing too hard to promote themselves.
5. Failure to admit a problem.
6. Failure to delegate and build a team.
7. Inability to select and develop a staff.
8. Inability to think strategically and broadly.
9. Unable to adapt to a superior with a different style.
10. Overdependence on superior or mentor.

JOINT LEARNING OF PSYCHOLOGY

Coasting, going through the motions, and rigidly following wornout procedures are no longer acceptable. Leaders and employees learn psychological ideas so that they can analyze their present way of working and develop more effective ones. They deepen their psychological understanding, strengthen their teamwork, and move toward a learning organization. They learn ideas by applying them to their own relationships; by applying ideas, they learn them. As Aristotle wrote, "For things we have to learn before we do them, we learn by doing them."

Reflection is the vital link between action and ideas. Ideas in this book can help leaders and employees understand each other and their relationships and make plans to work more effectively. However, they must experiment with these ideas and procedures, reflect and learn, and try again. Then they deepen their understanding of psychology and their capacity to lead and work with others. Without experimenting, the ideas of this book will remain abstract. Without reflection, they will not use their experience to improve their abilities.

Applying psychology to develop relationships needs to be a mutual process. It is risky for an employee to talk about feelings and relationships alone. She may look aggressive or be suspected of "playing games" and putting other people on the spot. One person cannot manage a conflict alone; it takes two to get entangled in a conflict and it takes two to get untangled. Leaders need to encourage joint discussion so that people talk openly and directly to develop a shared understanding of issues and a joint commitment to future improvements, and avoid gossiping and forming divisive coalitions behind closed doors.

Leaders and employees should strive for an ongoing, gradual approach to relationships, rather than quick fixes. They recognize the complexity and difficulties of working together effectively and appreciate there will be inevitable frustrations, misunderstandings, and conflict. These are not in themselves great obstacles; indeed, conflicts, when properly discussed, help them know each other better, develop more effective ways of working, and leave them feeling united and directed toward their vision.

Applying Psychological Ideas

Leaders and employees can use the ideas of shared vision, cooperative goals, mutual power, two-way communication, managing feelings and conflicts, and constructive controversy to focus on important aspects of their work. They understand that discussing psychological ideas will keep them on course, examine their work relationships, promote mutual benefit, and strengthen their abilities.

Leaders and employees have a great number of ways to reflect on their experience working together.[10] They may complete questionnaires, interview each other, and use observations. They may discuss the data and identify an action plan after a meeting, at a weekend retreat, or as a conflict arises. The structure may be formalized and the time set or spontaneous. They may do it with their own resources, or invite a consultant from the firm's human resource group or the outside to assist them. The concrete way to proceed will depend upon a great number of practical considerations as well as their particular styles and wishes. What is critical is that people create valid, useful data and together recognize their accomplishments and obstacles. Then they can celebrate their successes and deal with limitations and conflicts to strengthen their work relationships.

Strengths and Weaknesses

Often it is assumed that an organization should concentrate on its weaknesses, as if it can only learn from mistakes and limitations. But people improve by recognizing their accomplishments and abilities. They are aware of what they are capable of doing, and the persistence that it takes to succeed. Their greater confidence gives them more energy to pursue and makes them less defensive and more able to recognize the weaknesses they need to work on to be more effective. They believe they are on course and believe in each other. Success breeds success.

Teams should celebrate their accomplishments together. As Renn Zaphiropoulos, president and CEO at Versatec put it, "If you are going to give someone a check, don't just mail it. Have a celebration." The sense of common success and mutual congratulations makes the achievement more meaningful, and reinforces the sense of team confidence and competence. It is much more fun to share a victory than to have to blow one's own horn alone. Bryan Trottier from the Pittsburgh Hockey Team said, "When you are playing with a group of guys, as opposed to a single sport, it's different. You can play tennis and win a championship and know you've accomplished something. But when you can look in the eyes of teammates and can share that feeling, it's something you can't describe."

Leaders and employees need to face their weaknesses head on. Problems that they do not know about will do it in; those that it does not work on will paralyze them. They avoid blaming individuals and share the responsibility and dig into doing something about it. Although blaming is avoided, they hold each other accountable. They have a shared responsibility to help remove obstacles and provide the resources for individual and group success.

PROGRAM FOR ONGOING LEARNING

Leaders and employees should work to understand their situation and problems rather than jump quickly to a solution. They want to investigate the past, not to find fault but to analyze it and understand reasons why problems arose. They use available information and reasoning to dig into issues, understand their relationships, and identify barriers and obstacles. They compare their present skill and work relationships with

---

Performance Appraisal

Many organizations rely on performance appraisal as a major tool for employee development. Leaders and employees are to review material, information, and conclusions about performance, identify issues that are interfering, and plan how to improve. Making performance appraisal work requires cooperative, learning relationships between leaders and employees.

Performance appraisal provides a forum for collaborative problem solving and learning, but it does not necessarily create the needed climate and interaction. Employees who felt they had cooperative goals and were able to discuss their opposing views with their leaders felt they had learned from their performance appraisal, were more motivated to do their jobs well, and more accepting of the performance appraisal system.[11] With competitive, conflict-avoiding interaction, performance appraisal was demoralizing; not even a good performance rating and subsequent pay increase restored their confidence. Learning in performance appraisal, as in many other settings, is facilitated by effective interpersonal dynamics.

---

the ideals of shared vision, cooperative goals, communication and conflict skills. They develop a common understanding of their strengths and weaknesses. Then they are prepared to develop and implement plans. Throughout they are using important psychological skills and developing their confidence.

Collecting Data

There are various ways to collect information. What is critical is that leaders and employees are able to discuss their views, reach an agreement of the team's plan, and be mutually motivated to strengthen it.

Questionnaires are relatively inexpensive ways to indicate how people view the group's vision, cooperative goals, and conflict management. However, questionnaires ask for generalizations, and people may use much different paths to draw conclusions. They may also differ in their use of the rating scale; a rating of "very much" is unlikely to mean the same for everyone. Questionnaires provide general conclusions, but do not themselves give the specific behaviors and incidents behind them.

Interviews allow people to explain the specific behaviors and incidents that lie behind their perceptions and generalizations about relationships. Interviewing each other allows for a mutual, two-way communication and shared understanding. However, interviews require training, skill, and time, and the results are often difficult to summarize and feed back. (See Chapter 7 for an overview of interviewing skills.)

Observations describe the actual behaviors of people. A team member, an employee from another group, or an outside consultant report what they have seen going on in the group. The group gets a much better picture of its actual workings. Observations, like interviews, require training and time. Unlike interviewing, observation focuses on overt behavior, and does not directly tell how people think and feel about each other.

Leaders and employees can draw a portrait of their group. People, either together or separately, draw a picture of the group, a collage that represents the group, or decide what kind of animal the group resembles. This method can be a fun way to get an overview of the group, but does not provide direct evidence of behavior or feelings.

Sometimes confidentiality is useful. People complete questionnaires or are interviewed with the understanding that only group scores will be made public, and their own responses will not be attributable to them. This confidentiality can help people reveal their true feelings and beliefs when they fear that openly doing so is too risky. If confidentiality is extended, then it needs to be protected. However, people should work toward direct exchange of feelings and feedback. People will then get to know each other much better and deal more effectively with issues. Confidentially can still be maintained: People do not disclose events to outsiders that might embarrass each other.

The strengths and uses of these methods complement each other and can be used together. For example, after discussing questionnaire results, people interview each other to understand each person's thinking. Then in a general discussion, they relate their observations about how they see the group working.

Open Discussion

Open discussion is key to reflection and learning. All employees, regardless of their power and prestige, express their opinions and feelings and the information and reasoning that lie behind them. They don't just

---

Feedback

Leaders and employees have a variety of ways to give each other feedback:[12]

1. Each person has a sheet of newsprint on the wall. They each write on the sheets the things they want the person to (a) begin doing, (b) to stop doing, and (c) to keep doing.
2. People answer the same questions as above, but instead send notes to the person in an envelope.
3. Each person reviews how she views her performance in the team, and others confirm or disconfirm these views.
4. Leaders and employees complete a questionnaire, results are analyzed and distributed, and they confirm or contradict the diagnosis.
5. Each person asks for feedback to identify areas of effectiveness and weaknesses.
6. Each person suggests what others should do to improve team performance.

---

speak out and assert themselves, but use communication skills to help others talk about theirs. They listen carefully and paraphrase each other's comments to make sure they understand. They avoid pressures to conform and coalitions to protect subgroups. The team as a whole analyzes itself and reaches a consensus on its strengths and issues.

1. *Structure a suitable time and place.* Regular sessions—ten minutes at the end of the meeting, a semi-annual retreat—build in reflection. Leaders and employees do not catch each other off guard, but select a situation when both have the energy, time, and openness to discuss the problem.

2. *Put self in other's shoes.* Leaders and employees ask about and try to know each other's perspective so they appreciate the problem fully, understand all sides, and develop solutions that work for all. They stop defending their own views long enough to listen carefully to others, and demonstrate their understanding of the other's position and arguments.

3. *Define issues specifically.* People resolve concrete conflicts more easily than general principles and grand ideas. They identify specific behaviors and stick to the issue and main problem without bringing up tangential issues that diffuse and confuse. They avoid diversion to side issues by taking the discussion too personally, feeling indignant, or trying to save face.

4. *Describe perceptions and feelings about each other's behavior.* The emphasis is on sharing information and understanding, not evaluating. People talk about their feelings and reactions to the team and its members and describe what led them to draw their conclusions. They use "I" and "my" to emphasize that they are talking about their perspective.

5. *Minimize labeling and judgment.* Abstract labels tend to be confusing, evaluative, and difficult for the person to do something about. People who feel that they are being evaluated often become defensive and closed-minded. Specific behaviors coupled with clear ownership are less threatening and more useful than analysis. For example, instead of "You're compulsive," use "I'm annoyed and feeling untrusted because you asked me three times within an hour to get that report to you later today." People express feelings directly rather than through innuendo and evaluations.

Plan and Implement

A thorough, joint diagnosis is the basis for developing action plans and carrying through. Rather than fixed on original positions, opposing views are used to create workable, effective solutions. The best ideas, information, and reasoning are combined to formulate ways to improve work relationships and a solution that promotes everyone's interests is selected. The responsibility to implement the solution is shared so that all employees know how they should act to strengthen the team.

1. *Recognize the gains for resolving difficulties and the costs for not.* It takes two teams to get into a pickle, and it takes two to get out of it. When everyone realizes the costs and the benefits, discussion is apt to be fruitful and directed at implementing solutions.

2. *Use constructive controversy.* Leaders and employees invite various possibilities, avoid assuming that it has to be one person's way

---

Program for Ongoing Learning

1. *Build in reflection.* Leaders and employees recognize that they will have opportunities to discuss their feelings and deal with issues to strengthen their relationships and prevent deterioration.
2. *Use psychological ideas.* They try to improve their abilities to have a shared vision, develop cooperative goals, communicate openly, manage their feelings, use controversy, and manage conflict productively.
3. *Collect data through questionnaires, interviews, and observations.* A combination of methods provides a rich, broad understanding of dynamics.
4. *Dialogue.* All employees dig into the data and present their views of the team and their personal experiences.
5. *Deal with conflicts.* Making interpersonal frustrations public is often the most difficult part. Once identified, people can develop new ways of working that reduce frustrations and improve productivity.
6. *Use good feedback skills.* People describe their perceptions and feelings, and avoid labeling and judging.
7. *Search for a diagnosis.* Leaders and employees objectively assess their strengths and weaknesses.
8. *Use constructive controversy.* They openly discuss alternative positions about how to proceed and combine ideas into creative, workable solutions that are mutually acceptable. They avoid win-lose arguing.
9. *Celebrate strengths.* They appreciate and value their accomplishments and abilities. They understand that admitting and dealing with problems and weaknesses are valuable assets and signs of their competence.

---

or another's, and combine ideas. They elaborate their opposing views and ideas. They search to try to understand each other and the benefits and costs of different courses of action. They integrate their views to create mutually acceptable and beneficial solutions.

3. *Manage feelings.* The power of feelings can be misused. Some people use their anger to overpower. When confronted, they argue that they are just angry and no explanation is necessary or possible. They demand that others change or face continued hostility. But talking about feelings, clarifying others' intentions, re-interpreting events, and planning how to work in the future change feelings.

4. *Strive for ongoing improvement.* Relationships need time to develop, and some interpersonal problems are not easily solved. The goal should be to make progress through repeated discussions rather than to solve all issues quickly and become a completely successful team instantly. Open reflection and discussion should be a regular, accepted part of working. Open discussions are convincing evidence that the team is making progress. They celebrate small as well as major gains. While recognizing their weaknesses, they feel confident that they can cope with them and can get better with experience.

Diverse people and their complex interactions make organizations psychological laboratories for continuous learning. There is either growth or decay; organizations are either getting more effective or less effective; leaders and employees are either strengthening their relationships or letting them slide; individuals are either becoming more self-assured or more insecure. Developing learning relationships is not a one-time effort, but an ongoing process. Applying psychology together pays off not only in learning important ideas but developing the capacity for people to work together productively and creatively. Open, cooperative, mutually powerful, conflict-positive relationships are the basis for become a learning organization that is doing things right and doing the right thing.

14 PREPARING FOR THE FUTURE

> He that will not apply new remedies must expect new evils:
> for time is the greatest innovator.
>
> Sir Francis Bacon

Leaders and their organizations face a formidable challenge: how to get prepared for the future when the future cannot be predicted. Economists and futurists make predictions because they are asked, but the truth is that no one knows what products and services will be highly valued and how organizations will operate. Forecasts have lost credibility. Not many people and companies are very confident they know what they will be doing even in five years.

Although much about business and organizations will change, organizations will still have to deliver value to their customers and stakeholders to survive and flourish. They will have to innovate because what customers find valuable today they may not next year.

Ironically, uncertainty and rapid change have resulted in a return to the basics. People are increasingly recognized as an organization's greatest resource. The latest technology, a new marketing strategy, and a hot product become quickly outdated. People not only produce goods and services, but they develop the new products future customers will demand.

Organizations require nor only the talents, energy, and commitment of individuals but that they work together. A team of people incorporates new technological developments, listens to customers, and combines perspectives to innovate and prepare an organization to serve its customers in the future.[1] Seldom can an individual alone, regardless of how brilliant or hard-working, get extraordinary or even ordinary things done for organizations.

Rapid change has also reasserted the basic imperative for leadership. Divided, suspicious organizations and communities call out for leaders. Teamwork is not an alternative to leadership. The choice is not between being led or being self-directing. Individuals feel empowered and teams become capable of self-managing through effective leadership.

We want you can to use the psychological ideas and procedures described in earlier chapters to fulfill the need to lead. The specific ways to lead effectively in the future cannot be predicted because of changes in the work force and requirements of organizations. However, the principles of a shared vision, the value of cooperative goals and power, the need for two-way, open communication, the necessity to manage conflict, and utility of controversy to solve problems will continue to be effective guides.

LEARNING LEADERSHIP

Learning to lead is an investment in the future of managers and their organization. However, becoming a leader is an ongoing journey of self and team development. John Kotter concluded that it took 10 to 20 years to grow an effective leader.[2]

Leaders develop psychological maturity as they work with diverse people under the demands and pressures of today's organizations. They do not expect to handle the challenges of leading perfectly, but commit themselves to learning as they ask people to develop themselves and their organization. No one is simply born knowing how to develop an inspiring, practical bottom line and shared vision, foster cooperative unity, communicate effectively, manage feelings and conflicts, use controversy, and the many other psychological abilities needed to be an effective leader today.

Combining Experience and Psychological Ideas

Formal education alone is not enough to become a psychologically savvy leader. One manager put it this way: "The only goal I'd had in school was to do well and get good grades at whatever I was doing. But work was a rude shock. In college, if I made an 86 on an exam, it meant that I knew most of the right answers. But at work, I found out that knowing the right answer was only 10 percent of the battle: working with people was the other 90 percent. We hadn't learned that at school."[3]

Yet experience alone is not enough to learn to lead. Useful ideas are needed to confirm and bring out the lessons of experience. Mark Twain wrote, "We should be careful to get out of an experience only the wisdom that is in it—and stop there; lest we be like the cat that sits down on a hot stove lid. She will never sit down on a hot stove lid again—and that is well; but also she will never sit down on a cold one anymore." Managers need to apply valid psychological ideas and reflect on experience to become effective leaders.

Leaders need to be insightful to understand psychological ideas and credible and flexible in applying them. There is a lot of psychology in becoming a leader. Leadership is not a set of techniques, because leading is a performing art.[4] Leaders must know themselves and be known before employees will follow. They build upon their abilities and extend their sensitivity; they confront some of their values and habits; they develop new ways of working.

Leader Development Teams

Leadership is too important to be left to chance or a training program every three years. Too often the idea that leaders are born is used as an excuse for the failure of organizations to structure and support learning to lead. Applying psychology to be an effective leader is something too complex and precious for one person to do alone.

Learning teams are important vehicles to apply psychology and become a leader.[5] In these groups, managers turn to each other for intellectual probing, creative problem solving, and courageous risk-taking. Managers need the assistance of others to experiment with new ways to lead and learn from their experiences.

In leader development teams, people have professional discussions in which they talk directly and honestly about the challenges, frustrations, and opportunities of leadership. They talk in increasingly concrete and precise terms about the nature of people and teamwork and how psychological ideas can be applied. They use their shared, precise language to describe these ideas, distinguish one practice and its virtues from others, and integrate ideas and approaches. Through discussing, explaining, and teaching, they deepen their understanding and skills in leadership and teamwork.

Leaders together plan programs and activities to strengthen the abilities of their employees and themselves. They share the burden and excitement and learn from others' experience. As they put ideas in place, they clarify their understanding and get the encouragement needed to experiment with plans that are appropriate for their people and situation. Discussions about the effectiveness of previous attempts suggest how they can modify plans for future action.

Leaders observe and give each other feedback. Most managers are unsure of their impact on employees and believe that employees are reluctant to be direct and honest. Managers can visit each other's work place and give an outside, informed perspective on group dynamics and leadership. Observation and feedback should be reciprocal to underline that everyone is helping each other learn. Managers need to be respectful and, when pointing out shortcomings and problems, recognize that everyone has strengths and weaknesses and good and bad days.

Leaders should think developmentally, weigh toward success, and build upon small wins. They cannot expect to be full-flowered leaders quickly. They will experience frustrations and failures that should not be allowed to discourage and demoralize.

Leaders take a long-term perspective. People do not automatically know how to work together and manage their conflicts. It may take years before they are highly skilled and proficient. The point is to enjoy the progress toward becoming a leader, not be downcast about imperfections. Nurturing and ongoing improvement are their watchwords.

Leaders are committed yet flexible. They remain convinced they want to strengthen their approaches but are responsive to changes and new directions. They work to integrate, for example, cooperative teamwork with a new emphasis on quality improvement.

In addition to support from other managers committed to leadership, leaders, as described in Chapter 13, increasingly involve their employees in understanding and applying psychology ideas. They strive so that people throughout the organization are committed to building an organization that delivers to customers and to them.

BUILDING ON COMMON SENSE

Leaders are psychologists. They act upon their ideas about what drives and motivates people, what people want and how they plan to get it, what is healthy and effective and what is not, and how feelings should be expressed. They have developed skills to understand people and communicate their ideas and goals. Although continually applying and refining their ideas, they seldom articulate them in much detail. Indeed, their implicit theories about people are much more complex than the explicit theories of formal psychology.

The psychological ideas discussed in this book reinforce commonly held beliefs: Social support is critical for coping with stress and individual well-being, tapping into people's motives and needs builds commitment, improved communication pays off for relationships and productivity, and trust is needed for collaborative work. But psychological research has refined these beliefs. Trust is not just there in a relationship; cooperative goals where people believe they are on the same side helps people develop trust. Managing conflict for mutual benefit moves people away from assuming that co-workers are arrogant and untrustworthy to seeing them as reliable colleagues.

Research has clarified the debilitating confusion that working cooperatively and conflict are opposites. People with cooperative goals will conflict over the best approaches to reach their goals, a fair and effective way of dividing the labor and sharing the benefits of their common work. Surprisingly, competitive goals underline both escalating conflict and conflict avoidance.

People in organizations disagree about much. Unfortunately, too often what they do agree on as common sense is that they should avoid conflict. But conflict will not be pushed away and disappear. The result of conflict avoidance is that people feel irritated and powerless without a way to deal with grievances and frustrations. The organizations suffer as poor decisions are made and problems remain unsolved. There is no realistic, viable alternative to conflict management. But it takes courageous leadership to create the conflict-positive organization.

Applying psychological knowledge also requires common sense. The value of cooperative, open conflict does not mean that no conflict should ever be avoided. Knowledge that social support is critical does not mean that people must seek it all the time. Trust can not be just extended but people together have to develop and earn it.

We want you to build upon the ideas discussed in this book to deepen your understanding and sensitivity to people and their relationships. These ideas are living, and need to be refined and extended in light of new research and practice. Psychological ideas are personal. Each of us understands and applies them in our own ways. But these ideas can also be shared. Their real potential is realized when leaders and employees together study and apply them.

The future is exciting and foreboding. The intensely competitive international marketplace poses unimagined potentials and uncertain threats. The disarray in our families, the fragmentation of our organizations and communities, and the suspicion toward our leaders feed our difficulties and frustrate our response; they also make us appreciate our basic need for genuine, competent leadership.

Although optimism may not be justified, hope is essential.[6] We can recommit ourselves to use psychological ideas to strengthen our common bonds to confront our opportunities and predicaments. But first we need courageous, experimenting, cooperative leaders to show us how together we make a difference.

Notes

Introduction

1. Deming, W. E. (1993). *The new economics: for industry, government, education.* Cambridge, MA: Massachusetts Institute of Technology Center for Advanced Engineering Study.

2. Deutsch, M. (1990). Sixty years of conflict. *The International Journal of Conflict Management, 1,* 237–263.

Tjosvold, D. (1993). *Learning to manage conflict: Getting people to work together productively.* New York: Lexington Books.

Tjosvold, D. (1991). *The conflict-positive organization: Stimulate diversity and create unity.* Reading, MA: Addison-Wesley.

3. Deutsch, M. (1973). *The resolution of conflict.* New Haven, CT: Yale University Press.

Johnson, D. W., & Johnson, R. T. (1989). *Cooperation and competition: Theory and research.* Edina, MN: Interaction Book Company.

4. Baker, J., Tjosvold, D., & Andrews, I. R. (1988). Conflict approaches of effective and ineffective managers: A field study in a matrix organization. *Journal of Management Studies, 25,* 167–178.

5. Cusumano, M. A. (1988). Manufacturing innovation: Lessons from the Japanese auto industry. *Sloan Management Review, 20,* 29–39.

Jusela, G. E., Chairman, P., Ball, R. A., Tyson, C. E., & Dannermiller, K. D. (1987). Work innovations at Ford Motor. In Y. K. Shetty & V. M. Buehler (Eds.), *Quality productivity and innovation: Strategies for gaining competitive advantage.* New York: Elsevier, 123–145.

Chapter 1
Your Bottom-Line Goals

1. Rayner, B. (1992). Trial-by-fire transformation: An interview with Globe Metallurgical's Arden Smith. *Harvard Business Review,* May–June, 117–129.

2. Farnham, A. (1989). The trust gap. *Fortune,* December 4, 56–78.

3. Hogan, R., Curphy, G. J., & Hogan, J. (1994). What we know about leadership: Effectiveness and personality. *American Psychologist, 49,* 493–504. For a thorough and depressing account of managers' lack of credibility, see Kouzes, J. M., & Posner, B. Z. (1993). *Credibility: How leaders gain and lose it, why people demand it.* San Francisco: Jossey-Bass, especially pp. 33–36.

4. DeVries, D. L. (1992). Executive selection: Advances but no progress. *Issues & Observations, 12,* 1–15.

5. Boneau, C. A. (1992). Observations on psychology's past and future. *American Psychologist, 47,* 1586–1596.

6. Cascio, W. F., & Morris, J. R. (1990). A critical reanalysis of Hunter, Schmidt, and Coggin's (1988) "Problems and pitfalls in using capital budgeting and financial accounting techniques in assessing the utility of personnel programs." *Journal of Applied Psychology, 75,* 410–417.

7. Janz, T., & Tjosvold, D. (1985). Costing effective vs. ineffective work relationships: A method and first look. *Canadian Journal of Administrative Sciences, 2,* 43–51.

8. Hamilton, V. L., Hoffman, W. S., Broman, C. L., & Rauma, D. (1993). Unemployment, distress, and coping: A panel study of autoworkers. *Journal of Personality and Social Psychology, 65,* 234–247.

Vinokur, A. D., & van Ryn, M. (1993). Social support and undermining in close relationships: Their independent effects on the mental health of unemployed persons. *Journal of Personality and Social Psychology, 65,* 350–359.

9. Locke, E. A., & Laham, G. P. (1991). *A theory of goal setting and task performance.* Englewood Cliffs, NJ: Prentice-Hall.

Pritchard, R. D., Jones, S. D., Roth. P. L., Stuebing, K. K., & Ekeberg, S. E. (1988). Effects of group feedback, goal setting, and incentives on organizational productivity. *Journal of Applied Psychology, 73,* 337–358.

Chapter 2
Learning Psychology

1. Strayer, R. (1990). How I learned to let my workers lead. *Harvard Business Review,* November–December, 66–83.

2. Sisco, R. (1992, July). Put your money where your teams are. *Training,* 41–45.

3. Kouzes, J. M., & Posner, B. Z. (1987). *The leadership challenge.* San Francisco: Jossey-Bass, chapters 9 and 10.

4. McCall, M. W., Jr., Lombardo, M. M., & Morrison, A. M. (1988). *The lessons of experience: How successful executives develop on the job.* Lexington, MA: Lexington Books, 28.

5. Borman, W. C., Hanson, M. A., Oppler, S. H., Pulakos, E. D., & White, L. A. (1993). Role of early supervisory experience in supervisor performance. *Journal of Applied Psychology, 78,* 443–449.

Morrison, R. F., & Brantner, T. M. (1992). What enhances or inhibits learning a new job? A basic career issue. *Journal of Applied Psychology, 77,* 926–940.

6. Deming, W. E. (1993). *The new economics: for industry, government, education.* Cambridge, MA: Massachusetts Institute of Technology Center for Advanced Engineering Study.

7. Argyris, C. (1991). Teaching smart people how to learn. *Harvard Business Review,* May–June, 99–109.

8. Deutsch, M. (1992). Kurt Lewin: The tough-minded and tender-hearted scientist. *Journal of Social Issues, 48,* 31–43.

Marrow, A. J. (1969). *The practical theorist: The life and work of Kurt Lewin.* New York: Teachers College Press.

9. Lewin, K. (1943). *Forces behind food habits and methods of change: The problem of changing food habits.* (NRC Bulletin No. 108). Washington, DC: National Research Council: Committee on Food Habits.

10. Lewin, K., Lippitt, R., & White, R. K. (1939). Patterns of aggressive behavior in experimentally created "social climates." *Journal of Social Psychology, 10,* 271–299.

11. Lewin, M. (1992). The impact of Kurt Lewin's life on the place of social issue in his work. *Journal of Social Issues, 48,* 15–29.

12. Deutsch, M. (1992). Kurt Lewin: The tough-minded and tender-hearted scientist. *Journal of Social Issues, 48,* 31–43.

13. Deutsch, M. (1992). Kurt Lewin: The tough-minded and tender-hearted scientist. *Journal of Social Issues, 48,* 41.

14. Frey, R. (1993, September–October). Empowerment or else. *Harvard Business Review,* 80–94.

15. McCall, M. W., Jr., Lombardo, M. M., & Morrison, A. M. (1988). *The lessons of experience: How successful executives develop on the job.* Lexington, MA: Lexington Books, chapter 5.

16. Morrison, R. F., & Brantner, T. M. (1992). What enhances or inhibits learning a new job? A basic career issue. *Journal of Applied Psychology, 77,* 926–940.

17. Deutsch, M. (1993). Educating for a peaceful world. *American Psychologist, 48,* 510–517.

Johnson, D. W., Maruyama, G., Johnson, R. T., Nelson, D., & Skon, S. (1981). Effects of cooperative, competitive, and individualistic goal structures on achievement: A meta-analysis. *Psychological Bulletin, 89,* 47–62.

18. Johnson, D. W., & Johnson, R. T. (1989). *Cooperation and competition: Theory and research.* Edina, MN: Interaction Book Company, chapter 3.

19. Johnson, D. W., & Johnson, R. T. (1985). Motivational processes in cooperative, competitive, and individualistic learning situations. In C. Ames & R. Ames, (Eds.), *Attitudes and attitude change in special education: Its theory and practice,* New York: Academic Press, 249–286.

20. Argyris, C., & Schon, D. (1978). *Organizational learning.* Reading, MA: Addison-Wesley, chapters 1 and 2.

21. Hogan, R., Curphy, G. J., & Hogan, J. (1994). What we know about leadership: Effectiveness and personality. *American Psychologist, 49,* 493–504.

Levinson, H. (1994). Why the behemoths fell: Psychological roots of corporate failure. *American Psychologist, 49,* 428–436.

22. Senge, P. M. (1990). *The fifth discipline.* New York: Doubleday.

23. Kouzes, J. M., & Posner, B. Z. (1987). *The leadership challenge.* San Francisco: Jossey-Bass.

Chapter 3
Becoming Committed to Leading

1. Cohen, M. D., & March, J. B. (1974). *Leadership and ambiguity.* New York: McGraw-Hill.

Mintzberg, H. (1973). *The nature of managerial work.* New York: Harper & Row.

Sayles, L. (1979). *Leadership: What effective managers really do . . . and how they do it.* New York: McGraw-Hill.

Stewart, R. (1967). *Managers and their jobs: A study of the similarities and differences in the way managers spend their time.* London: Macmillan.

2. Pavett, C. M., & Lau, A. W. (1983). Managerial work: The influence of hierarchical level and functional speciality. *Academy of Management Journal, 26,* 170–177.

3. Brewer, E., & Tomlinson, J. W. C. (1964). The manager's working day. *The Journal of Industrial Economics, 12,* 191–197.

4. Dahl, T., & Lewis, D. R. (1975). Random sampling device used in time management study. *Evaluation, 2,* 20–22.

5. Coperman, G., Luijk, H., & Hanika, F. P. (1963). *How the executive spends his day.* London: Business Publications.

6. Kouzes, J. M., & Posner, B. Z. (1987). *The leadership challenge.* San Francisco: Jossey-Bass.

7. Stogdill, R. M. (1974). *Handbook of leadership.* New York: Free Press.

8. Bass, B. M. (1990). *Bass & Stogdill's handbook of leadership: Theory, research & managerial applications.* (3rd ed.) New York: The Free Press.

9. Hogan, R., Curphy, G. J., & Hogan, J. (1994). What we know about leadership: Effectiveness and personality. *American Psychologist, 49,* 493–504.

10. Klimoski, R., & Brickner, M. (1987). Why do assessment centers work? The puzzle of assessment center validity. *Personnel Psychology, 40,* 243–260.

11. Zaccaro, S. J., Foti, R. J., & Kenny, D. A. (1991). Self-monitoring and trait-based variance in leadership: An investigation of leader flexibility across multiple group situations. *Journal of Applied Psychology, 76,* 308–315.

12. Kouzes, J. M., & Posner, B. Z. (1993). *Credibility: How leaders gain and lose it, why people demand it.* San Francisco: Jossey-Bass, chapter 1 and Appendix.

13. Bass, B. M. (1990). *Bass & Stogdill's handbook of leadership: Theory, research & managerial applications.* (3rd ed.) New York: The Free Press.

14. Wofford, J. C., & Liska, L. Z. (1993). Path-goal theories of leadership: A meta-analysis. *Journal of Management, 19,* 857–876.

15. Falbe, C. M., & Yukl, G. (1992). Consequences for managers of using single influence tactics and combinations of tactics. *Academy of Management Journal, 35,* 638–652.

Yukl, G., & Tracey, J. B. (1992). Consequences of influence attempts used with subordinates, peers, and the boss. *Journal of Applied Psychology, 77,* 525–535.

16. Liden, R. C., Wayne, S. J., & Stilwell, D. (1993). A longitudinal study on the early development of leader-member exchanges. *Journal of Applied Psychology, 78,* 662–674.

Tjosvold, D. (1988). Interdependence and power between managers and employees: A study of the leader relationship. *Journal of Management, 15,* 49–64.

Tjosvold, D., Andrews, I. R., & Jones, H. (1983). Cooperative and competitive relationships between leaders and their subordinates. *Human Relations, 36,* 1111–1124.

17. Tjosvold, D., & Tjosvold, M. M. (1993). *The emerging leader: Ways to a stronger team.* New York: Lexington Books.

18. Tjosvold, D., & Tjosvold, M. M. (1991). *Leading the team organization: How to create an enduring competitive advantage.* New York: Lexington Books.

19. McCall, M. W., Jr., Lombardo, M. M., & Morrison, A. M. (1988). *The lessons of experience: How successful executives develop on the job.* Lexington, MA: Lexington Books, p. 26.

20. Kasser, T., & Ryan, R. M. (1993). A dark side of the American dream: Correlates of financial success as a central life aspiration. *Journal of Personality and Social Psychology, 65,* 410–422.

Peterson, B. E., & Stewart, A. J. (1993). Generativity and social motives in young adults. *Journal of Personality and Social Psychology, 65,* 186–198.

21. McClelland, D. C. (1975). *Power: The inner experience.* New York: Irvington.

McClelland, D. C., & Boyatzis, R. E. (1982). Leadership motive pattern and long-term success in management. *Journal of Applied Psychology, 67,* 737–743.

Spangler, W. D., & House, R. J. (1991). Presidential effectiveness and the leadership motive profile. *Journal of Personality and Social Psychology, 60,* 439–455.

22. Farnham, A. (1989). The trust gap. *Fortune,* December 4, 56–78.

23. Clymer, A. (1985, June 9). Low marks for executive honesty. *New York Times,* p. 1F.

24. Kouzes, J. M., & Posner, B. Z. (1993). *Credibility: How leaders gain and lose it, why people demand it.* San Francisco: Jossey-Bass, chapter 1 and Appendix.

25. Tjosvold, D., Andrews, I. R., & Jones, H. (1985). Alternative ways leaders can use authority. *Canadian Journal of Administrative Sciences, 2,* 307–317.

Tjosvold, D., & Deemer, D. K. (1980). Effects of control or collaborative orientation on participation in decision-making. *Canadian Journal of Behavioural Science, 13,* 33–43.

Chapter 4
Building Employee Commitment

1. Kouzes, J. M., & Posner, B. Z. (1987). *The leadership challenge.* San Francisco: Jossey-Bass, 248.

2. Wright, P. M., George, J. M., Farnsworth, S. R., & McMahan, G. C. (1993). Productivity and extra-role behavior: The effects of goals and incentives on spontaneous helping. *Journal of Applied Psychology, 78,* 374–381.

3. Organ, D. W. (1988). *Organizational citizenship behavior: The good soldier syndrome.* Lexington, MA: Heath.

4. George, J. M., & Brief, A. P. (1992). Feeling good-doing good: A conceptual analysis of the mood at work—organizational spontaneity relationship. *Psychological Bulletin, 112,* 310–329.

5. Hundley, J. (1987). J.C. Penney relies on people power. In Y. K. Shetty & V. M. Buehler (Eds.), *Quality productivity and innovation: Strategies for gaining competitive advantage.* New York: Elsevier, 81–101.

6. Lawler, E. E. (1992). *The ultimate advantage: Creating the high-involvement organization.* San Francisco: Jossey-Bass.

7. McClelland, D. C. (1987). *Human motivation.* New York: Cambridge University Press, 312–316.

8. McClelland, D. C., & Boyatzis, R. E. (1982). Leadership motive pattern and long-term success in management. *Journal of Applied Psychology, 67,* 737–743.

9. Winter, D. G. (1973). *The power motive.* New York: Free Press.

Winter, D. G., & Stewart, A. J. (1978). Power motivation. In H. London & J. Exner (Eds.), *Dimensions of personality.* New York: Wiley.

10. McClelland, D. C. (1987). *Human motivation.* New York: Cambridge University Press, chapters 9 and 10.

11. Slade, L. A., & Rush, M. C. (1991). Achievement motivation and the dynamics of task difficulty choices. *Journal of Personality and Social Psychology, 60,* 165–172.

Hollenbeck, J. R., Williams, C. R., & Klein, H. J. (1989). An empirical examination of the antecedents of commitment to difficult goals. *Journal of Applied Psychology, 74,* 18–23.

12. McClelland, D. C. (1975). *Power: The inner experience.* New York: Irvington.

McClelland, D. C. (1970). The two faces of power. *Journal of Affairs, 24,* 29–47.

13. Brown, J. D., & Smart, S. A. (1991). The self and social conduct: Linking self-representations to prosocial behavior. *Journal of Personality and Social Psychology, 60,* 368–375.

14. Ellis, R., & Taylor, M. (1983). Role of self-esteem within the job search process. *Journal of Applied Psychology, 68,* 632–640.

Shamir, B. (1986). Protestant work ethic, work involvement and the psychological impact of unemployment. *Journal of Occupational Behavior, 7,* 25–28.

15. Brockner, J. (1988). *Self-esteem: Theory, research, and practice.* Lexington, MA: Lexington Books.

16. Donahue, E. M., Robins, R. W., Roberts, B. W., & John, O. P. (1993). The divided self: Concurrent and longitudinal effects of psychological adjustment and social roles on self-concept differentiation. *Journal of Personality and Social Psychology, 64,* 834–846.

17. Parker, L. E. (1993). When to fix it and when to leave: Relationships among perceived control, self-efficacy, dissent, and exit. *Journal of Applied Psychology, 78,* 949–959.

Geringer, J. M., & Frayne, C. A. (1993). Self-efficacy, outcome expectancy and performance of international joint venture general managers. *Canadian Journal of Administrative Sciences, 10,* 322–333.

18. Mead, G. H. (1934). *Mind, self and society.* Chicago: University of Chicago Press.

Tice, D. M. (1992). Self-concept change and self-presentation: The looking glass self is also a magnifying glass. *Journal of Personality and Social Psychology, 63,* 435–451.

19. Bolger, N., & Eckenrode, J. (1991). Social relationships, personality, and anxiety during a major stress event. *Journal of Personality and Social Psychology, 61,* 440–449.

20. Kirmeyer, S., & Lin, T. (1987). Social support: Its relationship to observed communication with peers and superiors. *Academy of Management Journal, 30,* 138–151.

21. Fisher, C. D. (1985). Social support and adjustment to work: A longitudinal study. *Journal of Management, 11,* 39–53.

22. Eisenberger, R., Huntington, R., Hutchison, S., & Sowa, D. (1986). Perceived organizational support. *Journal of Applied Psychology, 71,* 500–507.

Eisenberger, R., Fasolo, P., & Davis-LaMastro, V. (1990). Perceived organizational support and employee diligence, commitment, and innovation. *Journal of Applied Psychology, 75,* 51–59.

23. Jecker, J., & Landy, D. (1969). Liking a person as a function of doing him a favor. *Human Relations, 22,* 371–378.

24. Vinokur, A. D., & van Ryn, M. (1993). Social support and undermining in close relationships: Their independent effects on the mental health of unemployed persons. *Journal of Personality and Social Psychology, 65,* 350–359.

25. Gurtman, M. B. (1992). Trust, distrust, and interpersonal problems: A circumplex analysis. *Journal of Personality and Social Psychology, 62,* 989–1002.

26. Kasser, T., & Ryan, R. M. (1993). A dark side of the American dream: Correlates of financial success as a central life aspiration. *Journal of Personality and Social Psychology, 65,* 410–422.

27. Seligman, M. (1988, October). Boomer blues. *Psychology Today, 22,* 50–55.

28. Dooley, D., & Catalano, R. (1988). Recent research on the psychological effects of unemployment. *Journal of Social Issues,* 1–12.

Hamilton, V. L., Hoffman, W. S, Broman, C. L., & Rauma, D. (1993). Unemployment, distress, and coping: A panel study of autoworkers. *Journal of Personality and Social Psychology, 65,* 234–247.

29. Whitbourne, S. K., Zuschlag, M. K., Elliot, L. B., & Waterman, A. S. (1992). Psychosocial development in adulthood: A 22-year sequential study. *Journal of Personality and Social Psychology, 63,* 260–271.

30. Johnson, D. W., Maruyama, G., Johnson, R. T., Nelson, D., & Skon, S. (1981). Effects of cooperative, competitive, and individualistic goal structures on achievement: A meta-analysis. *Psychological Bulletin, 89,* 47–62.

31. Hammer, M., & Champy, J. (1993). *Reengineering the corporation.* New York: HarperBusiness, chapters 10–13.

Michaelsen, L. K., Watson, W. E., & Black, R. H. (1989). A realistic test of individual versus group consensus decision making. *Journal of Applied Psychology, 74,* 834–839.

Tjosvold, D. (1993). *Teamwork for customers: Building organizations that take pride in serving.* San Francisco: Jossey-Bass.

Robertson, D., Tjosvold, D., & Tjosvold, M. M. (1989). Staff relations, job commitment, and acceptance of elderly in long-term care facilities. *Journal of Long-Term Care Administration,* Fall, 2–7.

32. *Business Week,* (1990, December 17) Sharpening minds for a competitive edge, 72–78.

33. Fernandez, J. P. (1991). *Managing a diverse work force: Regaining the competitive edge.* Lexington, MA: Lexington Books.

Thiederman, S. (1991). *Profiting in America's multicultural marketplace.* New York: Lexington Books.

34. Tjosvold, D. (1983). Social face in conflict: A critique. *International Journal of Group Tension, 13,* 49–64.

35. Tjosvold, D., Johnson, D. W., & Lerner, J. (1981). The effects of affirmation and acceptance on incorporation of an opposing opinion in problem-solving. *Journal of Social Psychology, 114,* 103–110.

Tjosvold, D. (1974). Threat as a low-power person's strategy in bargaining: Social face and tangible outcomes. *International Journal of Group Tensions, 4* 494–510.

36. Peters, T., & Waterman, R. (1982). *In pursuit of excellence.* New York: Harper & Row.

Chapter 5
Developing a Shared Vision and Purpose

1. Hundley, J. (1987). J.C. Penney relies on people power. In Y. K. Shetty & V. M. Buehler (Eds.), *Quality productivity and innovation: Strategies for gaining competitive advantage.* New York: Elsevier, 81–101.

2. Moukheiber, Z. (1993, April 12). Our competitive advantage. *Forbes,* 59–62.

3. Berry, L. L., Parasuraman, A., & Zeithaml, V. A. (1994). Improving service quality in America: Lessons learned. *Academy of Management Executive, 8,* 32–45.

4. Jackson, S. E., & Dutton, J. E. (1988). Discerning threats and opportunities. *Administrative Science Quarterly, 33,* 370–387.

5. Gronroos, C. (1991). *Service management and marketing: Managing the moments of truth in service competition.* Lexington, MA: Lexington Books.

Normann, R. (1984). *Service management.* New York: Wiley.

6. Brown, S. W., Gummesson, E., Edvardsson, B., & Gustavsson, B. (1991). *Service quality: Multidisciplinary and multinational perspectives.* Lexington MA: Lexington Books.

Buzzell, R. D., & Gale, B. T. (1987). *The PIMS principles: Linking strategy to performance.* New York: The Free Press.

7. Hammer, M., & Champy, J. (1993). *Reengineering the corporation.* New York: HarperBusiness.

8. Katzenbach, J. R., & Smith, D. K. (1993). *The wisdom of teams: Creating the high-performance organization.* Cambridge: Harvard Business School Press, chapter 3.

Locke, E. A., & Laham, G. P. (1991). *A theory of goal setting and task performance.* Englewood Cliffs, NJ: Prentice-Hall.

9. Masternak, R. L. (1991/1992, Winter). Gainsharing programs at two Fortune 500 facilities: Why one worked better. *National Productivity Review,* 71–86.

Miller, C., & Schuster, M. (1987). A decade's experience with the Scanlon Plan: A case study. *Journal of Occupational Behaviour, 8,* 167–174.

Schuster, M. (1984). The Scanlon Plan: A longitudinal analysis. *Journal of Applied Behavioral Science, 20,* 23–38.

10. Seashore, S. E. (1954). *Group cohesiveness in the industrial work group.* Ann Arbor, MI: Survey Research Center, Institute for Social Research.

Mullen, B., & Copper, C. (1994). The relation between group cohesiveness and performance: An integration. *Psychological Bulletin, 115,* 210–227.

11. Moukheiber, Z. (1993, April 12). Our competitive advantage. *Forbes,* 59–62.

12. Tjosvold, D. (1991). *Team organization: An enduring competitive advantage.* New York: Wiley, chapter 8.

13. Beckhard, R., & Harris, R. T. (1987). *Organizational transitions: Managing complex change.* Reading, MA: Addison-Wesley.

14. Banas, P. A. (1988). Employee involvement: A sustained labor/management initiative at the Ford Motor Company. In J. P. Campbell & R. J. Campbell (Eds.), *Productivity in organizations: New Perspectives from industrial and organizational psychology.* San Francisco: Jossey-Bass, 388–416.

15. Jusela, G. E., Chairman, P., Ball, R. A., Tyson, C. E., & Dannermiller, K. D. (1987). Work innovations at Ford Motor. In Y. K. Shetty & V. M. Buehler (Eds.), *Quality productivity and innovation: Strategies for gaining competitive advantage.* New York: Elsevier, 123–145.

16. Tjosvold, D. (in press). Cooperative teamwork and constructive controversy: The test of crisis. In R. A. Guzzo & E. Salas, (Eds.) *Team Effectiveness and Decision Making in Organizations.*

Tjosvold, D. (1984). Effects of crisis orientation on managers' approach to controversy in decision making. *Academy of Management Journal, 27,* 130–138.

17. Jusela, G. E., Chairman, P., Ball, R. A., Tyson, C. E., & Dannermiller, K. D. (1987). Work innovations at Ford Motor. In Y. K. Shetty & V. M. Buehler (Eds.), *Quality productivity and innovation: Strategies for gaining competitive advantage.* New York: Elsevier, 123–145.

Chapter 6
Cooperation and Competition

1. Adler, P. S. (1993). Time-and-motion regained. *Harvard Business Review,* 97–108.

2. Peters, T. (1992). *Liberation management: Necessary disorganization for the nanosecond nineties.* New York: Alfred A. Knopf.

3. Nichols, N. A. (1994, January–February). Scientific management at Merck: An interview with CFO Judy Lewent. *Harvard Business Review,* 89–99, quote p. 93.

4. Henderson, R. (1994, January–February). Managing innovation in the information age. *Harvard Business Review,* 100–105.

5. Kumar, S., & Gupta, Y. P. (1991, May). Cross-functional teams improve manufacturing at Motorola's Austin plant. *Industrial Engineering, 23,* 32–36.

6. Wagner, J. (1993, February). A-teams in residence. *CIO, 6,* 28–30.

7. Vasilash, G. S. (1993). Changing everything at Chrysler Manufacturing. *Production, 105,* 60–62.

8. Vasilash, G. S. (1992). Chrysler gets serious about success. *Production, 10,* 58–60.

9. Perry, T. S. (1990). Teamwork plus technology cuts development time. *IEEE Spectrum, 27,* 61–67.

10. Bailetti, A. J., Guild, T., & Paul, D. (1991). A method for projects seeking to merge technical advancements with potential markets. *R & D Management, 2,* 291–300.

11. Gleckman, H. (1993, June 14). The technology payoff. *Business Week,* 56–68.

12. Puri, S. J. (1992). Industrial vendors' selling center: Implications for sales management. *Journal of Business & Industrial Marketing, 7,* 59–69.

13. Deutsch, M. (1993). Educating for a peaceful world. *American Psychologist, 48,* 510–517.

Deutsch, M. (1990). Sixty years of conflict. *The International Journal of Conflict Management, 1,* 237–263.

Deutsch, M. (1985). *Distributive justice: A social-psychological perspective.* New Haven: Yale University Press.

Deutsch, M. (1980). Fifty years of conflict. In L. Festinger (Ed.), *Retrospections on social psychology*. New York: Oxford University Press, 46–77.

Deutsch, M. (1973). *The resolution of conflict*. New Haven, CT: Yale University Press.

Deutsch, M. (1949). A theory of cooperation and competition. *Human Relations, 2*, 129–152.

14. Johnson, D. W., & Johnson, R. T. (1989). *Cooperation and competition: Theory and research*. Edina, MN: Interaction Book Company.

Johnson, D. W., Johnson, R. T., & Maruyama, G. (1983). Interdependence and interpersonal attraction among heterogeneous and homogeneous individuals: A theoretical formulation and a meta-analysis of the research. *Review of Educational Research, 53*, 5–54.

Johnson, D. W., Maruyama, G., Johnson, R. T., Nelson, D., & Skon, S. (1981). Effects of cooperative, competitive, and individualistic goal structures on achievement: A meta-analysis. *Psychological Bulletin, 89*, 47–62.

15. Johnson, D. W., Johnson, R. T., Smith, K., & Tjosvold, D. (1990). Pro, con, and synthesis: Training managers to engage in constructive controversy. In B. Sheppard, M. Bazerman, & R. Lewicki (Eds.), *Research in Negotiations in Organization*, Vol. 2, 139–174. Greenwich, CT.: JAI Press.

Tjosvold, D. (1989). Interdependence and conflict management in organizations. In M. A. Rahim (Ed.), *Managing conflict: An interdisciplinary approach*. New York: Praeger, 41–50.

16. Helmreich, R. (1982). *Pilot selection and training*. Paper presented at the annual meeting of the American Psychological Association, August, Washington, DC.

Helmreich, R., Beane, W., Lucker, W., & Spence, J. (1978). Achievement motivation and scientific attainment. *Personality and Social Psychological Bulletin, 4*, 222–226.

Helmreich, R., Sawin, L., & Carsrud, A. (1986). The honeymoon effect in job performance: Temporal increases in the predictive power of achievement motivation. *Journal of Applied Psychology, 71*, 185–188.

Helmreich, R., Spence, J., Beane, W., Lucker, W., & Matthews, K. (1980). Making it in academic psychology: Demographic and personality correlates of attainment. *Journal of Personality and Social Psychology, 39*, 896–908.

17. Tjosvold, D. (1986). *Working together to get things done: Managing for organizational productivity.* Lexington, MA: Lexington Books, chapters 1 and 2.

18. Karau, S. J., & Williams, K. D. (1993). Social loafing: A meta-analytic review and theoretical integration. *Journal of Personality and Social Psychology, 65*, 681–706.

George, J. M. (1992). Extrinsic and intrinsic origins of perceived social loafing in organizations. *Academy of Management Journal, 35*, 191–202.

Williams, K. D., & Karau, S. J. (1991). Social loafing and social compensation: The effects of expectations of co-worker performance. *Journal of Personality and Social Psychology, 61*, 570–581.

19. Katzenbach, J. R., & Smith, D. K. (1993). *The wisdom of teams: Creating the high-performance organization.* Boston: Harvard Business School Press, p. 259–263.

20. Tjosvold, D. (1990). Flight crew collaboration to manage safety risks. *Group & Organization Studies, 15*, 11–191.

21. Judge, T. A., & Bretz, R. D., Jr. (1994). Political influence behavior and career success. *Journal of Management, 20*, 43–65.

22. Tjosvold, D. (1993). *Learning to manage conflict: Getting people to work together productively.* New York: Lexington Books, chapter 7.

23. Deutsch, M. (1973). *The resolution of conflict.* New Haven, CT: Yale University Press.

24. Katzenbach, J. R., & Smith, D. K. (1993). *The wisdom of teams: Creating the high-performance organization.* Cambridge: Harvard Business School Press, chapter 3.

Lewin, K. (1947). Group decision and social change. In T. M. Newcomb & E. L. Hartley (Eds.), *Readings in social psychology.* New York: Holt, Rinehart and Winston.

25. Sisco, R. (1992, July). Put your money where your teams are. *Training*, 41–45.

26. Johnson, D. W., & Johnson, R. T. (1989). *Leading the cooperative school.* Edina, MN: Interaction Book Company, chapters 1 and 4.

27. Petty, M. M., Singleton, B., & Connell, D. W. (1992). An experimental evaluation of an organizational incentive plan in the electric utility industry. *Journal of Applied Psychology, 77,* 427–436.

Ross, T. L., Hatcher, L., & Collins, D. (1992, Spring). Why employees support (and oppose) gainsharing plans. *Compensation & Benefits Management, 8,* 17–27.

28. Cheung, J. L. (1983). Interdependence and coordination in organizations: A role-system analysis. *Academy of Management Journal, 26,* 156–162.

29. Sisco, R. (1992, July). Put your money where your teams are. *Training*, 41–45.

Chapter 7
The Faces of Power

1. Semler, R. (1993). *Maverick: The success story behind the world's most unusual workplace.* Warner Books: New York.

Semler, R. (1994, January–February). Why my former employees still work for me. *Harvard Business Review,* 64–74.

2. Kanter, R. M. (1979). Power failure in management circuits. *Harvard Business Review,* 65–75.

Kanter, R. M. (1977). *Men and women of the corporation.* New York: Basic Books.

3. Dahl, R. P. (1957). The concept of power. *Behavioral Science, 2,* 201–218.

Emerson, R. M. (1962). Power-dependence relations. *American Sociological Review, 27,* 31–41.

Pfeffer, J. (1981). *Power in organizations.* Boston: Pitman.

Weber, M. (1947). *The theory of social and economic organization.* New York: Oxford University Press.

4. Tjosvold, D. (1986). *Working together to get things done: Managing for organizational productivity.* Lexington, MA: Heath, chapter 7.

5. McClelland, D. C. (1975). *Power: The inner experience.* New York: Irvington.

McClelland, D. C. (1970). The two faces of power. *Journal of Affairs, 24,* 29–47.

6. Thibaut, J. W., & Kelley, H. H. (1959). *The social psychology of groups.* New York: Wiley.

7. Tjosvold, D. (1990). Power in cooperative and competitive organizational contexts. *Journal of Social Psychology, 130,* 249–258.

8. Eisenhardt, K. M. (1989). Making fast strategic decisions in high velocity environments. *Academy of Management Journal, 32,* 543–576.

Eisenhardt, K. M., & Bourgeois, L. J., III. (1988). Politics of strategic decision making in high-velocity environments: Toward a midrange theory. *Academy of Management Journal, 31,* 737–770.

9. Bottger, P. C., & Yetton, P. W. (1987). Improving group performance by training in individual problem solving. *Journal of Applied Psychology, 72,* 651–657.

Tjosvold, D., Andrews, I. R., & Struthers, J. (1991). Power and interdependence in work groups: Views of managers and employees. *Group & Organization Studies, 16,* 285–299.

10. Tjosvold, D. (1981). Unequal power relationships within a cooperative or competitive context, *Journal of Applied Social Psychology 11,* 137–150.

Tjosvold, D. (1985). The effects of attribution and social context on superiors' influence and interaction with low performing subordinates. *Personnel Psychology, 38,* 361–376.

Tjosvold, D. (1985). Power and social context in superior-subordinate interaction. *Organizational Behavior and Human Decision Processes, 35,* 281–293.

Tjosvold, D., Johnson, D. W., & Johnson, R. T. (1984). Influence strategy, perspective-taking, and relationships between high and low power individuals in cooperative and competitive contexts. *Journal of Psychology, 116,* 187–202.

11. Tjosvold, D. (1990). Power in cooperative and competitive organizational contexts. *Journal of Social Psychology, 130,* 249–258.

Tjosvold, D., Andrews, I. R., & Struthers, J. (1991). Power and interdependence in work groups: Views of managers and employees. *Group & Organization Studies, 16,* 285–299.

Tjosvold, D., Andrews, I. R., & Struthers, J. (1991). Leadership influence: Goal interdependence and power. *Journal of Social Psychology, 132,* 39–50.

12. McClelland, D. C. (1975). *Power: The inner experience.* New York: Irvington.

McClelland, D. C. (1970). The two faces of power. *Journal of Affairs, 24,* 29–47.

McClelland, D. C., & Boyatzis, R. E. (1982). Leadership motive pattern and long-term success in management. *Journal of Applied Psychology, 67,* 737–743.

13. Cohen, A. R. (1958). Upward communication in experimentally created hierarchies. *Human Relations, 11,* 41–53.

Solomon, L. (1960). The influence of some types of power relationships and game strategies upon the development of interpersonal trust. *Journal of Abnormal and Social Psychology, 61,* 223–230.

14. Jones, E. E., & Wortman, C. (1973). *Ingratiation: An attributional approach.* Morristown, NJ: General Learning Press.

15. Alkire, A. A., Collum, M. E., Kaswin, J., & Love, L. R. (1968). Information exchange and accuracy of verbal communication under social power conditions. *Journal of Personality and Social Psychology, 9,* 301–308.

16. Kelley, H. H. (1951). Communication in experimentally created hierarchies. *Human Relations, 4,* 39–56.

17. Thomas, D. L., Franks, D. D., & Caolnica, J. M. (1972). Role taking and power in social psychology. *American Sociological Review, 37,* 605–614.

Tjosvold, D., & Fabrey, L. (1980). The effects of independence and dependence on cognitive perspective-taking. *Psychological Reports, 46,* 755–765.

Tjosvold, D., & Sagaria, S. D. (1978). Effects of relative power on cognitive perspective-taking. *Personality and Social Psychology Bulletin, 4,* 256–259.

18. Kelley, H. H. (1951). Communication in experimentally created hierarchies. *Human Relations, 4,* 39–56.

Tjosvold, D. (1979). The other's controlling strategy and own group's evaluation in intergroup conflict. *The Journal of Psychology, 100,* 305–314.

19. Tjosvold, D., & Deemer, D. K. (1980). Effects of control or collaborative orientation on participation in decision-making. *Canadian Journal of Behavioural Science, 13,* 33–43.

20. Tjosvold, D. (1988). Interdependence and power between managers and employees: A study of the leader relationship. *Journal of Management, 15,* 49–64.

Tjosvold, D., Andrews, I. R., & Jones, H. (1985). Alternative ways leaders can use authority. *Canadian Journal of Administrative Sciences, 2,* 307–317.

Tjosvold, D., Andrews, I. R., & Jones, H. (1983). Cooperative and competitive relationships between leaders and their subordinates. *Human Relations, 36,* 1111–1124.

21. Tjosvold, D. (1986). *Working together to get things done: Managing for organizational productivity.* Lexington, MA: Heath, chapter 11.

22. Judge, R. A., & Bretz, R. D., Jr. (1994). Political influence behavior and career success. *Journal of Management, 20,* 43–65.

23. McCall, M. W., & Lombardo, M. M. (1983). *Coping with an intolerable boss*. Greensboro, NC: Center for Creative Leadership.

24. Kouzes, J. M., & Posner, B. Z. (1987). *The leadership challenge*. San Francisco: Jossey-Bass, Part I.

Chapter 8
Effective Communication

1. Drucker, P. (1993). *Post-capitalist society*. New York: Harper-Collins, chapter 1.

2. Webber, A. (1993, January–February). What's so new about the new economy? *Harvard Business Review*, 24–42.

3. Wriston, W. (1992). *The twilight of sovereignty: How the information revolution is transforming our world*. New York: Scribner's Sons.

4. Raffio, T. (1992, Fall). Quality and Delta Dental Plan of Massachusetts. *Sloan Management Review*, 101–110.

5. Deutsch, M. (1990). Sixty years of conflict. *The International Journal of Conflict Management, 1*, 237–263.

Tjosvold, D., & McNeely, L. T. (1988). Innovation through communication in an educational bureaucracy. *Communication Research, 15*, 568–581.

6. Argyris, C., & Schon, D. (1978). *Organizational learning*. Reading, MA: Addison-Wesley.

7. Johnson, D. W. (1993). *Reaching out: Interpersonal skills and self-actualization*. Englewood Cliffs, NJ: Prentice-Hall, chapters 4–7.

8. Kipnis, D. (1976). *The powerholders*. Chicago: University of Chicago Press.

9. Tjosvold, D., & Sagaria, S. (1978). Effects of relative power on cognitive perspective-taking. *Personality and Social Psychology Bulletin, 4*, 256–259.

10. Tjosvold, D., & Johnson, D. W. (1989). Conflict and authority hierarchies. In D. Tjosvold & D. W. Johnson (Eds.) *Productive conflict management: Implications for organizations.* Minneapolis, MN: Team Media, 150–173.

11. Tjosvold, D., Andrews, I. R., & Jones, H. (1985). Alternative ways leaders can use authority. *Canadian Journal of Administrative Sciences, 2,* 307–317.

Tjosvold, D., & Deemer, D. K. (1980). Effects of control or collaborative orientation on participation in decision-making. *Canadian Journal of Behavioural Science, 13,* 33–43.

12. McCall, M. W., Jr., Lombardo, M. M., & Morrison, A. M. (1988). *The lessons of experience: How successful executives develop on the job.* Lexington, MA: Lexington Books, pp. 33–34.

13. Falk, D., & Johnson, D. W. (1977). The effects of perspective-taking and ego-centrism on problem solving in heterogeneous and homogeneous groups. *Journal of Social Psychology, 102,* 63–72.

Johnson, D. W. (1971). Role reversal: A summary and review of the research. *International Journal of Group Tensions, 1,* 64–78.

Long, E. C. J., & Andrews, D. W. (1990). Perspective taking as a predictor of marital adjustment. *Journal of Personality and Social Psychology, 59,* 126–131.

14. Unterman, I. (1988). *National negotiating style: Mexicans.* Paper, Academy of Management Meetings, Anaheim, CA.

Chapter 9
Feelings and Their Expression

1. Welch, J. F., Jr., & Hood, E. E., Jr. (1992). To our shareholders. *The General Electric Company 1991 Annual Report.*

2. Tichy, N. M., & Sherman, S. (1993). *Control your destiny or someone else will.* New York: Doubleday.

3. Welch, J. F., Jr., & Hood, E. E., Jr. (1992). To our shareholders. *The General Electric Company 1991 Annual Report.*

4. Tichy, N. M., & Sherman, S. (1993). *Control your destiny or someone else will.* New York: Doubleday.

5. Overman, S. (November, 1991). After the smoke clears. *HRMagazine,* 44–46.

   Overman, S. (November, 1991). You may not be able to deal with this. *HRMagazine,* 46–47.

6. Argyris, C. (1991). Teaching smart people how to learn. *Harvard Business Review,* May–June, 99–109.

7. Averill, J. R. (1982). *Anger and aggression: An essay on emotion.* New York: Springer-Verlag.

8. George, J. M. (1992). Extrinsic and intrinsic origins of perceived social loafing in organizations. *Academy of Management Journal, 35,* 191–202.

   Harkins, S. G., & Petty, R. E. (1982). The effects of task difficulty and task uniqueness on social loafing. *Journal of Personality and Social Psychology, 43,* 1214–1229.

   Jones, G. R. (1984). Task visibility, free riding, and shirking: Explaining the effect of structure and technology on employee behavior. *Academy of Management Review, 9,* 684–695.

   Kerr, N. (1983). The dispensability of member effort and group motivation losses: Free-rider effects. *Journal of Personality and Social Psychology, 44,* 78–94.

   Latane, B. (1986). Responsibility and effort in organizations. In P. S. Goodman (Ed.), *Designing Effective Work Groups.* San Francisco: Jossey-Bass, 277–304.

   Maruymana, G., Fraser, S. C., & Miller, N. (1982). Personal responsibility and altruism in children. *Journal of Personality and Social Psychology, 33,* 178–187.

   Sheppard, J. A., & Wright, R. A. (1989). Individual contribution to a collective effort: An incentive analysis. *Personality and Social Psychology Bulletin, 15,* 141–149.

Williams, K. D., & Karau, S. J. (1991). Social loafing and social compensation: The effects of expectations of co-worker performance. *Journal of Personality and Social Psychology, 61,* 570–581.

9. DePaulo, B. M. (1992). Nonverbal behavior and self-presentation. *Psychological Bulletin, 111,* 203–243.

10. Tichy, N. M., & Sherman, S. (1993). *Control your destiny or someone else will.* New York: Doubleday.

11. George, J. M., & Brief, A. P. (1992). Feeling good-doing good: A conceptual analysis of the mood at work—organizational spontaneity relationship. *Psychological Bulletin, 112,* 310–329.

Tjosvold, D. (1993). *Teamwork for customers: Building an organization that serves.* San Francisco, Jossey-Bass.

12. Diamond, E. L. (1982). The role of anger and hostility in essential hypertension and coronary heart disease. *Psychological Bulletin, 92,* 410–433.

13. Watson, D., & Clark, L. A. (1990). Self-versus peer ratings of specific emotional traits: Evidence of convergent and discriminate validity. *Journal of Personality and Social Psychology, 60,* 927–940.

14. Ambady, N., & Rosenthal, R. (1992). Thin slices of expressive behavior as predictors of interpersonal consequences: A meta-analysis. *Psychological Bulletin, 111,* 256–274.

15. Averill, J. R. (1982). *Anger and aggression: An essay on emotion.* New York: Springer-Verlag.

Ellis, A. (1987). The impossibility of maintaining consistently good mental health. *American Psychologist, 42,* 365–375.

Tangney, J. P. (1991). Moral affect: The good, the bad, and the ugly. *Journal of Personality and Social Psychology, 61,* 598–607.

Tangney, J. P., Wagner, P., Fletcher, C., & Gramzow, R. (1992). Shamed into anger? The relations of shame and guilt to anger and self-reported aggression. *Journal of Personality and Social Psychology, 62,* 669–675.

16. Baumeister, R. F., Stillwell, A., & Wotman, S. R. (1990). Victim and perpetrator accounts of interpersonal conflict: Autobiographical

narratives about anger. *Journal of Personality and Social Psychology, 59,* 994–1005.

Parrott, W. G., & Smith, R. H. (1993). Distinguishing the experiences of envy and jealousy. *Journal of Personality and Social Psychology, 64,* 906–920.

17. Katz, L., & Epstein, S. (1991). Constructive thinking and coping with laboratory-induced stress. *Journal of Personality and Social Psychology, 61,* 789–800.

Forgas, J. P. (1994). Sad and guilty? Affective influences on the explanation of conflict in close relationships. *Journal of Personality and Social Psychology, 66,* 56–68.

18. Johnson, D. W. (1993). *Reaching out: Interpersonal skills and self-actualization.* Englewood Cliffs, NJ: Prentice-Hall, chapter 5.

Miller, S., Nunnally, E., & Wachman, D. (1975). *Alive and aware: Improving communication in relationships.* Minneapolis, MN: Interpersonal Communication Programs.

19. Fitness, J., & Fletcher, G. J. O. (1993). Love, hate, anger, and jealousy in close relationships: A prototype and cognitive appraisal analysis. *Journal of Personality and Social Psychology, 65,* 942–958.

Gross, J. J., & Levenson, R. W. (1993). Emotional suppression: Physiology, self-report, and expressive behavior. *Journal of Personality and Social Psychology, 64,* 970–986.

20. Bornstein, R. F. (1992). The dependent personality: Developmental, social, and clinical perspectives. *Psychological Bulletin, 112,* 3–23.

Diamond, E. L. (1982). The role of anger and hostility in essential hypertension and coronary heart disease. *Psychological Bulletin, 92,* 410–433.

21. Friedman, H. W., & Miller-Herringer, T. (1991). Nonverbal display of emotion in public and in private: Self-monitoring, personality, and expressive cues. *Journal of Personality and Social Psychology, 61,* 766–775.

22. Averill, J. R. (1982). *Anger and aggression: An essay on emotion.* New York: Springer-Verlag.

23. DePaulo, B. M. (1992). Nonverbal behavior and self-presentation. *Psychological Bulletin, 111,* 203–243.

24. McCroskey, J., Larson, C., & Knapp, M. (1971). *Introduction to interpersonal communication.* Englewood Cliffs, NJ: Prentice-Hall.

25. Russell, J. A. (1994). Is there universal recognition of emotion from facial expression? A review of the cross-cultural studies. *Psychological Bulletin, 115,* 102–141.

26. Brown, J. D. (1991). Staying fit and staying well: Physical fitness as a moderator of life stress. *Journal of Personality and Social Psychology, 60,* 555–561.

27. Judge, R. A., & Locke, E. A. (1993). Effect of dysfunctional thought processes on subjective well-being and job satisfaction. *Journal of Applied Psychology, 78,* 475–490.

Tangney, J. P. (1991). Moral affect: The good, the bad, and the ugly. *Journal of Personality and Social Psychology, 61,* 598–607.

Tangeney, J. P., Wagner, P., Fletcher, C., & Gramzow, R. (1992). Shamed into anger? The relations of shame and guilt to anger and self-reported aggression. *Journal of Personality and Social Psychology, 62,* 669–675.

28. Ellis, A. (1987). The impossibility of maintaining consistently good mental health. *American Psychologist, 42,* 365–375.

29. Hewitt, P. L., & Flett, G. L. (1991). Perfectionism in the self and social contexts: Conceptualization, assessment, and association with psychopathology. *Journal of Personality and Social Psychology, 60,* 456–470.

30. Tjosvold, D. (1983). Social face in conflict: A critique. *International Journal of Group Tension, 13,* 49–64.

Chapter 10
Making Decisions

1. Johnson, P. T. (1993). How I turned a critical public into useful consultants. *Harvard Business Review,* January–February, 56–66.

2. Barnes, H. H., Jr. (1984). Cognitive biases and their impact on strategic planning. *Strategic Management Journal, 5,* 129–137.

Brockner, J., Houser, R., Birnbaum, G., Lloyd, K., Deitcher, J., Nathanson, S., & Rubin, J. Z. (1986). Escalation of commitment to an ineffective course of action: The effects of feedback having negative implications for self-identity. *Administrative Science Quarterly, 31,* 109–126.

Cyert, R. M., & March, J. G. (1963). *A behavioral theory of the firm.* Englewood Cliffs, NJ: Prentice Hall.

Schwenk, C. R. (1984). Cognitive simplification processes in strategic decision-making. *Strategic Management Journal, 5,* 111–128.

Tversky, A., & Kahneman, D. (1974). Judgement under uncertainty: Heuristics and biases. *Science, 185,* 1124–1131.

3. Smith, J. F., & Kida, T. (1991). Heuristics and biases: Expertise and task realism in auditing. *Psychological Bulletin, 109,* 472–489.

4. Aldag, R. J., & Fuller, S. R. (1993). Beyond fiasco: A reappraisal of the groupthink phenomenon and a new model of group decision processes. *Psychological Bulletin, 113,* 533–552.

Janis, I. L. (1972). *Victims of groupthink.* Boston: Houghton Mifflin.

Wanous, J. P., & Yountz, M. A. (1986). Solution diversity and the quality of group decisions. *Academy of Management Journal, 29,* 149–1559.

5. Tetlock, P. E., Armor, D., & Peterson, R. S. (1994). The slavery debate in antebellum America: Cognitive style, value conflicts, and the limits of compromise. *Journal of Personality and Social Psychology, 66,* 115–126.

Nutt, P. C. (1993). Flexible decision styles and the choices of top executives. *Journal of Management Studies, 30,* 697–721.

6. Tjosvold, D., Meredith, L., & Weldwood, R. M. (in press). Implementing relationship marketing: A goal interdependence approach. *Journal of Business & Industrial Marketing.*

Tjosvold, D. (1993). *Learning to manage conflict: Getting people to work together productively.* New York: Lexington Books.

Tjosvold, D. (1991). *The conflict-positive organization: Stimulate diversity and create unity.* Reading, MA: Addison-Wesley.

Tjosvold, D. (1989). *Managing conflict: The key to making your organization work.* Minneapolis, MN: Team Media.

7. Leana, C. R., Ahlbrandt, R. S., & Murrell, A. J. (1992). The effects of employee involvement programs on unionized workers' attitudes, perceptions, and preferences in decision making. *Academy of Management Journal, 35,* 861–873.

Tjosvold, D., Wedley, W. C., & Field, R. H. G. (1986). Constructive controversy, the Vroom-Yetton model, and managerial decision making. *Journal of Occupational Behaviour, 7,* 125–138.

8. Driskell, J. E., & Salas, E. (1991). Group decision making under stress. *Journal of Applied Psychology, 76,* 473–478.

9. Tjosvold, D. (1987). Participation: A close look at its dynamics. *Journal of Management, 13,* 739–750.

10. Dennis, A. R., & Valacich, J. S. (1993). Computer brainstorms: More heads are better than one. *Journal of Applied Psychology, 78,* 531–537.

Hill, G. W. (1982). Group versus individual performance: Are N + 1 heads better than one? *Psychological Bulletin, 91,* 517–539.

Kelley, H. H., & Thibaut, J. W. (1968). Group problem solving. In G. Lindzey & E. Aronson, *Handbook of social psychology.* Reading, MA: Addison-Wesley, 3, 1–105.

Laughlin, P. R., VanderStoep, S. W., & Hollingshead, A. B. (1991). Collective versus individual induction: Recognition of truth, rejection of error, and collective information processing. *Journal of Personality and Social Psychology, 61,* 50–67.

Martell, R. F., & Borg, M. R. A comparison of the behavior rating accuracy of groups and individuals. *Journal of Applied Psychology, 78,* 43–50.

Strasser, G., & Stewart, D. (1992). Discovery of hidden profiles by decision-making groups: Solving a problem versus making a judgment. *Journal of Personality and Social Psychology, 63,* 426–434.

Walton, W., Michaelsen, L., & Sharp, W. (1991). Member competence, group interaction, and group decision making: A longitudinal study. *Journal of Applied Psychology, 76,* 803–809.

11. Smith, J. F., & Kida, T. (1991). Heuristcs and biases: Expertise and task realism in auditing. *Psychological Bulletin, 109,* 472–489.

Tjosvold, D. (1985). Implications of controversy research for management. *Journal of Management, 11,* 21–37.

12. Pasmore, W. W., & Friedlander, F. (1982). An action-research program for increasing employee involvement in problem-solving. *Administrative Science Quarterly, 27,* 343–362.

Richter, F., & Tjosvold, D. (1981). Effects of student participation in classroom decision-making on attitudes, peer interaction, motivation, and learning. *Journal of Applied Psychology, 65,* 74–80.

13. Diehl, M., & Stroebe, W. (1991). Productivity loss in idea-generating groups: Tracking down the blocking effect. *Journal of Personality and Social Psychology, 61,* 392–403.

Gigone, D., & Hastie, R. (1993). The common knowledge effect: Information sharing and group judgment. *Journal of Personality and Social Psychology, 65,* 959–974.

Goodman, P. S., & Leyden, D. P. (1991). Familiarity and group productivity. *Journal of Applied Psychology, 76,* 578–586.

Katzenbach, J. R., & Smith, D. K. (1993). *The wisdom of teams: Creating the high-performance organization.* Boston: Harvard Business School Press.

Libby, K. R., Trotman, K. T., & Zimmer, I. (1987). Member variation, recognition of expertise, and group performance. *Journal of Applied Psychology, 72,* 81–87.

Sheppard, J. A. (1993). Productivity loss in performance groups: A motivation analysis. *Psychological Bulletin, 113,* 67–81.

Strasser, G., & Stewart, D. (1992). Discovery of hidden profiles by decision-making groups: Solving a problem versus making a judgment. *Journal of Personality and Social Psychology, 63,* 426–434.

Weldon, E., Jehn, K. A., & Pradhan, P. (1991). Processes that mediate the relationship between a group goal and improved group performance. *Journal of Personality and Social Psychology, 61,* 555–569.

Watson, W. E., Kumar, K., & Michaelsen, L. K. (1993). Cultural diversity's impact on interaction process and performance: Comparing homogeneous and diverse task forces. *Academy of Management Journal, 36,* 590–602.

14. Janis, I. L. (1972). *Victims of groupthink.* Boston: Houghton Mifflin.

15. Kruglanski, A. W. (1986). Freeze-think and the Challenger. *Psychology Today,* August, 48–49.

16. Foushee, H. C. (1984). Dyads and triads at 35,500 feet: Factors affecting group process and aircrew performance. *American Psychologist, 39,* 886–893.

17. Eisenhardt, K. M. (1989). Making fast strategic decisions in high velocity environments. *Academy of Management Journal, 32,* 543–576.

Eisenhardt, K. M., & Bourgeois, L. J., III. (1988). Politics of strategic decision making in high-velocity environments: Toward a midrange theory. *Academy of Management Journal, 31,* 737–770.

18. Tjosvold, D. (1982). Effects of the approach to controversy on superiors' incorporation of subordinates' information in decision making. *Journal of Applied Psychology, 67,* 189–193.

Tjosvold, D., & Deemer, D. K. (1980). Effects of controversy within a cooperative or competitive context on organizational decision making. *Journal of Applied Psychology, 65,* 590–595.

Tjosvold, D., & Field, R. H. G. (1983). Effects of social context on consensus and majority vote decision making. *Academy of Management Journal, 26,* 500–506.

Tjosvold, D., & Field, R. H. G. (1984). Managers' structuring cooperative and competitive controversy in group decision making. *International Journal of Management, 1,* 26–32.

Tjosvold, D., & Field, R. H. G. (1985). Effect of concurrence, controversy, and consensus on group decision making. *Journal of Social Psychology, 125,* 355–363.

Tjosvold, D., & Johnson, D. W. (1977). The effects of controversy on cognitive perspective taking. *Journal of Educational Psychology, 69*, 679–685.

Tjosvold, D., & Johnson, D. W. (1978). Controversy within a cooperative or competitive context and cognitive perspective taking. *Contemporary Educational Psychology, 3*, 376–386.

Tjosvold, D., Johnson, D. W., & Fabrey, L. (1980). The effects of affirmation and acceptance on incorporation of an opposing opinion in problem-solving. *Psychological Reports, 47*, 1043–1053.

Tjosvold, D., Johnson, D. W., & Lerner, J. (1981). The effects of affirmation and acceptance on incorporation of an opposing opinion in problem-solving. *Journal of Social Psychology, 114*, 103–110.

Tjosvold, D., Wedley, W. C., & Field, R. H. G. (1986). Constructive controversy, the Vroom-Yetton model, and managerial decision making. *Journal of Occupational Behaviour, 7*, 125–138.

19. Driskell, J. E., & Salas, E. (1991). Group decision making under stress. *Journal of Applied Psychology, 76*, 473–478.

Kruglanski, A. W., & Webster, D. M. (1991). Group members' reactions to opinion deviates and conformists at varying degrees of proximity to decision deadline and of environmental noise. *Journal of Personality and Social Psychology, 61*, 21–225.

Tjosvold, D. (in press). Cooperative teamwork and constructive controversy: The test of crisis. Chapter, In R. A. Guzzo & E. Salas, (Eds.), *Team Effectiveness and Decision Making in Organizations*.

Tjosvold, D. (1984). Effects of crisis orientation on managers' approach to controversy in decision making. *Academy of Management Journal, 27*, 130–138.

20. Smith, K., Johnson, D. W., & Johnson, R. (1981). Can conflict be constructive? Controversy versus concurrence seeking in learning groups. *Journal of Educational Psychology, 73*, 651–663.

Tjosvold, D., & Johnson, D. W. (1977). The effects of controversy on cognitive perspective taking. *Journal of Educational Psychology, 69*, 679–685.

21. Tjosvold, D. (1985). Implications of controversy research for management. *Journal of Management, 11,* 21–37.

22. Tjosvold, D. (1988). Cooperative and competitive interdependence: Collaboration between departments to serve customers. *Group & Organization Studies, 13,* 274–289.

Tjosvold, D., & McNeely, L. T. (1988). Innovation through communication in an educational bureaucracy. *Communication Research, 15,* 568–581.

Tjosvold, D. (1990). Cooperation and competition in restructuring an organization. *Canadian Journal of Administrative Sciences, 7,* 48–54.

Tjosvold, D. (1990). Making a technological innovation work: Collaboration to solve problems. *Human Relations. 43,* 1117–1131.

Chapter 11
Managing Conflict

1. Insko, C. A., Schopler, J., Hoyle, R. H., Dardis, G. J., & Graetz, K. A. (1990). Individual-group discontinuity as a function of fear and greed. *Journal of Personality and Social Psychology, 58,* 68–79.

2. Baker, J., Tjosvold, D., & Andrews, I. R. (1988). Conflict approaches of effective and ineffective managers: A field study in a matrix organization. *Journal of Management Studies, 25,* 167–178.

Pahl, J. M., & Roth, K. (1993). Managing the headquarters-foreign subsidiary relationship: The roles of strategy, conflict, and integration. *International Journal of Conflict Management, 4,* 139–165.

Tjosvold, D., Tjosvold, M. M., & Tjosvold, J. (1991), *Love & anger: Managing family conflict.* Minneapolis, MN: Team Media.

3. Klass, B. S., Heneman, H. G., III, & Olson, C. A. (1991). Effects of grievance activity on absenteeism. *Journal of Applied Psychology, 76.*

4. Deutsch, M. (1993). Educating for a peaceful world. *American Psychologist, 48,* 510–517.

Etherington, L., & Tjosvold, D. (1992). *Managing budget conflicts: A goal interdependence approach.* Canadian Association for Management Accountants: Toronto.

Tjosvold, D. (1991). Rights and responsibilities of dissent: Cooperative conflict. *Employee Rights and Responsibilities Journal, 4,* 13–23.

Deutsch, M. (1994). Constructive conflict resolution: Principles, training, and research. *Journal of Social Issues, 50,* 13–32.

Fisher, R. J. (1994). Generic principles for resolving intergroup conflict. *Journal of Social Issues, 50,* 47–66.

Johnson, D. W., & Roger, R. T. (1994). Constructive conflict in schools. *Journal of Social Issues, 50,* 117–137.

Post, F. R., & Bennett, R. J. (1994). Use of the collaborative collective bargaining process in labor negotiations. *International Journal of Conflict Management, 5,* 34–61.

Rouhana, N. N., & Kelman, H. C. (1994). Promoting joint thinking in international conflicts: An Israeli-Palestinian continuing workshop. *Journal of Social Issues, 50,* 157–178.

5. Tjosvold, D. (1993). *Learning to manage conflict: Getting people to work together productively.* New York: Lexington Books.

Tjosvold, D. (1991). *The conflict-positive organization: Stimulate diversity and create unity.* Reading, MA: Addison-Wesley.

6. Deutsch, M. (1973). *The resolution of conflict.* New Haven, CT: Yale University Press.

7. Kouzes, J. M., & Posner, B. Z. (1993). *Credibility: How leaders gain and lose it, why people demand it.* San Francisco: Jossey-Bass, p. 99.

8. Tjosvold, D., Dann, V., & Wong, C. L. (1992). Managing conflict between departments to serve customers. *Human Relations, 45,* 1035–1054.

Weingart, L. R., Bennett, R. J., & Brett, J. M. (1993). The impact of consideration of issues and motivational orientation on group negotiation process and outcome. *Journal of Applied Psychology, 78,* 504–517.

9. Johnson, D. W., & Johnson, R. T. (1989). *Cooperation and competition: Theory and research.* Edina, MN: Interaction Book Company.

10. Johnson, D. W., Maruyama, G., Johnson, R. T., Nelson, D., & Skon, S. (1981). Effects of cooperative, competitive, and individualistic goal structures on achievement: A meta-analysis. *Psychological Bulletin, 89,* 47–62.

11. Fisher, R., & Ury, W. (1981). *Getting to yes.* New York: Harper & Row.

Pruitt, D. G., & Lewis, S. A. (1975). Development of integrative solutions in bilateral negotiations. *Journal of Personality and Social Psychology, 31,* 621–633.

Pruitt, D. G., & Syna, H. (1989). Successful problem solving. In D. Tjosvold & D. W. Johnson, (Eds.), *Productive conflict management: Perspectives for organizations.* Minneapolis, MN: Team Media, 69–90.

12. Johnson, D. W. (1971). Role reversal: A summary and review of the research. *International Journal of Group Tensions, 1,* 64–78.

13. Bazerman, M. H., & Neale, M. A. (1992). *Negotiating rationally.* New York: Free Press.

14. Thompson, L. (1990). An examination of naive and experienced negotiators. *Journal of Personality and Social Psychology, 59,* 82–90.

15. Lim, R. G., & Carnevale, P. J. D. (1990). Contingencies in the mediation of disputes. *Journal of Personality and Social Psychology, 58,* 259–272.

16. Tjosvold, D. (1993). *Learning to manage conflict: Getting people to work together productively.* New York: Lexington Books.

Johnson, D. W., & Johnson, R. T. (1987). *Creative conflict.* Edina, MN: Interaction Book Company.

Chapter 12
Moving to Self-Directing Teams

1. Pasmore, W., Francis, C., Haldeman, J., & Shani, A. (1982). Sociotechnical systems: A North American reflection on empirical studies of the Seventies. *Human Relations, 35,* 1179–1204.

2. Lawler, E. E., Mohrman, S. A., & Ledford, G. E., Jr. (1992). *Employee involvement and total quality management: Practices and results in Fortune 1000 companies.* San Francisco: Jossey-Bass.

3. Cohen, S. G. (in press). Designing effective self-managing teams. In M. Beyerlein (Ed.), *Research on Self-Managing Teams,* Greenwich, CT: JAI Press.

Goodman, P. S., Devadas, R., & Griffith-Hughson, T. L. (1988). Groups and productivity: Analyzing the effectiveness of self-managing teams. In J. P. Campbell & R. J. Campbell (Eds.), *Productivity in organizations: New Perspectives from industrial and organizational psychology.* San Francisco: Jossey-Bass, 295–327.

4. Wall, T. D., Kemp, N. J., Jackson, P. R., & Clegg, C. W. (1986). Outcomes of autonomous workgroups: A long-term field experiment. *Academy of Management Journal, 29,* 280–304.

5. Wall, T. D., Kemp, N. J., Jackson, P. R., & Clegg, C. W. (1986). Outcomes of autonomous workgroups: A long-term field experiment. *Academy of Management Journal, 29,* 280–304.

6. Corderey, J. L., Mueller, W. S., & Smith, L. M. (1991). Attitude and behavioral effects of autonomous group working: A longitudinal field study. *Academy of Management Journal, 34,* 464–476.

7. Cohen, S. G., & Ledford, G. E., Jr. (in press). The effectiveness of self-managing teams: A quasi-experiment. *Human Relations.*

8. Goodman, P. S. (1979). *Assessing organizational change: The Rushton quality of work experiment.* New York: Wiley-Interscience.

Walton, R. E. (1982). The Topeka work system: Optimistic visions, pessimistic hypotheses, and reality. In R. Zager, & M. P. Rosnow (Eds.), *The innovative organization: Productivity programs in action.* Elmsford, NY: Pergamon Press.

9. Beekun, R. I. (1989). Assessing the effectiveness of sociotechnical interventions: Antidote or fad? *Human Relations, 47,* 877–897.

Guzzo, R. A., Jette, R. D., & Katzell, R. A. (1985). The effects of psychologically based intervention programs on worker productivity: A meta-analysis. *Personnel Psychology, 38,* 275–291.

Macy, B. A., Bliese, P. D., & Norton, J. J. (1991). *Organizational change and work innovation: A meta-analysis of 131 North American field experiments—1961–1990.* Paper, Academy of Management, Miami.

10. Pritchard, R. D., Jones, S. D., Roth, P. L., Stuebing, K. K., & Ekeberg, S. E. (1988). Effects of group feedback, goal setting, and incentives on organizational productivity. *Journal of Applied Psychology, 73,* 337–358.

Tjosvold, D. (in press). Knowledge to empower self-managing teams: Research on cooperation and controversy. In M. Beyerlein (Ed.), *Research on Self-Managing Teams,* Greenwich, CT: JAI Press.

11. Manz, C. C., & Angle, H. (1986). Can group self-management mean a loss of personal control? Triangulating a paradox. *Group & Organization Studies, 11,* 309–334.

Manz, C. C., & Sims, H. P., Jr. (1982). The potential for 'groupthink' in autonomous work groups. *Human Relations, 35,* 773–784.

12. Alder, S. J. (1993). *Goal interdependence, interaction, and work outcomes in self-directed work teams.* Ph.D. Dissertation, University of Minnesota.

13. Goodman, P. S., Devadas, R., & Griffith-Hughson, T. L. (1988). Groups and productivity: Analyzing the effectiveness of self-managing teams. In J. P. Campbell & R. J. Campbell (Eds.), *Productivity in organizations: New perspectives from industrial and organizational psychology.* San Francisco: Jossey-Bass, 295–327.

14. Latane, B. (1986). Responsibility and effort in organizations. In P. S. Goodman (Ed.), *Designing effective work groups.* San Francisco: Jossey-Bass, 277–304.

15. Tjosvold, D., & Tjosvold, M. M. (1991). *Leading the team organization: How to create an enduring competitive advantage.* New York: Lexington Books.

Chapter 13
Becoming a Learning Organization

1. Greco, R. B. (1992, September–October). From the classroom to the corner office. *Harvard Business Review,* 54–63.

2. Argyris, C., & Schon, D. (1978). *Organizational learning.* Reading, MA: Addison-Wesley.

Senge, P. M. (1990). *The fifth discipline.* New York: Doubleday.

3. Hammer, M., & Champy, J. (1993). *Reengineering the corporation.* New York: HarperBusiness, chapter 7.

4. Garvin, D. A. (1993, July–August). Building a learning organization. *Harvard Business Review,* 78–91.

5. Womack, J. P., & Jones, D. T. (1994, March–April). From lean production to the lean enterprise. *Harvard Business Review,* 93–103.

6. Forgas, J. P. (1994). Sad and guilty? Affective influences on the explanation of conflict in close relationships. *Journal of Personality and Social Psychology, 66,* 56–68.

7. McCall, M. W., Jr., Lombardo, M. M., & Morrison, A. M. (1988). *The lessons of experience: How successful executives develop on the job.* Lexington, MA: Lexington Books.

8. Argyris, C. (1991). Teaching smart people how to learn. *Harvard Business Review,* May–June, 99–109.

9. McCall, M. W., Jr., & Lombardo, M. M. (1983). *Off the track: Why and how successful executives get derailed.* (Technical Report No. 21). Greensboro, NC: Center for Creative Leadership.

10. Dyer, W. G. (1987). *Team building: Issues and alternatives.* Reading, MA: Addison-Wesley, chapters 5 and 6.

11. Tjosvold, D., & Halco, J. A. (1992). Performance appraisal: Goal interdependence and future responses. *Journal of Social Psychology, 132,* 629–639.

12. Dyer, W. G. (1987). *Team building: Issues and alternatives.* Reading, MA: Addison-Wesley.

Chapter 14
Preparing for the Future

1. Katzenbach, J. R., & Smith, D. K. (1993). *The wisdom of teams: Creating the high-performance organization.* Cambridge: Harvard Business School Press.

2. Kotter, J. P. (1982). *The general managers.* New York: Free Press.

3. McCall, M. W., Jr., Lombardo, M. M., & Morrison, A. M. (1988). *The lessons of experience: How successful executives develop on the job.* Lexington, MA: Lexington Books, p. 22.

4. De Pree, M. (1989). *Leadership is an art.* New York: Doubleday.

Kouzes, J. M., & Posner, B. Z. (1987). *The leadership challenge.* San Francisco: Jossey-Bass.

5. Johnson, D. W., & Johnson, R. T. (1989). *Leading the cooperative school.* Edina, MN: Interaction Book Company.

6. Drucker, P. (1993). *Post-capitalist society.* New York: Harper-Collins.

Index